AF541180

The Policy Pivot

The Policy Pivot

Inside India's Strategic Shift

Edited by

Ajay Khanna and
Rahul Sharma

JUGGERNAUT BOOKS
C-I-128, First Floor, Sangam Vihar, Near Holi Chowk,
New Delhi 110080, India

First published by Juggernaut Books 2025

10 9 8 7 6 5 4 3 2 1

P-ISBN: 9789353458652
E-ISBN: 9789353459437

Typeset in Adobe Caslon Pro by R. Ajith Kumar, Noida

Printed at Thomson Press India Ltd

I started not alone, but with the values of my family – my wife, children and parents – who keep me grounded, steady and moving forward. And along the way, many, many people joined me in this journey.

To Renu – my partner in every sense, whose love and quiet strength have carried me through every turn.

To our children – Surbhi and Ankur – who keep encouraging, questioning and gently pushing me to write, reflect and grow.

To my parents – whose silent sacrifices and steadfast values are the foundation of all I am and hope to be.

To every friend, colleague, mentor and fellow traveller – thank you for walking alongside me, in ways big and small.

– AJAY KHANNA

To Vandana, my wall to lean on and constant source of strength and laughter.

My sons, Siddharth and Shantanu, who have lived across several countries, embraced diverse cultures, and have grown into remarkable human beings. Thank you both for always being honest, kind and helpful.

My parents, who taught me to read, think, take risks, live the way I wanted to and, most importantly, laugh at life and get on with it. And to all those who have helped me learn, change, challenge, adjust, re-calibrate, re-invent and enjoy what I do – friends, colleagues, past and present – and well-wishers, both known and unknown.

– RAHUL SHARMA

Contents

Foreword xi
Introduction xvii

The Beginning

1. Public Affairs Landscape: Transformation and Today 3
AJAY KHANNA

2. Playing a Role in Policy: My Experiences 15
NANDAN NILEKANI

Society

3. Why Do We Need Social Policy? 25
SHUBHASHIS GANGOPADHYAY

4. Economic Development through Grassroots Social Change 35
SHASHANK MANI

5. Capacity Building for Policymaking 45
LUIS MIRANDA

6. The Entertainment and Arts Industry 51
SANJOY K. ROY

7. How Indian Philanthropy Needs to Evolve for Higher Return on Investment 65
ASHISH DHAWAN, PRAVEEN KHANGHTA, SWAGATO GANGULY

8. Developed by 2047: Flawed Narratives and Reality 75
LAVEESH BHANDARI

9. The Missing Seat at the Table: Engaging India's Youth in Policymaking – An Imperative for Viksit Bharat 85
APARAJITA BHARTI

Economy

10. Evolution of Policy Paradigms: Transitions and Continuity 97
A.K. BHATTACHARYA

11. It's a Matter of Policy 115
AMITABH KANT

12. A Ringside View of Policymaking: From State and Centre to Global 123
CHANDRAJIT BANERJEE

13. India's Policy Priority: Promoting Private Enterprise 135
RAJIV KUMAR

14. Policy in Transition: Navigating the Past, Present and Future of Public Affairs in India 147
CHETAN KRISHNASWAMY

15. Policy to Boost Trade in the Current Environment 157
T.S. VISHWANATH AND ADHIRAJ GUPTA

16. Reforms in the Financial Market Regulation in India 169
AJAY TYAGI

17. Unlocking India's Economic Potential: Women's Workforce Participation as a Critical Driver of Viksit Bharat 179
POOJA SHARMA GOYAL

Diplomacy

18. A Yogic Foreign Policy for a Fractured World 199
AJAY BISARIA

19. A Journey beyond Borders: The Story of the Indian Diaspora 211
VIJAY CHAUTHAIWALE

20. Towards a Developed Nation 221
NAVDEEP SURI

Future

21. Energy Security for a Viksit Bharat: Analysing the Evolutionary Journey of India's Public Policy 235
HARDEEP S. PURI

22. State-Level Business Reforms in India: Laboratories for Growth 247
RICHARD ROSSOW

23. Digital Swaraj: Accommodating Aspirations for Inclusive Growth 259
ANIL PADMANABHAN

24. How Public Policy and Public Affairs Can Propel India to Developed-Nation Status by 2047 269
SUNIL KANT MUNJAL

25. The Role of Institutions in Promoting Economic Growth 277
T.K. ARUN

Notes 286

Acknowledgements 292

A Note on the Contributors 294

A Note on the Editors 309

Foreword

The Policy Pivot: Inside India's Strategic Shift comes at a critical juncture for India. As the fastest-growing fourth-largest economy, India has achieved multiple seemingly impossible milestones. It now enjoys increasing global recognition, but it still has a long way to go in its quest to become a developed economy; an aspiration that, according to the World Bank, means increasing its per capita income from $2,878 to $20,000. This represents an eightfold increase between now and 2047.

India faces multiple challenges, but similar transformations have been achieved before and can be replicated to the country's advantage. This book comes at a time when new challenges have emerged.

First and foremost, there has been an almost complete destruction of the post-World War economic and social order. The institutions that were created for development are in retreat. The United Nations itself, whether in its ability to forge consensus for orderly transitions, or the international financial architecture, going beyond the multilateral development banks to include international institutions, are equally in disarray.

Second, the broad understanding between major powers in the post-World War era has been overtaken, initially by plurilateral arrangements and now increasingly by bilateral and transactional relationships – a form of mercantilism we have not witnessed in a long time.

The reform of the international financial architecture has eluded consensus. Much was expected from the recent 4th United Nations Conference on Financing for Development, held in Seville, Spain, this year. However, apart from reiterating old commitments by way of platitudes, there were no tangible outcomes.

On the reforms of the multilateral development banks, aimed at making them more purposive as well as better, bolder and bigger, progress has been halted. Thirty important recommendations were approved by the G20 in a broad-ranging report submitted by Lawrence Summers and myself, on behalf of the Independent Expert Group. Action has begun in a halting manner. The most important area where progress remains elusive is the participation of the private sector in enabling more purposeful leveraging of capital.

The United States has become increasingly reluctant to inject additional capital for the recapitalization of the World Bank institutions. As a result, the enhanced financing that was expected is unlikely to materialize. Similarly, the convergence and cohesiveness in the policies of other multilateral development institutions, apart from the World Bank, have fallen far short of the expected financing needs.

Added to this is the existential crisis facing humanity: global warming and climate change. Despite repeated commitments by the Annual Meeting of the Conference of the Parties – now numbering thirty – and based on the recommendations of the UNFCCC, progress has been far from satisfactory. An orderly transition from an era of fossil fuels to renewable sources of energy, including the development of a vibrant carbon market, remains a distant goal. We now look ahead to COP30 in Belém, Brazil, scheduled for later this year. Yet on all these issues, despite the urgency, the necessary political will remains elusive. The United States, having reneged on the Paris Agreement undertaken in 2015 for a second time, has suffered a serious setback. Of course, the world is larger than the commitment of any single country, but commensurate action by others will require more purposive coherence than is currently evident.

There is a sense that the world is turning inward, becoming more protectionist and moving rapidly away from an integrated global value-added chain based on productivity and efficiency, fostered through the migration of capital, technology, freer movement of people and the transition of skills to maximize global good.

These arrangements were originally embedded in the General Agreement on Tariffs and Trade, and later formalized through the charter of the World Trade Organization, endorsed by all participating countries. The recent trend of moving towards individual tariff decisions through bilateral reciprocal arrangements represents a complete perversion of the original objectives of making trade a key engine of growth.

The new proliferation of Free Trade Agreements between major economies does not align with the multilateral framework. Nevertheless, there is hope that this abundance of bilateral trade agreements will, in due course, be integrated into a broader multilateral structure. Until that happens, the use of tariffs and trade agreements as instruments for larger political objectives, coercing nations into accepting terms dictated by major G7 countries, stands in direct opposition to the post-World War vision of economic cooperation.

After all, the philosophy of international cooperation is not compatible with the principle that might is right. Tariffs cannot be legitimized as tools for advancing unrelated political or strategic goals. This concern extends beyond current US policies. In fact, under earlier regimes, the weaponization of reserve currencies and banking arrangements for collateral purposes was inconceivable. Even during broader global conflicts, currency and financial channels were not manipulated as instruments to enforce ideological or geopolitical objectives.

This book, in more senses than one, encapsulates these far-reaching changes in multiple ways. The Public Affairs Forum of India (PAFI) has made a valuable contribution in bringing out this policy pivot through 25 essays by domain experts engaged in shaping public policy in its multiple facets. It will enhance awareness and shape the quality of public discourse.

This is entirely consistent with the priorities of the PAFI, set up in 2008 with the broad objective of creating a robust platform for public affairs professionals to engage in dialogue, promote transparency and contribute to policy formulation through constructive advocacy and stakeholder engagement.

One important overarching factor for the future of policymaking is the ethical use of artificial intelligence (AI). While AI substantially enhances human productivity, it also raises serious moral and ethical concerns. The fear that the advancement of super intelligence may replace human intelligence and decision-making, regenerating and recreating itself through autonomous processes beyond human oversight, would usher in a dangerous world.

In a somewhat sceptical vein, it is now being argued that while there is no escaping the fact that AI will perform multiple functions currently carried out by human societies, perhaps only wisdom and emotions will remain outside the scope of its rapidly evolving reach.

The consequences for the orderly functioning of human society and the emergence of alternative gainful occupations remain challenging. Harmonizing the productivity gains from AI with ethical imperatives and aligning them with the creative potential of human beings is an emerging challenge for which there are no obvious answers.

The world, therefore, is in a state of flux, and this book touches on many of these complex dynamics, where the last word is far from being said. These essays, however, serve as valuable pointers across multiple domains – human society, the evolving global economy, intricate diplomacy and an uncertain future – and are designed to rekindle fresh thinking.

The essays significantly enhance our understanding of the far-reaching contemporary economic changes, the dynamics of these shifts and the challenges involved in realizing India's vision for 2047.

This book will help shape public discourse and is an inescapable read for those interested in India's past and present opportunities, its challenges and a glimpse into its future.

N.K. Singh
September 2025
New Delhi

Introduction

It was a quiet yet defining moment. At one of the early annual meetings of the Public Affairs Forum of India (PAFI), in a packed room of policy professionals, industry leaders and bureaucrats, a senior minister from Prime Minister Narendra Modi's first cabinet stood up to speak. 'We're open to feedback,' he said. 'We're listening. But only if two conditions are met – your ideas must serve the public good, and they must not drain the exchequer.'

There was a pause. The room absorbed the weight of what was said – and, perhaps more significantly, what was unsaid. It was a signal. A door had opened. After years of policy inertia and silos, the government was inviting engagement – but on terms that prioritized national interest and fiscal prudence. It was no longer about lobbying behind closed doors. It was about earning trust through facts, fairness and foresight.

That moment encapsulated the pivot this book seeks to explore.

The Winds of Change

Not too long ago, public policy in India felt like a black box – opaque, slow-moving, often disconnected from those it claimed to serve. The term 'policy paralysis' wasn't just a media headline – it was a lived experience for many. Entrepreneurs struggled to launch, innovators were stifled by red tape and citizens were often the last to be heard.

Then something shifted.

What followed wasn't always loud or dramatic. It was, more often, the quiet recalibration of how change really happens in India. A startup founder lobbying for digital payment reforms didn't stage protests – she spent months presenting data to NITI Aayog, refining her pitch with feedback from the Reserve Bank of India (RBI) officials and bringing civil society allies on board. Today, her early efforts echo in every UPI transaction across the country.

A seasoned public affairs professional recalled the day they walked into a ministry with not just a complaint – but a coalition. 'We've brought five competitors together,' they told the joint secretary. 'We're not asking for favours. We're asking for clarity.' That clarity eventually became policy. Not because it was easy – but because it was rooted in shared interest and structured dialogue.

There are countless such stories – of persistence, of principle, of people working across boundaries to nudge the system forward. A health NGO that helped reframe rural vaccination as a digital challenge, not just a medical one. A logistics executive who, during the pandemic, worked 20-hour days to align truck routes with changing state border rules – so essential supplies could keep moving.

None of these stories made headlines. But they moved the needle.

What This Book Hopes to Capture

Public policy in India is not linear. It's a monsoon river – full of energy, sometimes messy, but capable of carving new landscapes when guided well. It's also deeply human – shaped by relationships, values and the ability to listen.

This book is both a celebration and an exploration of that dynamic space. It marks 18 years of the PAFI's journey – not just as an organization, but as a movement committed to ethical advocacy, institutional trust and collaborative reform.

This book brings together 25 essays by practitioners who have lived these realities – policymakers, diplomats, public affairs professionals, economists, entrepreneurs, philanthropists and thinkers. Their voices are diverse, but their goal is shared: to reflect on how India's policymaking has changed, why it matters and where we go from here.

Why Now?

India stands at a rare crossroads. With the world's largest youth population, rapid digital transformation and an expanding global footprint, the country has a unique opportunity – not just to grow, but to lead with purpose. But that promise will remain unfulfilled unless we reimagine how policies are shaped: smarter regulation, deeper collaboration, stronger institutions and more responsive governance.

This book arrives at a time when the need for such reimagination is urgent. Policymaking today unfolds at lightning speed – on Twitter threads, in Cabinet meetings, through parliamentary debates and Zoom consultations with think tanks. Citizens are more informed. Industry is more vocal. The state is more visible.

In this ecosystem, the role of public affairs professionals has evolved dramatically. They are no longer mere interpreters of regulation – they are navigators of complexity, translators of trust and architects of consensus.

Yet their work often goes unacknowledged. This book seeks to make that labour visible.

The Shape of the Book

The volume is organized into five thematic sections:

- Foundations of Public Affairs – How it all began: tracing the origins and evolution of public affairs in India.
- Social and Economic Policy – Essays on education, healthcare, philanthropy, startups and skilling.
- Geoeconomics and Foreign Policy – Perspectives on India's Free Trade Agreement strategies, global alliances, diaspora diplomacy and more.
- Institutions and Governance – Reflections on administrative reform, regulatory frameworks and state capacity.
- The Road to 2047 – Bold ideas for India's future: from artificial intelligence (AI) and sustainability to inclusive development.

These are not academic treatises. They are grounded reflections, shaped by hard-won experience and animated by lived conviction. They offer not just insights – but blueprints.

Trust, Collaboration and the Next Frontier of Reform

One of the clearest lessons from India's recent policy evolution is that sustainable reform depends on building trust – across government, business, civil society and citizens. That trust is not transactional; it is earned through transparency, predictability, humility and shared responsibility.

The policymaking process must become more open, consultative and pragmatic. Today's challenges – from employment generation and urbanization to climate resilience and data governance – cannot be solved by any one actor alone. Governments need the innovation of startups, the reach of corporates, the credibility of civil society and the lived insights of citizens. When diverse stakeholders are engaged early and meaningfully, policies are more robust, inclusive and future-ready.

Crucially, the next generation of reforms must deepen India's federal fabric. Many of the most transformative levers – healthcare, skilling, housing, sustainability, education – lie with states. Empowering states with fiscal tools, technical capacity and policy flexibility is no longer optional – it is essential. Competitive federalism should now evolve into collaborative federalism, where innovation is encouraged, successes are scaled and the whole becomes greater than the sum of its parts.

The future of policymaking in India will rest not just on ideas, but on the ability to build consensus, cultivate mutual respect and work across boundaries.

Looking Ahead

India's journey to 2047 – the centenary of its Independence – will be defined by the choices we make now. Will our cities become engines of inclusion or islands of inequality? Will digital governance bridge divides or deepen them? Will our institutions inspire trust or merely compliance?

Answering these questions will require courage. But also collaboration. And, above all, commitment.

It will also require a renewed focus on economic development as the foundation of national strength. India must continue to unlock productivity, generate quality jobs and expand opportunity across sectors and states. This demands bold deregulation, the removal of outdated laws and bureaucratic friction and the creation of policy environments that reward innovation, efficiency and enterprise.

Equally critical is a ruthless approach to corruption. In an age of global transparency and real-time perception, even isolated lapses can undermine investor confidence and citizen trust. Integrity must be built into systems – not left to individual discretion. Accountability, auditability and the rule of law must be non-negotiable.

As the world transitions into a new economic era – defined by digitalization, green growth, resilient supply chains and AI-driven productivity – India must position itself as a smart economy: open, nimble and future-ready. Infrastructure must be intelligent, regulations agile and institutions adaptive. We are not just competing with legacy systems – we are competing with nations. And in that race, capital goes where it is welcomed, talent goes where it is respected and innovation goes where it is enabled.

Just as we welcome global capital and celebrate foreign investment, we must also value and respect India's own wealth creators. Entrepreneurs, industrialists and family businesses – many of whom have grown in the face of extraordinary challenges – deserve not only policy support but public legitimacy. Domestic investment must be celebrated as much as the FDI. We must offer the same red carpet to Indian investors as we do to those from abroad.

If India is to rise as an economic leader, it must ensure that its own industrialists, innovators and job creators feel invested in its future – not just through capital, but through commitment. Retaining them – encouraging them to build, scale and give back within India – will be just as important as attracting the next global unicorn.

The Policy Pivot is not just a book. It is an invitation – to think deeper, act smarter and engage better. To move from noise to nuance. From short-term lobbying to long-term nation-building.

And to recognize that public affairs, when done right, is not about power – it is about purpose.

The evolution of public affairs from its narrow origins in informal lobbying to its present role as a strategic, ethical and multistakeholder function central to governance and policymaking defines the present. **Ajay Khanna** outlines how global developments, ranging from post-World War II institutionalization of civil society to the rise of globalization, technological advances and growing demands for transparency, have redefined public affairs as a discipline grounded in dialogue, evidence and accountability. In the Indian context, the transition from the opaque 'license raj' era to a liberalized, participatory governance model underscores this shift, with public affairs maturing into a forward-looking function driving national reform agendas, building coalitions and aligning public and private priorities.

The chapter emphasizes that public affairs now require deep domain knowledge, data-driven advocacy and the ability to foster institutional trust across government, industry and civil society. It explores how the COVID-19 pandemic catalysed this transformation further, positioning public affairs as a central pillar of crisis response and collaboration. The rise of younger professionals adept at digital tools, and the need for cross-sectoral partnerships all point to a new era where public affairs play a vital role in shaping inclusive, sustainable and democratic policy outcomes. As the lines between business and policy blur, public affairs professionals are called to act not just as advocates, but as bridge-builders and strategic advisers guiding the future of governance.

In this reflective essay, derived from his PAFI Annual Lecture, **Nandan Nilekani** shares his decades-long experience in shaping public policy across sectors such as technology, urban development, identity infrastructure and digital payments. He emphasizes that good policy is long-term in nature, driven by public interest and requires collaboration across stakeholders. Drawing from his involvement with initiatives like the software industry's early growth through NASSCOM, the Bangalore Agenda Task Force and Aadhaar, Nilekani explains how thoughtful advocacy, coalition building and bipartisan support are essential for policy success. He views policy as a tool to generate large-scale positive impact by creating jobs, improving governance and addressing systemic inefficiencies.

Nilekani also explores how major events often act as catalysts for reform. He illustrates this through examples like the launch of FASTag following early work on RFID-based tolling, the rise of digital payments after demonetization and the COVID-19 pandemic and direct benefit transfers born out of a tragedy involving subsidy-related violence. The chapter underscores that effective policymaking requires vision, patience and readiness to act when windows of opportunity open. Nilekani concludes by stressing the importance of broad-based coalitions, public trust and a clear articulation of national benefit as the foundation for impactful and enduring policy change.

Shubhashis Gangopadhyay presents a compelling argument for the necessity of robust and inclusive social policy as the foundation of a good society. Using education and healthcare as central examples, he challenges the notion that economic growth must precede social development. Drawing from international experiences, such as Finland, Sweden and South Korea, he demonstrates that nations often become prosperous *because* they first invested in universal education and healthcare, not the other way around. He distinguishes between 'rights' and 'policies', arguing that while rights like the Right to Education establish intent, effective policies focus on measurable outcomes. A well-designed policy, he notes, must consider not just inputs and outputs but also the social context, behavioural incentives and long-term impacts on communities.

The chapter also introduces the economic concept of externalities to explain why individual choices in areas like health and education often fall short of optimal social outcomes. Positive externalities from education and healthcare justify government intervention to correct market failures and ensure collective welfare. Gangopadhyay calls for a shift toward universalism in social provisioning, where quality education, healthcare, sanitation and security are seen not as services for the poor, but as essential rights for all citizens. Human capital, built through inclusive social policy, is the true driver of a nation's prosperity and cohesion.

A vision for India's journey towards becoming *Viksit Bharat* by 2047, rooted in citizen-led development and grassroots enterprise, is what **Shashank Mani** argues for in his essay. He argues that true economic transformation must be inclusive, sustainable and culturally resonant, one that reflects India's civilizational values while embracing innovation. Rather than relying solely on top-down models or metropolitan growth, the chapter emphasizes empowering India's 'Middle of the Diamond', 800 million citizens in Tier 2 and Tier 3 districts, as the real engine of progress. This emerging middle class, filled with aspirations and potential, must be supported through decentralization, public participation and context-driven policies that reflect dignity, opportunity and ownership.

Mani advocates for enterprise as the central driver of employment and local prosperity, proposing a three-pronged approach: a national campaign to celebrate entrepreneurship, the creation of local enterprise institutions and systemic realignment of financial and policy structures to support grassroots innovation. Drawing from the success of initiatives like Jagriti Yatra and the Jagriti Enterprise Centre in Deoria, he showcases how sustainable ecosystems of entrepreneurship can spark economic renewal in underserved regions. Framed as the 'Banyan Revolution', this model combines civilizational wisdom with modern tools to offer a globally relevant alternative to extractive development.

Luis Miranda makes a strong case for the urgent need to strengthen policymaking capacity across government, business and civil society. He begins by highlighting the limited exposure to formal public policy education among India's civil servants and the shortage of institutions offering relevant training. Citing initiatives such as the Capacity Building Commission and Mission *Karmayogi*, Miranda underscores the importance of equipping India's 1.5 crore government officials with lifelong learning tools to navigate increasingly complex governance challenges. The chapter also references the Indian School of Public Policy's efforts, including its report on administrative reforms and courses developed for platforms like iGOT, as key steps in addressing structural and competency gaps within the system.

Miranda then turns to the private and social sectors, arguing that an understanding of public policy is equally essential for business leaders and nonprofit practitioners. As companies interact more frequently with the government in roles ranging from regulator to partner, public affairs professionals become critical connectors. He emphasizes the need for greater cross-sectoral mobility to facilitate knowledge transfer, urging corporates, governments and non-profits to recruit talent from each other. This exchange of skills and perspectives, he suggests, will foster a more collaborative and capable policy ecosystem that can respond to India's development needs more effectively.

The transformative potential of India's creative sector as a powerful engine for economic growth, cultural identity and social cohesion is what **Sanjoy Roy** focuses on. He outlines the sector's growing impact, with digital media and live entertainment showing double-digit growth and contributing significantly to job creation and GDP. Roy emphasizes the breadth of the creative economy, encompassing everything from traditional artisans and performers to tech-enabled artists and experience-based industries. Despite being governed by 21 ministries, the sector suffers from policy fragmentation and a lack of structured support. He calls for comprehensive mapping of the creative workforce and a more coordinated policy effort to harness its potential, including through public–private partnerships, infrastructure development, tourism integration and arts-based education.

Roy also explores how culture, technology and inclusive policy can transform communities and boost innovation. Citing examples like the economic impact of Durga Puja in Bengal and cultural districts in cities worldwide, he illustrates how festivals, heritage sites and creative hubs can stimulate local economies. He advocates for a 360-degree policy approach that includes fiscal incentives, investment in education and digital infrastructure and national coordination across ministries while highlighting the need for safeguarding creators, enabling access to technology and developing research-backed digital strategies to expand the cultural ecosystem.

Ashish Dhawan, Praveen Khanghta and **Swagato Ganguly**, explore how Indian philanthropy can become a more powerful force for systemic change. They outline the limitations of current philanthropic efforts, especially the dominance of short-term, fragmented or community-oriented giving. The authors argue for a shift toward patient, flexible capital that can fund ambitious, long-term solutions to India's development challenges. They highlight how partnerships with government – given its scale and mandate – are essential for interventions to achieve population-level impact. They make a case for a 'systems change' approach, which involves seeding innovative models, piloting scalable programs and strengthening institutions that can work in sync with public systems.

Central to this vision is the work of The Convergence Foundation (TCF), whose three-pillar approach focuses on accelerating economic growth, enhancing human capital and advancing development enablers. The authors draw on examples from TCF network, such as support for foundational literacy and partnerships with state governments, to illustrate how philanthropy can achieve exponential returns. The Convergence Foundation's belief in building high-quality institutions echoes the legacy of the Tata philanthropic model, which helped shape modern India.

Economist **Laveesh Bhandari** presents a sharp critique of the idea that India cannot achieve developed nation status by 2047. He acknowledges the serious challenges India faces, including low investment levels, inflexible policymaking and inefficiencies in the judicial system. However, he argues that these are not insurmountable. The greater barrier, in his view, is the widespread acceptance of limiting narratives that have shaped public policy and diminished national confidence. Ideas such as the poverty trap, the Hindu rate of growth and the middle-income trap have created an undue reliance on government intervention and a belief that progress must come through global validation rather than internal capability.

Bhandari calls for a shift in mindset that recognizes the momentum already building in India's digital services, global capability centres and labour exports. These areas have expanded with minimal government interference and demonstrate the ability of market forces to overcome institutional constraints. He draws on India's success in the IT and service sectors to make the case that growth can be driven by entrepreneurship, innovation and a strong private sector. While long-term systemic reforms are still needed, he argues that India's development trajectory should be shaped by its own strengths rather than constrained by outdated or externally imposed narratives.

How can India's youth be included in the country's policy debates and changes, asks **Aparajita Bharti**. She uses the Digital Personal Data Protection Act to illustrate how crucial legislation affecting consent and privacy was shaped with little input from the youth. Bharti argues that policies on education, reproductive treatments and marriage rights deeply affect young lives, yet existing consultation mechanisms fail to capture the diversity and scale of India's youth. This marginalization not only silences fresh ideas but also traps policymakers in outdated paradigms.

To fix this anomaly, Bharti calls for mandatory prelegislative consultations that include youth voices, expanded fellowships and internships in government, and the establishment of dedicated youth advisory councils. She urges the adoption of digital engagement tools and robust data systems to track evolving youth needs. By institutionalizing these measures and encouraging intergenerational dialogue, India can unlock its young cohort's potential and accelerate progress towards becoming a developed nation by 2047.

A.K. Bhattacharya offers a detailed examination of the shifts in India's economic policy since Independence, illustrating how political leadership, crises and global developments have influenced policymaking over the decades. It begins by critiquing the early statist model championed by Nehru and Indira Gandhi, which prioritized state control and import substitution, but yielded limited growth. The liberalization era, beginning in the 1980s and accelerating with the 1991 reforms under P.V. Narasimha Rao and Manmohan Singh, marked a decisive turn towards market-oriented policies. Subsequent administrations, including those led by Atal Bihari Vajpayee, Manmohan Singh and Narendra Modi, maintained a reformist momentum with varying emphasis, from rights-based entitlements to regulatory, fiscal and digital infrastructure reforms.

The chapter also addresses missed opportunities and the rollback of reforms in key areas such as land acquisition, labour laws and agriculture due to political resistance. It argues that sustainable growth requires not only bold policymaking but also an enabling political economy that fosters open dialogue, regulatory independence and administrative capacity. Highlighting India's demographic potential and current structural challenges, the author calls for a renewed focus on exports, manufacturing, vocational training and private investment. The central message is clear –

consistent, inclusive and forward-looking policy reforms remain vital to unlocking India's economic future.

It is extremely important to underscore the pivotal role of visionary policy in driving India's transformation, and **Amitabh Kant** does this well. He opens with India's landmark initiatives under Prime Minister Modi – Startup India, Make in India and Digital India – which have generated jobs and boosted transparency. Ambitious climate strategies such as the Green Hydrogen Mission and National Solar Mission further reinforce India's leadership in sustainable energy. Drawing on his decades in the Indian Administrative Service, Kant illustrates how targeted interventions in Kerala from beach-level auctions for fisherfolk to community-funded airport expansion, exemplify the power of participatory governance to deliver inclusive growth.

Reflecting on his tenure at the Ministry of Tourism, DIPP and as CEO of NITI Aayog, Kant traces the evolution of flagship programmes like Incredible India, Ease of Doing Business, the Production Linked Incentive scheme and the Aspirational Districts Programme. He highlights the importance of evidence-based design, public–private partnerships and data-driven monitoring in achieving rapid results. As G20 Sherpa, he demonstrates how skilful consensus building on the global stage can advance the Global South's interests. Kant concludes with an exhortation to India's youth: public policy offers an unparalleled avenue to create lasting impact by listening to citizens, fostering innovation and planning decades ahead.

The role of industry bodies that build strong and effective coalitions to influence policy change cannot never be overlooked.

Chandrajit Banerjee outlines CII's journey since 1895, from colonial advocacy to a pivotal policy stakeholder. He highlights CII's bottom-up model, based on industry councils and data-driven research, that influenced liberalization in 1991 and subsequent initiatives such as the National Manufacturing Policy, Make in India, Startup India and the Production Linked Incentive scheme.

He then examines CII's interventions in manufacturing policy, ease of doing business, decriminalization of business laws, state-level advocacy during COVID-19 and global engagement through trade delegations and the India–US Initiative on Critical and Emerging Technologies. Banerjee distils the CII playbook of consistent government engagement, representative policy inputs, supported by research and non-partisan partnership. He concludes that credible, inclusive and participatory policy making remains vital to realizing India's development goals.

Rajiv Kumar celebrates India's post-liberalization ascent from USD 1.98 trillion in 2014 to USD 3.9 trillion in 2024, noting the fall in multidimensional poverty from 29.17 per cent in 2013–14 to 11.28 per cent in 2022–23 and a reduction in absolute poverty (under USD 3.65 per day) from 61.8 per cent in 2011–12 to 28.1 per cent in 2022–23. He credits the JAM (JanDhan, Aadhaar, Mobile) trinity with extending over 323 direct benefit schemes and saving ₹3.48 lakh crore in leakages. Kumar also underlines the expansion of highways, railways, airports and power infrastructure as vital to job creation and productivity gains.

Looking ahead, Kumar asserts that sustaining above 8 per cent growth is essential to avoid the middleincome trap before the demographic dividend wanes. He argues for a governance overhaul that transforms regulators into enterprise promoters and sketches four corporate adaptations to heavy regulation: full compliance, evasion, association-based lobbying and privileged access. He warns that failure to reform will drive talent offshore and urges PAFI and think tanks to forge coalitions offering innovative, complementary policies for climate, agriculture and industry built on trust and accountability.

The key to finding solutions is to know what and who went ahead. Past, therefore, is as important as the present. **Chetan Krishnaswamy** describes how India's policymaking moved from opaque, connections-based processes to an open, expertise-driven model. Drawing on three decades at the intersection of journalism, technology firms and government, he shows how liberalization and digital adoption led to routine publication of draft regulations, widespread consultations and the creation of regulatory sandboxes. The emergence of Digital Public Infrastructure (Aadhaar, UPI and DigiLocker) exemplifies a mobile-first leap that delivered services at scale.

Looking forward, Krishnaswamy argues that effective policy will combine technological tools (such as AI sentiment analysis and data analytics) with human judgement to build trust and manage complex stakeholder relationships. He highlights the rise of specialist policy teams in corporate boardrooms and the deepening of public–private partnerships evident in platforms like CoWIN. He concludes that tackling emerging challenges will demand foresight, empathy and genuine multistakeholder collaboration.

T.S. Vishwanath and **Adhiraj Gupta** describe today's paradox of deep global interconnection alongside rising protectionism. They note India's record export performance of USD 825 billion in

FY 2024–25 and argue that sustaining this momentum requires deft navigation of fragmented supply chains, new nontariff standards and a weakened multilateral system. The authors outline key policy responses such as the Foreign Trade Policy 2023–28's shift to remission-based incentives, digitization of clearances, district export hubs and proactive Free Trade Agreements with partners including the UAE, Australia and the UK. These measures aim to streamline processes and diversify markets.

Their chapter then assesses India's competitive levers in services, manufacturing and green technology, while acknowledging constraints in logistics, MSME integration, quality standards and workforce skills. The authors propose a strategic roadmap to 2047 that accelerates digital trade, focuses on niche global value chain segments, aligns trade accords with security objectives and embeds resilience, inclusivity and ESG into planning. They conclude that, with well-targeted reforms and strategic partnerships, India can turn current headwinds into an opportunity window for Viksit Bharat by its centenary.

Robust, independent regulation is essential for a healthy financial sector, argues **Ajay Tyagi**. He highlights the need for financial regulators to enjoy budgetary autonomy, clear statutory mandates and arm's length relationships with government. Tyagi examines conflicts within the Reserve Bank of India, which combines monetary policy, debt management and market infrastructure ownership and the central bank's dual role as operator and regulator of the UPI-led payment system. He also critiques overlapping oversight in public-sector banks and calls for greater clarity in roles and conversion of statutory banks into companies under the Companies Act.

To strengthen governance, Tyagi recommends a transparent selection process via a specialist appointments committee, with mixed government and private sector expertise bound by a reinforced code of conduct. He outlines a due process model for drafting subordinate regulations through public consultation and board approval. Finally, he urges direct parliamentary oversight by the Finance Committee, with biannual reviews, actiontaken reporting and eventual sanctioning of regulator appointments to ensure accountability.

Pooja Sharma Goyal brings to light the paradox of India's rapid social progress alongside persistently low female workforce participation. Despite improvements in girls' education, maternal health and a rise in the female labour force participation rate (FLFPR) from 27 per cent in 2022 to 41.3 per cent in 2024, only 18 per cent of women now engage in the formal economy. Goyal argues that closing this gap is vital to realizing India's demographic dividend and achieving its desire to be a developed nation by 2047. She notes key public commitments, including gender-tagged budget allocations of 8.9 per cent, the G20 emphasis on women-led development and a goal of 70 per cent FLFPR by 2047, as foundations for change.

Drawing lessons from South and Southeast Asia, she outlines three policy pillars: integrating gender into governance and planning, supporting childcare and return-to-work transitions, and incentivizing employers to recruit and retain women. Goyal calls for a systems level approach combining inclusive job and workspace design with gender-smart infrastructure and catalytic policy measures such as targeted subsidies and mandatory workforce data. She concludes that only a coordinated, data-driven partnership of government, industry and civil society can unlock the full potential of India's women and power sustainable growth.

The post–Cold War order has shifted from a brief unipolar moment to a fragile multipolarity disrupted by geopolitical rivalry, economic coercion and nontraditional threats such as pandemics and climate change, writes **Ajay Bisaria**. He argues that old hierarchies have eroded without a stable new equilibrium emerging. India has responded with pragmatic resilience and strategic autonomy, balancing partnerships with the West, Russia and regional neighbours while managing tensions with China and Pakistan.

Bisaria proposes a yogic foreign policy that is calm yet agile, enabling India to navigate complexity with foresight. He highlights India's multialigned posture through platforms like the Quad, G20 presidency, Vaccine Maitri and digital diplomacy. As a bridging power, India must shape global norms in trade, climate and technology rather than simply follow them. By combining composure, flexibility and principled engagement, India can not only survive but influence the evolving world order leading up to its centenary in 2047.

From the trading caravans of the sixteenth century to today's Silicon Valley leaders, **Dr Vijay Chauthaiwale** traces how Indians first ventured to Central Asia, the Caucasus and beyond, and how indentured Girmityas endured hardship to lay the roots of diaspora communities in Mauritius, Fiji and the Caribbean. Post-Independence, thousands more emigrated as students, professionals and entrepreneurs, forging influential diasporas across North America, Europe, the Middle East and Southeast Asia.

The chapter then examines India's evolving diaspora diplomacy under Prime Minister Narendra Modi – landmark gatherings such as Howdy Modi, the lifesaving Vande Bharat Mission and Vaccine Maitri, and enhanced programmes like the Pravasi Bharatiya

Samman and Know India Programme. Chauthaiwale shows how overseas Indians now drive remittances, investments and soft power, serving as vital partners in nation building. He concludes that by 2047 the global Indian family will remain an essential force in realizing the vision of *Viksit Bharat*.

Navdeep Suri opens by recalling India's centuries-old maritime and commercial links with the Gulf, noting how post-Independence neglect gave way to a strategic reset when Prime Minister Modi's visit to Abu Dhabi in August 2015 rekindled relations. He describes the swift personal rapport with Sheikh Mohamed bin Zayed and three subsequent visits that cemented a Comprehensive Strategic Partnership. Politically, the UAE's invitation of India to the OIC foreign ministers' meeting and its early support for India's decisions on Kashmir demonstrate a profound shift in regional dynamics.

Turning to economic and strategic dimensions, Suri highlights the UAE's commitment to invest up to USD 75 billion, sovereign fund anchors in India's infrastructure, the 2022 CEPA zero tariff agreement and the pioneering India–UAE Virtual Trade Corridor. He also examines India's energy ties via Lower Zakum stakes and strategic reserves, the launch of IIT Delhi's Abu Dhabi campus, deepening intelligence and maritime cooperation, and the integration of RuPay UPI payments. He concludes with caveats on state-level policy misalignments, legacy legal inflexibilities and communal tensions that risk undermining this dynamic template for Viksit Bharat.

Minister Hardeep Puri traces the development of India's public policy from Independence to its current trajectory, arguing that effective policy choices have enabled national progress despite resource constraints and external scepticisms. He examines the arc from early idealism and Nehruvian socialism, through the stagnation of the licence raj, to the liberalization triggered by the 1991 crisis, crediting Prime Minister Narendra Modi's tenure with decisively shifting Indian governance toward data-driven, digitally enabled, citizen-centric frameworks.

A central focus is India's evolving energy policy. The author details the transition from biomass reliance to oil import dependence and recent efforts to secure domestic exploration, expand refining and diversify suppliers. Energy security is framed not only as an economic imperative but as a geopolitical and strategic necessity. The essay outlines reforms in renewable energy, ethanol blending, hydrogen and critical minerals, emphasizing balance and pragmatism over ideology.

Minister Puri underscores the complexity of policymaking in an unpredictable global order, urging continued boldness, institutional resilience and investment in human capital. He presents India's policy evolution as adaptive rather than perfect, but fundamentally successful in steering the country toward becoming a leading global power.

India's economic trajectory is increasingly influenced by reform efforts at the state level, argues **Richard Rossow**. While the central government provides direction, states wield control over crucial levers such as land, electricity and labour regulations. This results in a diverse investment environment, where regions like Tamil Nadu, Gujarat and Maharashtra have become manufacturing hubs, while others lead in agriculture or services.

The chapter highlights how progressive states are enacting policy innovations to attract investment in emerging sectors such as semiconductors, drones and data centres. However, frequent political turnover can disrupt policy continuity, diminishing investor confidence. Rossow also draws attention to cities as the next frontier for economic reforms, noting that despite contributing a large share of GDP, urban centres lack adequate autonomy and fiscal power. He concludes that India's economic future will depend on empowering sub-national governments, building institutional stability and tailoring engagement strategies to local contexts. For investors and policymakers alike, understanding the reform momentum in state capitals such as Gandhinagar, Lucknow and Hyderabad is now more important than ever.

Anil Padmanabhan examines how India's homegrown Digital Public Infrastructure (DPI) has reshaped inclusion and growth. Padmanabhan opens with the striking rise of UPI from 29,000 transactions in November 2016 to 18.6 billion in May 2025 – highlighting its reach into low-value payments and its impact on financial inclusion. He details how Aadhaar, JanDhan accounts and mobile integration (JAM) have democratized access to banking and benefits for over half a billion previously unbanked citizens.

Padmanabhan then explores the broader DPI ecosystem including Aadhaar, DigiLocker, CoWIN and the upcoming Universal Lending Interface – showing how open protocols drive interoperability, transparency and scale. He notes the global endorsement via the 2024 G20 declaration and illustrates how these digital building blocks enable targeted direct benefit transfers, reduce corruption and pave the way for easier credit to underserved Micro, Small and Medium Enterprises (MSMEs). This chapter synopsis underscores how India's digital revolution not only lifted millions out of poverty but is also reshaping political engagement and economic aspirations.

Sunil Kant Munjal opens with India's remarkable transformation since 1991 when its GDP was under USD 300 billion, noting that today UPI processes a similar value each month. Munjal highlights that India now has more internet users than Europe, e-KYC costs have fallen from ₹100 to ₹5, and the Direct Benefit Transfer system saved about USD 42 billion in 2024 by removing leakages. He celebrates infrastructure gains such as expressways halving travel times and freight corridors reducing logistics bills by 10 to 15 per cent while setting the goal of developed nation status by 15 August 2047 with quadrupled per capita income and gender-balanced workforce participation.

The author argues that achieving this vision requires public policy and public affairs to work in concert, embedding empathy in lawmaking so remote farmers benefit from frictionless trade portals and underprivileged children gain quality education. Munjal calls for smarter regulation, sustained R&D investment and robust citizen engagement to ensure accountability. He likens policy to scaffolding and public affairs to the mortar that cements progress, emphasizing the need for transparent dialogue, dynamic feedback mechanisms and seamless governance platforms to realize India's Viksit Bharat ambition.

The role of institutions is critical in promoting economic growth, and **T.K. Arun** examines how the quality of institutions fundamentally shapes a nation's economic trajectory. Drawing on the work of Nobel laureates Acemoglu, Johnson and Robinson, he contrasts prosperity levels in the border town of Nogales, split between Mexico and the United States, to illustrate the power of inclusive versus extractive institutions. He argues that in India, weak enforcement, corruption, judicial delays and social exclusion systematically hinder economic potential.

The chapter critiques exclusionary systems rooted in caste, inequality and poor governance, which inhibit innovation, entrepreneurship and competition. From flawed public education to patronage-based political financing and regulatory opacity, the author presents a landscape where institutional dysfunction stifles growth. He calls for parliamentary accountability of regulators, university-led research reform and greater private investment in research and development. Ultimately, he asserts that societal coherence and political mobilization are critical to achieving institutional transformation that supports inclusive and sustainable growth.

Ajay Khanna and Rahul Sharma

The Beginning

1

Public Affairs Landscape: Transformation and Today

AJAY KHANNA

Public affairs, once narrowly equated with lobbying, has undergone a profound transformation. What began as a focused effort to influence specific legislative outcomes has matured into a strategic, inclusive and multistakeholder discipline. This evolution is a direct reflection of seismic shifts in our global political and economic landscape. We live in an era shaped by dynamic changes in governance models, breathtaking technological innovation, ever-increasing global interdependence and a public demanding more from its institutions – governmental, corporate and civic.

This fundamental redefinition of public affairs responds to a broader societal imperative: a fervent call for accountability, transparency and trust in governance. Simultaneously, it acknowledges the rise of civil society as a powerful force in public discourse, reshaping decision-making and policy formation. For policymakers, understanding this evolution is crucial for effective governance; for the general public, it sheds light on how their voices and concerns navigate the complex machinery of policy. This chapter will trace the journey of public affairs, providing both a historical narrative and an analytical framework for understanding it today.

Tracing the Historical Evolution of Public Affairs: From Influence to Engagement

The roots of modern public affairs can be traced back to the post-World War II era. This pivotal period witnessed the unprecedented institutionalization of civil society. Think tanks and organizations dedicated to research and advocacy proliferated, alongside the establishment of multilateral bodies like the United Nations (UN) and numerous non-governmental organizations (NGOs). These entities played a pivotal role in shaping public policy, bringing issues like human rights, labour laws and environmental protection to the forefront of public and political debate. Their principled approach, often direct and focused on moral suasion or direct appeals, significantly impacted the landscape of advocacy.

By the 1970s and 1980s, the advocacy landscape began its journey towards professionalization, particularly within liberal democracies. Governments recognized the growing complexity of societal issues and the increasing demands for public input. These led to the introduction of formal public consultation mechanisms. This marked a crucial step, embedding civic participation within policy frameworks and moving beyond informal lobbying to structured dialogues. Consider, for instance, the emergence of formal legislative committees holding public hearings or government departments creating designated channels for receiving feedback from various stakeholders. These nascent mechanisms signified a clear shift towards acknowledging external input as a legitimate part of policymaking.

The advent of globalization in the 1990s and 2000s dramatically expanded the scope of advocacy. Local initiatives became increasingly linked with transnational movements. Issues such as climate change, trade liberalization and international migration demanded sophisticated global advocacy networks. At the same time, multinational corporations, facing complex international regulations and diverse public opinions, systematically institutionalized public affairs departments. These departments were no longer just about crisis management or regulatory compliance. They became strategic hubs designed to navigate and influence intricate global regulatory landscapes.

India, a nation of immense diversity and complexity, mirrored this global trend with its own profound paradigm shift. For decades following Independence, India operated under the rigid, state-controlled 'license raj' era. Policymaking was largely a technocratic, top-down function, with the state holding tight reins over economic and social life. Lobbying, though always present, was often informal, opaque and driven by personal connections rather than public discourse. However, with the economic liberalization of the 1990s, India's governance embraced stakeholder engagement, setting the stage for a new era of public policy where the lines between government, industry and civil society began to blur.

Over the past three decades, India's industry underwent a transformative shift from a command economy to a market-driven one. This transformation coincided with the exponential growth of the advocacy landscape. Powerful industry bodies, a burgeoning ecosystem of NGOs, influential research institutions and newly formed think tanks emerged as influential players, actively shaping national policy agendas. Initially, policy advocacy in India was reactive, responding to proposed legislation or addressing immediate concerns. However, it has matured significantly into a proactive, forward-looking discipline. Today, tools such as meticulously crafted long-term policy roadmaps, detailed stakeholder mapping, strategic coalition building and rigorously evidence-based policy briefs have become standard instruments in the advocacy toolkit, reflecting a sophisticated approach to shaping India's future.

Understanding Policy Advocacy: A Multidimensional Discipline

At its core, policy advocacy is a multifaceted discipline that operates across interrelated dimensions. It is far more than simply asking the government to do something; it is a strategic endeavour to influence the public agenda. This dimension involves bringing pressing societal issues to the forefront, thereby advocating for governmental action. It's about raising awareness, building consensus and demonstrating the urgency and importance of a particular challenge. Consider a campaign to raise awareness about mental health, initially focused on individual well-being, but gradually demonstrating its broader societal and economic impact. This demonstrates how the campaign can push it onto the legislative agenda for increased funding or policy changes.

Policy advocacy provides a crucial platform for diverse viewpoints, giving voice to various stakeholders in the public discourse. This includes businesses, environmental groups, labour unions, social justice organizations and citizen collectives. It ensures that policymaking is informed by the broad spectrum of society's needs and concerns, rather than being confined to a select few. For instance, an industry association might advocate for specific tax incentives not just for corporate gain, but by demonstrating how those incentives foster job creation and technological innovation, aligning with national economic goals.

Strategic advocacy involves the methodical application of evidence and targeted interventions to shape policymaking. It moves beyond mere persuasion to intelligent design, leveraging data, research and analytical rigour. Strategic advocates understand the political landscape, identify key decision-makers and craft messages that resonate with their priorities. A research institution, for example, might publish a white paper meticulously detailing the economic benefits of a particular renewable energy policy, using robust data to build an irrefutable case for its adoption.

Traditionally, business perspectives were often seen as pitted against environmental or social concerns, creating a zero-sum game where corporate profit was perceived as a societal cost. However, progressive enterprises now increasingly view stakeholder alignment as not just ethical but essential to long-term success.

Modern public affairs, on the other hand, recognizes that influence extends far beyond legislative chambers. It involves actively engaging with private actors, international organizations and civil society groups. This multistakeholder approach acknowledges that policy outcomes are often shaped by a complex interplay of forces, not just government decrees. Consider a global health initiative where an NGO partners with pharmaceutical companies to develop affordable vaccines, while simultaneously lobbying international bodies and national governments for equitable distribution policies.

This paradigm shift between then and now has transformed public affairs, moving beyond lobbying to creating shared value and promoting inclusive growth models where business success directly contributes to societal well-being.

Evolving Public Affairs: The Shifting Dynamics

Public affairs has evolved from a mere lobbying function to a high-level strategic function that integrates stakeholder collaboration, proactive public trust-building and a clear articulation of corporate purpose. It now emphasizes influencing policy through knowledge, dialogue and ethical engagement to promote equity and inclusive development.

Public affairs now touches almost every domain of an organization's interaction with the public sphere, including internal and external communications, robust NGO engagement, sophisticated risk and reputation management, nuanced political analysis and intricate regulatory strategy. Governments have also evolved, institutionalizing stakeholder consultations and often mandating public disclosure and impact assessments for proposed policies. This has rendered policy processes far more transparent, inviting broader participation and scrutiny.

The pandemic has marked a turning point in public affairs, highlighting the need for a more collaborative and ethical approach to addressing societal challenges. The COVID-19 pandemic acted as an unprecedented catalyst, fundamentally reshaping and accelerating shifts in public policy engagement globally. In this crisis, public affairs emerged as a critical, central pillar of response, not an auxiliary function. Professionals coordinated government relations, delivered clear, consistent and empathetic communications to a worried public, mobilized corporate social responsibility (CSR) initiatives on a massive scale and shaped strategic narratives to foster national unity and resilience.

In India, the pandemic presented a unique, unifying moment. For the first time in recent memory, the Indian government, diverse industries and the general public found themselves unified in a truly collaborative policy effort. Siloed approaches, often characteristic of pre-pandemic interactions, gave way to integrated, multisectoral responses. This unprecedented cooperation underscored the immense value of public affairs in orchestrating complex, cross-sector solutions during times of profound national crisis. For instance, industry bodies worked swiftly with the government to scale up oxygen production and pharmaceutical companies collaborated on vaccine distribution logistics, all facilitated by public affairs teams navigating complex regulatory landscapes and fostering trust amid urgency.

Notably, the professionalization of public affairs in India had already gained significant traction even before the pandemic hit. The role had matured significantly, evolving from the traditional 'liaison officer', often perceived as a mere go-between, to strategic advisers who engage on equal footing with policymakers. India's post–license raj reforms systematically dismantled opaque lobbying frameworks, replacing them with institutional mechanisms for transparent, industry-wide consultation. This marked a profound evolution in India's democratic policymaking ethos, where closed-door advocacy increasingly gave way to structured, transparent dialogues based on merit and evidence.

Modern advocacy requires professionals to think far beyond reactive lobbying or crisis management. Their mandate is to frame sectoral concerns within broader public interest narratives, demonstrating how specific industry or organizational goals align with societal well-being. The exponential rise of data analytics and artificial intelligence (AI) has profoundly enhanced the capacity for evidence-driven advocacy, moving beyond intuition to empirically supported arguments. Long-term success now demands a deep combination of domain knowledge, continuous engagement with stakeholders and an intimate understanding of complex policy ecosystems.

Public affairs has evolved from a mere reactive function to a core corporate and governmental capability. Its role is now pivotal in fostering trust between government and industry, advocating for transformative reforms that benefit both the economy and society and aligning national priorities with business strategies. Take, for instance, the ongoing discussions around data privacy and AI regulation. Public affairs teams here don't merely react to proposed laws; they proactively engage, often drawing on global best practices and technological insights to shape sensible, forward-looking policies that protect citizens while promoting innovation.

The expanding scope of public affairs is also evident in the increasingly blurred lines between economic and strategic policy. Geopolitical tensions, intensified technology rivalries and evolving security concerns now directly impact global trade, investment flows and domestic regulatory frameworks. Consequently, public affairs professionals navigate a complex landscape that demands balancing national priorities with international obligations and aligning corporate strategies with critical Environmental, Social and Governance (ESG) and Diversity, Equity and Inclusion (DEI) commitments. This necessitates highly integrated approaches that consider political, economic, social and technological dimensions simultaneously. Public affairs professionals now serve as crucial strategic advisers, interpreting global developments to inform both national policy responses and corporate positioning on the world stage.

Fostering Trust and Institutional Dialogue

In current times, public affairs revolves around fostering trust and building enduring institutional dialogue. Corporate public affairs departments have integrated previously disparate functions – communications, CSR, advocacy and government relations – into cohesive, holistic strategies. Their ultimate goal is to establish durable, trust-based partnerships across government, industry and civil society. This marks a significant cultural shift, transitioning from transactional, often opaque lobbying to relationship-driven, transparent engagement built on shared values and mutual understanding.

Governments, recognizing the expertise of the private sector and civil society, increasingly encourage collaboration in policy design. Regular consultations, open public hearings and the submission of white papers and expert testimonies have become integral to the policymaking process. Today, highly skilled policy professionals participate in these discussions alongside senior bureaucrats and elected officials, marking a departure from older, more hierarchical interaction models. States within federations have also embraced this participatory approach, actively collaborating with policy experts and industry bodies to promote investment, skills development and sustainability, leading to a more collaborative and responsive federal dynamic.

In a knowledge-driven economy, thought leadership has become the foundation of policy influence. Successful public affairs professionals combine deep sectoral expertise with robust research capabilities and compelling storytelling skills. While one-off meetings still hold value, meticulously researched white papers, well-reasoned position notes and analytical reports have increasingly replaced them as primary tools of influence. The ability to articulate complex ideas clearly, backed by evidence, is paramount.

India, for instance, is currently undergoing significant regulatory reform to enhance the ease of doing business. Archaic laws are being streamlined, compliance processes simplified and enforcement mechanisms rationalized. Public affairs professionals play a crucial role in helping organizations navigate this rapidly changing terrain by connecting the dots between central government policies, state-level regulations and local governance structures. They act as interpreters and navigators of this dynamic landscape.

Companies are now recognizing the strategic importance of public affairs not just as a cost centre, but as a value driver, and are institutionalizing it within their core business functions. These integrated departments are responsible for managing relationships, reputations, risks and regulations cohesively and consistently, aligning external engagement with overall corporate strategy.

The Contemporary Public Policy Professional: Strategic, Informed, Agile

The demands on modern public affairs professionals are rigorous and diverse. They must be strategic in their thinking, deeply informed about their domain and the broader policy environment and highly agile in adapting to rapid change. Successful advocacy begins with clearly defined goals, a meticulous understanding of the policy environment and, crucially, a clear alignment with broader public interests.

Stakeholder engagement is not merely a task; it's a core competency. Public affairs professionals must identify and collaborate effectively with government officials, regulators, civil society organizations and industry bodies. Trust and impeccable ethical behaviour form the bedrock of sustainable influence. Effective advocacy is inherently evidence-based and data-driven, with its messaging tailored for maximum impact. Timing, messaging and the ability to build effective coalitions are all critical ingredients for success.

The industry is shifting from influence primarily driven by personal networks to leadership rooted in knowledge and expertise. While connections still matter, content expertise, analytical rigour and the ability to navigate complex issues are far more valuable in earning the respect of policymakers and the public. Younger professionals, particularly those skilled in digital communications, social media engagement and data analysis, are playing an increasingly vital role in modern advocacy, leveraging new platforms to shape public opinion and policy. The public affairs function is becoming more integrated, with direct involvement from senior leadership and cross-functional teams, reflecting its strategic importance across the enterprise.

Conclusion: Public Affairs at a Turning Point

India's public affairs ecosystem, like the global landscape, stands at an inflexion point. Technological innovation, the imperative for inclusive governance and the urgency of sustainability are converging. Public policy is evolving to be more responsive, accountable and globally aligned, reflecting the interconnectedness of our world.

As the line between public and private interests blurs – a trend accelerated by global challenges and technological shifts – public affairs professionals must rise to an even higher challenge. Their role is no longer merely to advocate for their specific interests but to actively build: consensus across diverse stakeholders, trust between sometimes disparate entities and ultimately, the future of policy through inclusive, informed and deeply ethical engagement.

Every day offers a new opportunity for this kind of meaningful, impactful advocacy, shaping not just outcomes but the very fabric of how decisions are made in a democratic society.

2

Playing a Role in Policy: My Experiences

NANDAN NILEKANI

Policymaking is about what we can do to make the country a better place. It's about how it will advance the country, how it will create more jobs, how all this will create a better future for young people while ensuring we have a safety net for the vulnerable. Good policies take time to come into play; it's mostly like running a marathon, not a sprint.

I have been a business leader and worked in government. I have also worked with the government from the outside on different policy and technology issues and led an NGO that is trying to do something on a large-scale. My learnings span three decades.

I have always approached policy as things that have positive network effects, positive externalities. And all the work I have done on policy – whether it is from the private sector or as a government person or from an NGO – has been from the angle of how does policy make the country better, and I think that's a very important thing in policy. Policy is not lobbying; policy is about figuring out what's good for the country and then making sure you articulate that and make it effective.

My first encounter with policy, so to speak, was back in 1991. Those were the early years of the software industry. The National Association of Software and Service Companies (NASSCOM) was set up as a policy advocacy group for the software industry sometime in 1988. One of the reasons for setting it up was that the earlier technology association was not representing the software interests. That there was a possibility of a huge opportunity in software exports became apparent in 1990–91 at the time of economic liberalization and reforms. We then had technology, and it became possible to use earth stations for remote developments.

NASSCOM leaders worked very closely with the government and especially with Mr N. Vittal, the fantastic secretary of the Department of Electronics. A lot of the policy framework that led to the accelerated growth of India's technology industry was laid at that time. Those included liberalization of software technology parks, tax breaks, imports of the latest equipment and installation of earth stations. That was possible because the industry came together and said here's something that is going to create millions of jobs, here's something that can earn India a huge amount of foreign exchange, which was then a critical need after the government was forced to pledge its gold to raise money to run the economy. The government also realized the value of software.

Today, thanks to that concerted effort in policymaking, we have an industry that has hundreds of billions of dollars in revenue, employs several million people and really impacts the world through technology. It's a great example of how a policy, which was brought together by the industry working with the government in a very trusted manner, has become a flagship industry for India. The software industry is one of India's biggest foreign exchange earners to the extent that our software surpluses are contributing to our current account surplus.

Another example of policy, which I was involved with, was on urbanization. In 2001, I worked on something called the Bangalore Agenda Task Force. The aim was to make Bangalore a better place to work and live. In 2004, when the UPA came to power, we presented some of those ideas to the government, saying how cities can be improved upon and many of those ideas became part of the national-level urban renewal mission. This was important because until then, cities in India had not been given the right importance. The whole perception was that India was more in the villages, and cities could take care of themselves.

I think that was the first time that cities started getting importance in the scheme of things. Today, after two decades, cities have become central to India's growth and its economic vitality. There again, I think many of the ideas and policies on urbanization that we had proposed were helpful. So that again shows that if you are able to bring a good set of ideas to the table, you can actually change the direction of things.

My biggest experience with policy was with Aadhaar, of course. I was given the job to give an identity to everyone, and while it was a technology project, it was also a huge policy advocacy project, which is sometimes not fully appreciated because people see it as an extremely high-tech product. But actually, the bigger job for me was advocacy. When this project started in July 2009, it took us 14 months to build the tech platform. In those 14 months, I went and visited every state in the country. I met the chief ministers and the chief secretaries and told them about this identity project and how it would benefit the state, and how it would help them deliver benefits better. I talked the same story to Parliament, I did it to journalists, to activists, to lawyers, to external agencies, to the world – everyone.

I realized that if you want to bring a huge change in a country, you have to articulate it well and make it widely known. And that evangelization and that advocacy, which I did, helped to actually deal with a lot of the challenges that we faced. So when the thing was actually rolled out 14 months later, it was very easy to scale up. By the time I quit government in 2014, 600 million people had been issued the Aadhaar number. Today, it covers India's entire population. I also learnt how to deal with political uncertainty because the project was started at the time of the UPA government, and it has been continued with renewed vigour under Prime Minister Narendra Modi's BJP government. So fundamentally, a lot of policies are also about how you make sure you get bipartisan support across political lines, as that ensures the policy remains consistent and is not reversed every time the government changes.

Coming back to what I said earlier, it is also important to realize that policy is a marathon game, it's not a sprint. Sometimes, it takes years and years for policies to mature. However, if you do it right, policies which have value for society will emerge sooner or later. When I was chairman of the UIDAI, I was asked by the then road transport minister to find ways to simplify the collection of tolls on our highways. A committee I headed came out with an idea of having an RFID tag-based system. This was in 2010. The report laid the complete framework of the process involving the RFID tags, digital payments and ways to let trucks and cars go through highways without stopping.

Today, the FASTag has become the universal way of tolling roads, and a great success. Everyone is now able to go on highways and doesn't have to stop to pay the toll. The other good thing about this has been the increase in revenues, making it viable to invest in tolls. Something that was conceived 15 years ago has today become mainstream. So, policy is something which you have to be patient about, you must articulate it, you must put your weight behind it.

Another very important aspect of policy is being prepared with whatever policies you have in mind, because events trigger changes. A good example is the Disaster Management Act of 2005, which came into life because of the massive tsunami in 2004, which killed thousands of people in Tamil Nadu. It was based on this Act that the government set up the National Disaster Management Authority (NDMA), which also came into play during the COVID pandemic. Similarly, the horrific 26/11 terrorist attack on Mumbai led to the formation of the National Investigation Agency (NIA) as well as the Unlawful Activities Prevention Act, 2019.

The third example is, of course, the Nirbhaya case in Delhi, which was the horrific rape case which led to the Nirbhaya Act on matters of sexual assault. The point I am making is that policy is a consequence of an event happening. And, therefore, it is important that we recognize that events lead to policies. If a particular event happens, it also creates what is known as a policy window. The idea of a policy window is that there is a problem, there is a possible solution and there is political will or political appetite to find a solution because of some event.

I encountered this policy window in my work on benefit transfer and subsidy reform, and it was a very unusual thing because sometime exactly 14 years back, on 25 January 2011, an additional collector in Nashik district was burnt to death by the kerosene mafia and that led to obvious outrage. Later on, investigations discovered additional complexities and created a huge outcry to reform our subsidy and direct cash transfer. Mr Pranab Mukherjee was the finance minister then, and he asked me to lead a group to come up with a reform structure.

That whole effort led to the formation of the Aadhaar-based direct cash transfer. Direct benefit transfer (DBT), which was applied to energy reform, allowed cooking gas to be sold at market price, so the cash transfer was done. Kerosene could be sold at market price, too, and Aadhaar also allowed things like pensions and scholarships to be electronically credited. That single tragic incident of one person being burnt to death by the so-called kerosene mafia gave the political impetus to reforms. This infrastructure of DBT came extremely handy during the COVID crisis because the government was able to transfer to millions of people emergency money using instant credit to their bank accounts.

The RBI had set up the NPCI in 2008 to transform retail payments. After I stepped down from government, I became the Advisor on Innovation and Public Policy to NPCI and contributed to conceptualizing an advanced payments system called Unified Payments Interface (UPI). The Reserve Bank of India was also very supportive of the move.

The UPI was launched in May 2016, but there was not much traction because people were not using it. In October 2016, it was doing barely 1,00,000 transactions a month. Today, it is entirely a different story. There were two events which accelerated digital payments. One, the withdrawal of currency notes in November 2016 led to the realization that there was a need for an alternative to cash. Second, the COVID pandemic, when people couldn't move out but needed to make monetary transactions, further propelled the shift and led to a massive acceleration in digital payments. Given that the policy windows were small, the government had to move quickly and we saw many policy changes during those periods. However, many of those policy changes had already been conceptualized. They got tremendous traction because of events. The message in all that is that you have to be patient, you have to think about various policy changes and make sure that they are there in the system. It is also necessary to take them forward.

Another good policy change from the business side is work from home. For many years, we have had software technology parks and special economic zones (SEZs). The fundamental rule in both these cases is that you work inside a physical area. A software technology park or SEZs have computers inside, people come there and work, and that was considered as software export. But COVID changed this dramatically, and again, the government moved at lightning speed and allowed work from home to be considered for software export, allowing computers to be moved to people's homes from campuses so that they could work from there. This was a great act of good faith by the government. So again, COVID led to the policy changes that changed the whole concept of software technology parks, bonded warehouses and SEZs.

The other important thing in policy, which I mentioned briefly in the beginning, is coalition building. First of all, the intent should be good. The intent should be for a policy which is in the public interest; a policy which will expand the market, create more jobs and help the country grow. And it should be a policy which has many beneficiaries, and, therefore, you have to create a coalition of those potential beneficiaries. If you want to bring change through policy, then many people must believe in that change; it's not just you or your company or even the association that you represent. You must look at a larger coalition and find other stakeholders who have an interest in that policy if you really want to make it successful. I have found that people are very open-minded if you are able to put forth a policy that is beneficial to the country. They are willing to go along and build coalitions, evangelize and create a network of allies if they believe it is important.

Coalitions do a good job because they are not just about corporate leaders. They could include state governments, enlightened politicians and a lot of others to build a consensus around a policy. Putting a lot of different people behind an idea is always the key to success.

(The essay is an edited version of the PAFI Annual Lecture delivered by Nandan Nilekani, co-founder and chairman of Infosys, and founding chairman, UIDAI [Aadhaar] on 29 January 2021.)

Society

3

Why Do We Need Social Policy?

SHUBHASHIS GANGOPADHYAY

It may be worthwhile to begin with a list of what we term as social policies. These would include policies on education, health, poverty alleviation, water supply, sanitation, access to energy, law and order, old-age pensions, insurance against uncontrollable shocks, etc. Social policies define the society we live in. A good society is one where people want to stay.

This raises two questions. First, what is a good society? Second, does a good society evolve randomly, or is it the result of deliberate attempts by the collective? Let us take the second question first. Do we need a social policy for, say, education? Every parent knows the importance of education and will get their children educated if they can. The significantly high school dropout rates in India (as high as 40 per cent in Bihar and increasing even in developed states like Karnataka) are explained away as being because parents cannot afford to keep children in school.[1] This leads to the following conclusion: once the country becomes rich enough, every child will finish school. India, therefore, needs to focus on policies that increase national income, or the nation's gross domestic product (GDP).

In this way of looking at things, one is looking at 'getting educated' as nothing more than 'buying an iPhone'. Just as one buys costlier phones as one's income increases, one will be educated if one can afford it. This then implies that a poor country can wait till it gets rich to ensure that every child is educated. Putting it plainly, a rich country can attain universal public schooling, while a poor country cannot. This sort of reasoning is flawed, both theoretically and empirically.

Empirically, countries have grown rich because their children were educated, rather than their children receiving education only after they were rich enough to afford it. Finland and Sweden are two countries whose school education systems are widely celebrated. Both were extremely poor countries when they introduced free and compulsory education for their children. After a crippling famine in 1868–69, Finland aggressively implemented a policy of educating their children; so much so that the youth had to pass a literacy test before they were allowed to marry!

Sweden, another very poor country at the time, made education free and compulsory in 1882. South Korea, perhaps, is a better example for us. India and South Korea started their journeys at around the same time. In fact, India was comparable to (some may say slightly ahead of) South Korea in economic indicators like GDP and share of world trade at the start of the 1950s. South Korea implemented mandatory and free schooling from 1 June 1950. Former UN Secretary General Ban Ki-moon, a South Korean, held education to be the one factor behind 'Korea's growth in just a single century'.[2] Our transactional and engineering approach to policymaking has completely ignored this aspect of Korea's development policy and focused entirely on how Korea's economic policies brought about their transition to a developed economy.

In 2023, more than half of the Indian population above the age of 25 did not go beyond primary school, and many of them, of course, were illiterate.[3] In 2004, we passed the Right to Education (RTE) Act, hoping that this would ensure school education for every child. As the official dropout rates discussed above show, we are still unable to get every child educated up to class ten. RTE is not a 'sufficient' policy for India. Its purpose was to ensure that every child has the right to schooling. The problem with a right like this, even if it is a fundamental one, is that the focus shifts to the (enforcement) process rather than the actual outcome.

A 'policy', on the other hand, is a commitment by the government to achieve some outcomes during its tenure. This enables focus on the outcomes promised rather than the 'effort' put in by the government. The RTE, therefore, led to a series of (administrative) notifications, for example, those to (private) schools to ensure that they reserved a proportion of seats for children who come from economically weaker sections of society. There was little or no effort to ensure (near) zero school dropouts, for instance. In other words, social policy needs to focus on the word 'policy' as well as the word 'social'.

Otherwise, it becomes a simple exercise in administering rules regardless of the outcome. Policy is an intervention in the individual space. Through such interventions, we attempt to bring about outcomes that people by themselves will be unable to achieve. When we design interventions in the individual space, we conceptualize the logical framework, or the 'log frame', as a sequence of causal steps. This logical sequencing describes the process through which policy objectives are to be achieved. It starts with 'inputs' (financial and human resources), followed by planned 'activities', after which comes the 'output'.

These are followed by two more consequential steps: 'outcome' and then 'impact'. Till the level of output, things should be under the control of the interventionist. In other words, the performance parameters set up till this level in the design and implementation stage must be attained in a well-designed and well-implemented policy intervention. This is what government administration is expected to fulfil.

What distinguishes a good policy from a not-so-good one is what happens after the 'output' stage. Outcomes are different from outputs in that the former are no longer in the control of the planner, administrator or policymaker. Take, for example, teaching in a school. The school administration can create phenomenal infrastructure, make sure students attend classes, assignments are regularly handed out by teachers and handed in on time by students, etc. All of these are measures of output. Outcome, on the other hand, is not measured by the number of class hours or the amount of reading the students were tasked with or the grades they obtained. It is measured in what the students have learnt and that depends on the effort put in by them. The school and its teachers can induce or cajole students to put in the effort, but the amount of concentrated and systematic effort put into learning the syllabus is up to the students.

If the school designs its curriculum, student activities and teaching in a way that encourages the students to put in the effort, then and only then is the school good. For this, one needs to understand how the students would react to what the school is implementing.

Similarly, in policymaking, it is necessary to understand the context in which the policy intervention will play out. How will the people respond to the policy? Will they respond positively? If not, should we induce them with a carrot or use the stick to make them comply?

Do we know why the people are not behaving the way the policy wants them to? These issues are fundamental in the discussions on social policy. Dowry and child labour continue to plague our society despite all the laws made to stop these practices. When it comes to economic policymaking, we are confronted by two extreme views. For example, before 1991, the standard argument was that the government needed to intercede in markets to ensure desirable outcomes. Post 1991, many have started to espouse the exact opposite, that is, governments cannot do better than what markets can. When it comes to social policy, should we have a similar debate? This brings me to the theoretical reasoning behind the need for a policy on education.

To understand why we need an education policy, we need to understand the significance of education in society. Most of our discussions on education are centred around how important it is for an individual to be educated. However, education is not only valuable to those who get educated; it also adds value to those around the educated. A trained computer scientist, working with a trained physicist and medical researcher, could develop medical instruments for the provision of better healthcare. Two of these experts make the third expert more productive than she would have been without them.

Forgetting experts, the quality of life around educated people is better than that around uneducated people. Some time ago, the India Development Foundation (IDF) had undertaken an evaluation of an adult literacy programme. One of our findings was that adult women spent more time discussing school with their children after they went through the literacy programme. Since children, especially the younger ones, spend more time with their mothers, this improves the quality of time spent by the children with their mothers.

In economics, we use the term 'externality' to describe situations when (economic) interactions between two parties affect a third party, unrelated to the transaction.[4] Externality could be negative (harms the third party, as happens with carbon emissions) or positive (benefits the third party, as in education). This externality is also evident in health – if I am the carrier of an infectious disease, you better beware. Similarly, improper sanitation in my neighbour's house not only affects them, but it probably would also affect me. Economists have successfully argued that the presence of externalities makes the market inefficient. So, if people are left to make individual choices and transactions in sectors where there are externalities, the outcome for each is worse than what each could get if they made joint decisions or, as we say, collective decisions.

And such collective decisions are exactly what policies attempt to implement. If we look at education the same way as we view the individual's purchase of mobile phones, we would be creating similar degrees of inefficiency. Aggregate activity level resulting from the sum of private individual actions overshoots optimum aggregate levels in the presence of negative externality; similarly, aggregate activity level for education and healthcare would undershoot the optimum aggregate. Our adult literacy programme was a transaction between those implementing the project and the erstwhile illiterate adult women. Literacy not only helped the women but also their children (the third party).

Given that education has positive externalities, if left to individual choices, society would be less educated than what is desired. What is true of education is even more true of healthcare. This is for two reasons. First, unlike iPhones, people do not want to buy healthcare, but are forced to do so when they have health issues. Second, they do not get to choose the treatment regimen. This treatment regimen is chosen by the healthcare provider, namely the doctor, who knows more about both – what ails the patient as well as what will work. Purchasing healthcare is, therefore, not the same as buying a box of cornflakes or an iPhone or a car. In economics, a situation where one side of the market (the healthcare provider) has more information than the other side (the healthcare demander) is described as one with asymmetric information. Markets are never efficient by themselves in such situations.

What compounds the problem is that when ill, one cannot avoid healthcare. That is why we need a health policy. Our global experiences with universal schooling and universal provision of healthcare point to the significance of social policies in these areas. Social policies are governed by our visions of the society we want to live in. For example, in some societies, a lot of effort goes into ensuring that schools are of uniform quality. This implies strict government control of how schools are run. Finland, for example, does not encourage privately run schools, fearing that richer kids going to private schools will be trained 'differently' from those unable to afford private schools.

Indeed, there are only a handful of private schools in Finland, and they are not independent of the government. Controlled and uniform curricula are the norm in all the Scandinavian countries. These are countries that strive to create an egalitarian society when it comes to opportunities within a market-driven capitalist system. For them, it is important that children's access to good education is not dependent on how well-off their parents are.

Contrast this with our situation. Our government schools lag far behind in infrastructure, the number of trained teachers and attendance. This creates a gap between the rich and the poor kids at the very beginning of their lives, making social mobility within a generation that much more difficult. This is something that has evolved over the years in India. In my own experience, I did not have to pay for my schooling, and the majority of the top ten schools of that time, in all lists, were government schools.

In fact, we have never envisioned the society we want to live in. Social policies have little to do with society and more with the individual's material welfare. Let me give an example. Given the law and order situation in many Indian cities, it is customary to cordon off an area – a colony – and restrict entry into the area to those who are residents of the area or are 'approved' as legitimate visitors by the residents. Indeed, Indian cities are fast becoming 'gated communities' linked by motorable roads. These communities are havens of peace, tranquillity and safety.

Within the gates, there are clubs, pubs, gyms and stores – everything you would need to survive daily. If one has to meet people from other communities, one gets into one's car and drives into another of these communities. So, our cities are essentially nothing more than high-rise communities connected by roads. Unfortunately, a significantly large section of our population continues to believe that private initiatives in meeting our social objectives will take us to where we want to be!

The phrase 'target beneficiaries' has seeped into almost all our policy discussions. Any discussion about a policy invariably ends up trying to identify those the policy will target. Invariably, these are the poor or otherwise vulnerable sections of society. Our obsession with this term has led us to only discuss policies that benefit a sub-section of the citizens. If there are target beneficiaries of a policy, there must be others who are not expected to benefit from the said policy. This inevitably leads to an 'us versus them' conflict in society and its consequent fragmentation. Policies that affect 'everyone' never get the focus they need.

That is the reason why we never discuss universal healthcare or education. Social policy can be broadly divided into two groups: those that are relevant for people when they face a shock outside their control, for example, social insurance, or those that form part of the universal access programmes of the society, for example, water, sanitation, and so on. Do we want a society where education and health are two important parts of the universal access set of programmes or do we want the rich and connected to get state-of-the-art healthcare (and education) while the poor go to quacks (or send their children to non-functional government schools)?

As pointed out at the very beginning of this piece, such universal and easy access does not happen when countries get rich; countries become rich because they implement these social goals. After all, a country's most important asset is its human capital, and that is the result of a systematic approach to social policy.

4

Economic Development through Grassroots Social Change

SHASHANK MANI

Towards Viksit Bharat: A Grassroots Vision

India's aspiration to become Viksit Bharat (Developed India) by 2047 requires transformative economic growth – growth that is equitable, sustainable and deeply rooted in our social and cultural contexts. This goal, aligned with the centenary of India's Independence, demands a citizen-led movement that can become the largest nation-building exercise in human history. The nature of this transformation must go beyond conventional metrics; it must reach into the aspirations and day-to-day realities of the common Indian citizen.

Grassroots-led transformation is not merely a conceptual ideal – it is a pragmatic necessity. For development to be lasting, it must involve those it seeks to uplift. Local participation ensures contextual relevance and community ownership, making progress both meaningful and enduring. This inclusive growth model embodies the principles of decentralization, self-reliance and community stewardship, all of which are embedded in our civilizational fabric.

This transformation offers an alternative development model for the Global South – democratic, inclusive and sustainable. Unlike China's top-down approach or colonial exploitation, India's model must be participatory and culturally resonant. It should reflect our traditions while embracing innovation and modernity. This path offers a refreshed 'Indian modernity', rooted in a 5,000-year-old civilization that values coexistence, decentralization and civilizational wisdom.

A key challenge is ensuring that this new development model is neither elitist nor exclusionary. The real energy of India lies in its villages and small towns, where resilience and ingenuity flourish amid constraints. These regions must not be afterthoughts; they must become the nucleus of our economic renaissance. Achieving this requires a fundamental reimagining of public policy, development paradigms and institutional focus.

The Middle of the Diamond: India's Emerging Majority

India's socio-economic structure has evolved from the 'bottom of the pyramid' to a 'middle of the diamond', where around 800 million people form the emerging middle class. Concentrated in 240 Tier 2 and Tier 3 districts, this Middle India is central to our developmental aspirations. It represents the dreams and struggles of everyday Indians seeking dignity, opportunity and upward mobility.

For decades, national focus and resources were skewed toward metropolitan centres – remnants of a colonial, extractive economy. These cities, though important, cannot be the sole engines of development. This oversight must be corrected by empowering Middle India with citizen-centric institutions and infrastructure. Economic policies, cultural investments and technological interventions must now prioritize this neglected middle. The potential of this demographic segment is enormous – it holds the key to unlocking widespread prosperity.

Prime Minister Narendra Modi, himself a product of Middle India, has refocused national attention on this real India – Bharat. Inspired by the Integral Humanism of Deendayal Upadhyaya, the prime minister has prioritized Antyodaya – uplifting the last citizen – through campaigns like Swachh Bharat Mission, Jal Jeevan Mission and Ayushman Bharat. His mantra of 'Sabka Prayas' and 'Jan Bhagidari' underscores a collaborative development model. These initiatives emphasize dignity, participation and shared responsibility.

In this Middle India, we find a rich confluence of traditional wisdom and youthful energy. Empowering this population is not merely an economic strategy; it is a moral imperative that affirms our democratic ethos. With rising aspirations and increasing access to education and technology, this section of society is poised to lead India's development in a manner that is both inclusive and sustainable.

Enterprise as the Engine of Employment

Creating employment at scale demands a shift in national narrative: enterprise must be seen as the primary engine of job creation. Employment must not be viewed as the responsibility of the state alone, but as a national movement driven by empowered individuals and responsive institutions. While flagship initiatives like Startup

India are commendable, we must extend this entrepreneurial ethos to every district and foster a decentralized economy that promotes local self-sufficiency.

Three critical steps can enable this:

1. **National Campaign for Enterprise**: Promote entrepreneurship through targeted campaigns that elevate the status of local entrepreneurs. Like Swachh Bharat, this should be a national movement designed to alter social attitudes and institutional priorities. The image of the entrepreneur must evolve into one of a community builder and national contributor. Education, media and policy must work together to shift this perception. Awareness programmes, entrepreneurial education in schools and recognition of grassroots entrepreneurs through awards and storytelling platforms can catalyse this transformation.
2. **Local Enterprise Institutions**: Build institutional support systems across Tier 2 and Tier 3 districts. Jagriti, through its hub in Deoria and spokes in adjoining districts, exemplifies this approach. Using a structured 7M model, it supports entrepreneurs with mentorship, market access and funding. These institutions should also include training centres, incubators, innovation labs and platforms for cross-sectoral collaboration. Local governments, academic institutions and industry must collaborate to provide end-to-end support for entrepreneurs. Plans for a national ecosystem, including a 'middle of diamond' institute in Mumbai, are underway to conduct research, share best practices and develop replicable models.
3. **Systemic Realignment**: Encourage financial institutions, CSR initiatives and policymakers to integrate enterprise-led development into their core agendas. Move beyond charity to strategic collaboration that addresses the real problems of real

India. CSR can catalyse infrastructure, but mainstream investment is needed for long-term impact. Furthermore, tax incentives, venture funds and blended finance models must be designed to reward impact-driven entrepreneurship in underserved regions. Banks and non-banking financial companies (NBFCs) need to develop products tailored for micro and small entrepreneurs, ensuring that finance is an enabler, not a barrier.

Enterprise-led development creates not just jobs but also local role models. It builds confidence in communities and restores pride in local economies. It can transform social structures, reduce migration pressures and deepen democratic participation. More importantly, it allows individuals to shape their futures with agency and purpose, aligning economic activity with social transformation.

Examples from Jagriti Yatra and Jagriti Enterprise Centre

There are many inspiring stories of individuals and groups taking on the task of local incubation and innovation. Some of this has been catalysed by Jagriti Yatra, a national moving platform for enterprise and innovation, which itself has gone global. In recent years, this has also been seen in and around Deoria, my constituency, where a local ecosystem has been created for nurturing entrepreneurs, in what was once a backward area of Uttar Pradesh. It is also significant to note that with just under 40 international participants every year, the Jagriti Yatra has been replicated in five countries, including the US.

Jagriti Yatra was founded in 2008 and has now been going for 17 years, including two digital versions during COVID. This journey on a specially chartered train takes 500 young leaders, carefully selected from over 15,000 applicants, on a national adventure to learn from change makers, innovators and entrepreneurs. Over an 8,000 km journey of 15 days, that starts from Mumbai, goes south, curves up north, hugging the eastern coast up to Nalanda, before turning west towards Deoria. At Deoria, all 500 participants stay in a village that is defined by a mighty banyan, where we have located the Jagriti Enterprise Centre. After spending a night here, the train goes to New Delhi, before returning via Sabarmati Ashram to Mumbai. The train has created over 9,000 leaders, and many have started companies as a result of their association during the travels.

One such example is Get My Parking, a company now in its third round of venture capitalist (VC) funding. Both Chirag Jain and Rasik Pansare came on the journey and, more than India, they discovered each other. The bond that was formed encircling the country has now endured for over a decade, and the company is scaling new heights in India and overseas. Both founders credit the journey for their association and the large national Jagriti ecosystem for giving them a network which benefited them with talent and ideas even after the journey.

A similar but more regional ecosystem has been created at the Jagriti Enterprise Centre, next to the banyan tree in Deoria, where over 240 small and large enterprises have been incubated over the past few years in an area that now includes six adjoining districts. This ecosystem is powered by a unique cadre of people we call Udyam Corps and Udyam Mitra. They are seen as gardeners of this ecosystem, tending and pruning, acting as mentors and connectors to the entrepreneurs they support. This ecosystem has inspiring stories of incubation, like Malti Yadav, an entrepreneur who has created an enterprise that makes pickles and has the potential to employ more than 100 women. Similarly, Arvind Rai, a local innovator from Kushinagar, created an electric utility bike that can support the livelihoods of milkmen and washermen with a design suited to their needs.

It is such groups of citizen builders, learning horizontally from each other, that will create local, regional and national ecosystems that will power Viksit Bharat. Ecosystem creation is not easy, as results do not show for the first few years. But once they get to critical mass, several activities start happening naturally, without the constant exertion of a programme management team. The ecosystem builds from within and, over a period of time, is sustainable, both economically and environmentally.

Sustainability and Global Relevance

Grassroots enterprise development that is local and believes in a regional economy is inherently sustainable. The Jagriti Enterprise Centre in Deoria, for instance, incorporates a Bio-Regional Centre of Excellence focused on circular economy principles. The constituency's 10-year growth plan also balances GDP growth with environmental preservation. The emphasis on decentralized, resource-sensitive growth aligns with India's traditional ecological philosophies.

This Banyan Revolution, as we call it, resonates beyond India. With nearly 5 billion people globally in the emerging middle class, there is a hunger for democratic development models. India can meet this demand, offering a scalable, sustainable alternative to infrastructure-heavy, environment-blind approaches like China's Belt and Road initiative. These models often neglect human capital and environmental consequences – India's alternative prioritizes human well-being and ecological balance.

An international cadre of Udyam Corps – Udyamita Sans Frontieres – can help export this model, strengthening global partnerships and people-to-people ties. These trained professionals can serve as grassroots consultants, capacity builders and cultural ambassadors who spread the vision of inclusive, bottom-up development. This network could be supported through bilateral cooperation, philanthropic foundations and international development agencies.

Furthermore, this model can contribute to global climate goals by emphasizing low-carbon growth pathways. It can also serve as a bulwark against authoritarian development paradigms, offering a humane and replicable alternative. By demonstrating success at home, India can provide moral and practical leadership in shaping a new world order grounded in democracy, dignity and diversity.

A Civilizational Imperative

India's future must reconnect with its civilizational strengths. From the urban planning of the Harappan civilization to today's entrepreneurial innovations, our history showcases a legacy of resilience and creativity. As we unshackle ourselves from colonial, socialist and capitalist ideologies, a new Indian thought is emerging – inspired by Integral Humanism and centred on the citizen.

This perspective sees the economy as a means to human well-being rather than just material accumulation. It calls for spiritual and emotional dimensions to be integrated into development. Art, tradition, community and environment must be respected alongside science, technology and finance. This holistic approach ensures that progress is not achieved at the cost of identity, cohesion or sustainability.

Viksit Bharat must reflect GDP growth, equity and a cultural foundation that empowers 1.4 billion citizens to become agents of change. Our prime minister stands as a role model in this journey of atmanirbharta (self-reliance) and swavalamban (self-sufficiency). Together, we must embrace this national challenge and build a nation worthy of its past and future. Our approach must not mimic the West or the East, but instead craft an original Indian paradigm that prioritizes harmony and human dignity.

By building on our civilizational continuity and cultural coherence, we can create a model of development that is enduring and adaptable. The task is to synthesize ancient wisdom with contemporary tools, forging a path that is uniquely Indian and universally relevant.

Conclusion

The Banyan Revolution is not just a policy shift; it is a cultural and economic renaissance. Through grassroots enterprise and citizen-led development, India can achieve inclusive growth and offer a global template for democratic prosperity. It demands unity of purpose across political lines, institutional reforms with compassion and long-term patience.

Let us rise to this moment and co-create a Viksit Bharat rooted in heritage, driven by enterprise and inspired by the dreams of a billion citizens. Let every town become a centre of innovation, every youth an architect of progress and every citizen a torchbearer of this generational movement. In doing so, we will not only fulfil the dreams of our freedom fighters but also carve a path for the world to follow – a path that is democratic, equitable and truly sustainable.

This is a time for resolve, renewed imagination and bold experimentation. The seeds of Viksit Bharat have already been sown – now it is upon all of us to nurture them with wisdom, effort and unity. Let the banyan grow, deep-rooted and ever-expanding, sheltering a billion dreams beneath its shade.

5

Capacity Building for Policymaking

LUIS MIRANDA

The need for better-qualified people in various parts of the Indian economy has been talked about for decades. This problem is a serious constraint on our country's growth. Educational and skilling institutions are working with the government on this. The Economic Survey 2025 continues to refer to the need for appropriate skilling and education.[4]

This chapter talks about the need for capacity building in policymaking. This is required in all sectors of the samaaj, sarkaar and bazaar.

The Government

Shri Hasmukh Adhia, former finance secretary, Government of India, wrote an op-ed in 2023 titled, 'India needs public policy education'. He wrote, 'Only a small percentage of policymakers – civil service officers – are exposed to the formal study of public policy and public administration.'[5] Only 130 institutions teach public administration, and only 29 teach public policy, according to data from the All-India Council for Technical Education. One of the main reasons, according to Shri Adhia, for this low capacity is the limited number of jobs available after completing these courses.

More importantly, he adds, even civil servants are not taught how to make good policies during their initial training. The need is huge, with 1.3 lakh Group A officers in the Government of India. He suggested that public management (public administration and public policy) be made a compulsory subject for civil service examinations. This way, those who study for the civil service examinations will have some prior formal education in public management.

The government set up the Capacity Building Commission, which went live in April 2021, to enable lifelong learning for civil servants.[6] The mandate was to create a dedicated programme for the capacity building of civil servants. 'Today, our civil servants are solving complex problems in an increasingly dynamic, connected and technologically driven world … "Mission Karmayogi" will aim to transform approximately 1.5 crore government officials across the Centre, the States and the local bodies.'[7] Karmayogi Bharat is a crucial part of the government's capacity-building framework. An online platform has been set up for civil service officials, which 'guides learning, hosts discussions, manages careers and conducts reliable assessments to showcase officials' competency effectively'.[8] Over 1 crore civil servants have been onboarded onto the mission's platform – iGOT (Integrated Government Online Training) – which offers nearly 300 courses.

There are around 10 lakh active monthly users. Many institutions have prepared online courses for iGOT. Recently Shri Rajeev Kapoor, professor of Practice at the Indian School of Public

Policy (ISPP), former secretary in the Government of India and former director of the Lal Bahadur Shastri National Academy of Administration, created a course entitled, 'Introduction to Public Policy' on iGOT to 'equip learners with the essential knowledge and analytical frameworks needed to navigate and contribute effectively to governance and policy processes'.

Finally, ISPP's first flagship report was titled 'Administrative Reforms for a Viksit Bharat'. It talks about 'changes needed in the structure of the administrative system, its work culture, the ability to take risks and innovate and its staffing patterns'. It made recommendations in six specific areas:

1. Improve internal collaboration.
2. Strengthen collaboration with external players.
3. Strengthen risk-taking ability in the government.
4. Ensure competent staffing.
5. Strengthen institutional mechanisms for integrated visioning, oversight and implementation.
6. Strengthen the economic development focus in the current urban planning systems.

Capacity building is key to helping us grow faster. Some recommendations include assigning officers to a specific domain at the time of empanelment as joint secretary, using performance reviews to improve performance rather than to find fault, establishing exchange programmes for civil servants and experts outside the government, reducing the selection period at higher levels, emphasizing economic development in urban planning and scaling up public–private partnerships.

The Private Sector

The private sector has increasingly seen a larger role for the government in its work. The government shows up as a regulator, a competitor, a supplier, a customer or a partner. This is besides ensuring personal safety within the country and at our borders, ensuring that we have a functioning rule of law and addressing the needs for appropriate education and healthcare. At the same time, the role of markets is needed to help the economy grow faster.

This has resulted in making running a business more complex, and the ability to deal with the government is still critical today. Globally, lobbyists play this role. In India, the Public Affairs Forum of India is playing a large role in building out the ecosystem. Some of the recent publications include 'Public Affairs in India: An Evolving Landscape' and 'Measuring Policy Response and Action: A Guide for Practitioners'.

But knowing how to deal with the government is a skill that should not be restricted only to a public affairs professional. Every chief experience officer (CXO) must be comfortable dealing with the government at different levels. It is akin to saying that finance is only to be handled by the finance team or that legal issues are to be handled only by the legal team. Various parts of the organization need to be familiar with the financial and legal aspects of what they are doing – be it purchases, manufacturing or sales. Similarly, the public affairs team helps the company deal with the government and assists various departments of the company to better understand the nuances of dealing with the government.

The key responsibilities of a public affairs person include advocacy, stakeholder engagement, risk mitigation, issue monitoring and management, corporate social responsibility and public relations, and it is important for the rest of the company to be aware that these skills reside within the company. If the Pre-Legislative Consultation Policy of 2014 (which was meant to help bring in more transparency, inclusivity and responsiveness into policymaking) is implemented properly, the role of the public affairs representative will be further strengthened.

The 2024 report by Public Affairs Forum of India (PAFI) on the evolving landscape of the sector highlighted the need for a higher level of training of public affairs personnel.[9] Companies headquartered overseas trained their employees more frequently. Another challenge faced by public affairs professionals in India is poor metrics to demonstrate value. Of the respondents, 47 per cent listed it as the biggest difficulty for policy professionals. In 2025, PAFI accordingly published a report, 'Measuring Policy Response and Action – a Guide for Practitioners'. It highlighted the critical role of this function in enabling businesses to deal with a dynamic and multifaceted environment and serve as a bridge between the business community and policymakers. Their research revealed that 38 per cent of respondents said policy changes have been disruptive to their organization, and 45 per cent believed that the impact was moderate.

To address these challenges, PAFI partnered with the ISPP to co-create and deliver a series of short courses to build the capacity of public affairs professionals and other professionals in the corporate sector. These cover topics like understanding government, stakeholder management, geopolitics, digital advocacy and building coalitions. Other institutions also address the training needs of the sector, like the Takshashila Institution, which focuses on defence and geopolitics.

It is also important for companies to recruit people who have been trained in public policy. The ability to understand economics, use data for decision-making, think critically and know how to design a policy appropriately are important skills for a public affairs person. Many public policy schools have recently started across the country, and public affairs teams should recruit and train alumni from these schools.

The Social Sector

The social sector is the third pillar of civil society and plays a critical role in India's development. They also need to understand better how to deal with the government and the corporate sector, beyond just fundraising or advocacy. The social sector plays a very critical role in policymaking by representing the voice of the communities being affected by these policy changes. Educational institutions have started running courses for the social sector to build capacity there also.

Finally, it is critical for these three pillars of civil society to recruit from each other. Corporates have successfully recruited people from the government, and the government has also seen the need to recruit from the corporate sector. Similarly, with the non-profit sector. These lateral movements help capacity building by transferring valuable skills and perspectives that are sometimes difficult to grow in-house. The ability to understand the perspective of others is very important. Institutions like Indian Leaders for Social Sector help corporate leaders to cross over to the social sector by running courses that help them transition. It will be useful to have more training courses to help others also make their crossover moves more effective.

6

The Entertainment and Arts Industry

SANJOY K. ROY

Overview

The Indian creative sector has the potential of being a sunshine sector in the coming years if policy, foresight and vision can nurture and provide much-needed incentives for it to realize its full potential. As per the EY FICCI Media and Entertainment report 2025, the creative sector grew a modest 3 per cent to cross ₹2.5 trillion with a projected growth rate of 7.2 per cent in 2025–26. Television shows a negative compounded annual growth of -0.6 per cent from 2024 to 2027 and print will only grow marginally at +0.9 per cent in the same period. All other sectors showed significant growth, including digital media at 11.2 per cent and live entertainment at 18.2 per cent, thanks to augmented revenues from ticketed events, government and corporate spending. This segment is projected to grow at 18 per cent to reach ₹167 billion by 2027. Imagine the potential that's waiting to be unlocked, and the jobs and skills needed to address the demand.

The experience economy, which includes travel and tourism, food and drink, arts and culture and events and festivals, is transforming the way businesses operate, creating new opportunities for growth and innovation across different economic segments. Apart from the top 10 metro cities, it's the 40 additional B and C towns which are expected to see phenomenal growth in the coming years with a growing middle class and a larger proportion of disposable income or accessible credit. The gap between rural and urban per-capita income has reduced to 70 per cent, down from 84 per cent. The rise in women in the workforce, which has increased to 42 per cent from 30 per cent, means a whole lot of new consumers reaching out for more equitable and inclusive experiences.

Creating Wealth

Intervention through the arts creates wealth in a sustained manner, allowing people and their communities to find new ways of overcoming odds and finding unique solutions. Governments, who believe that supporting the creative arts is about handouts, need to reassess their policies and invest in the future of their people and provide for sustained arts education, design and aesthetics and civic sensibilities. Violence-scarred regions should use the arts to anchor the young and old to their traditions and history and allow for inclusive dialogue and dissent, much needed in any society riven by contradictions.

Creating Jobs

It's estimated that over 400 million people in India depend on their primary or secondary income from the creative and cultural sector. From the ragis in the gurdwaras to the pandal makers of Kolkata, from the glass bead makers of Firozabad to the Kumartoli sculptors in Kolkata who build idols of the Goddess Durga, from the itinerant Bahrupiyas to the Langas and Manganiyars of Rajasthan, from the weavers of Benaras, Kota, Maheshwar, Kanchipuram and Odisha to the cotton pickers and tie-and-dye karigars and from chefs and servers to film-makers and animators – they are all part of this sector, which in India is governed by 21 ministries giving rise to contradictions in policies, duplications and overall confusion.

An urgent need to define policy is to map this burgeoning sector and include this in the census for 2027, and determine how many rural and urban families are involved in the creative sector. Creating millions of sustainable jobs in this industry needs a focused policy, inter-ministerial coordination and long-term vision.

The Economic Proposition

In India, tourism and culture can contribute a greater share to GDP. Both of these represent an opportunity to create jobs locally in a way that is sustainable. We need focused upskilling and training, redevelopment and conservation funds for local heritage sites and basic facilities such as toilets, cafes and green transportation. India has a million heritage sites all waiting to be rediscovered and leveraged. The public–private partnership model, as demonstrated by Avantika and Puneeta Dalmia in their adoption of the Red Fort heritage site, has been a path-breaking initiative.

Annual creative festivals and daily cultural shows against the backdrop of a heritage monument, purpose-built space or open-air auditorium, allow tourists an opportunity to stay an additional night, boost local taxes and grow the associated food, hospitality, retail and transport sector. Much of the income can be ploughed back into the development of special heritage and cultural prescient.

Entertainment districts like Broadway contributed $14.7 billion to New York's economy pre-COVID as per the 2019 report, and the West End in London contributed £4.44 billion to London's economy and sustains over 2,30,000 jobs. The United Nations Educational, Scientific and Cultural Organization's (UNESCO) World Heritage City of Edinburgh hosts an annual festival that lasts for more than three weeks. In 2022, its economic impact was pegged at £492 million, and the total impact on Scotland was pegged at £620 million, generating £33 for every £1 invested by its government.

In India, every locality, town, city and village can boast of a unique contribution through built, tangible or intangible heritage. Creating platforms for these through local heritage centres, historical tours and community craft centres will provide jobs in local communities, improve services, help clean up the area and boost local economies.

The 'Mapping the Creative Economy' report on the contribution of Durga Puja has shown that this five-day celebration contributes ₹32,377 crore, or 2.58 per cent, to Bengal's local economy and provides employment for over 2.5 million gig workers. With the addition of experiential walks through pandals before the commencement of the religious ceremonies, tourists and art lovers can explore and experience the most amazing thematic presentations that convert this megacity into one large art installation. A cohesive approach and marketing effort can pivot this city into a must-visit for the world, increasing tourist traffic, celebrating India's art and creativity and looking at the export of our design and creative sector services.

While Vivid Sydney and Lyon's Fête de Lumière host annual light festivals, India has a multitude of occasions – from weddings and family celebrations to traditional and religious occasions including

Diwali, Kali Puja, Onam and Dusshera – to light up their cities in a democratic way where citizens take on the onus of creating beautiful imaging rather than this being a responsibility of the state or art curators. The lone Chandannagar lighting craftsperson has given way to enhanced LED gates and fantastical projections which illuminate streets, buildings and entire cities. This proliferation of creativity, with millions of people taking their initiative depending on their budgets, provides an opportunity for innovation and creation of new experiences which can be experienced by millions of people.

Creativity, Inclusivity and Equity

We need to study and credit the direct contribution that the intervention of art makes to marginalized communities. The arts provide young people with an opportunity to express and develop their views, ideas and confidence. At Salaam Baalak Trust (SBT), an organization providing support services for street and working children in Delhi since 1988, continues to lay great emphasis on theatre, music, dance and visual arts as a therapeutic tool. Vicky Roy, a young lad who grew up at the SBT, was part of a photography workshop. A year later, having apprenticed with a leading photographer, he was awarded a fellowship to record the rebuilding of the World Trade Center in New York. Today, his work appears in museum collections across the world and his speaking appearances at TED are much sought after. Yuva Ekta Foundation's work in Delhi's remand home, Place of Safety and Special Home for Boys in Majnu Ka Tila, has created a platform to allow for the integration of these minor offenders into mainstream life.

A Policy of Investment

The government, through its urban development programmes, needs to build sustainable projects which include theatres, museums, rehearsal spaces, experimental studios, galleries, digital labs, craft centres, digital museums, and do this in a spirit of public–private partnership. The world over, city centres and community spaces are earmarked in master plans, and these are provided at a discounted price or on a longer lease to those wishing to invest in the arts and community spaces. The New Delhi Municipal Council, in its inception, created Mandi House as an arts hub by leasing out land to corporates like the Sri Ram Family to set up Kamani, Shri Ram Centre, Little Theatre Group, and itself, then created the Sangeet Natak Akademi, National School of Drama, etc.

Post the COVID-19 pandemic, a slew of new venues invested in by private players are opening up. The most celebrated of these is the NMACC in Mumbai, a state-of-the-art multiarts space which has created a whole new ecosystem in the Bandra Kurla Complex area. The Prestige Centre for Performing Arts in Bengaluru, the Kiran Nadar Museum and Sunil Munjal-driven The Brij are other examples of excellent intervention and investment in the arts.

The investment in a multipurpose stadium for sports and concerts in Ahmedabad and Mumbai paid off. The three-day Coldplay concert series in Ahmedabad, Gujarat, generated ₹72 crore in additional GST taxation and an estimated ₹670 crore in additional revenue to the city as per a 2025 Ernst & Young (EY) report.

The EY 2025 report on the creative sector states that there has been a 25 per cent growth in the registration of intellectual properties this last financial year, with a slew of concerts, festivals, art events, food festivals and craft platforms burgeoning across the country and seeing exponential growth in ticketing income. Teamwork-based arts has experienced a 30 per cent increase in ticketing, delegate and other non-sponsorship driven revenue across its many festivals, including the Jaipur Literature Festival, Mahindra Kabira Festival and Sleepwell's Sacred Amritsar festival.

Possible Examples

Brazil has created a multitude of neighbourhood cultural centres, funded from a 1 per cent local tax on retailers who, in turn, have access to the shows and events in their neighbourhood and get the additional benefit of run-off sales when audiences throng to their theatres and community spaces.

The UK's lottery fund, which invests in capital assets for the creative sector, is another instance of creating a funding mechanism whilst regulating the lottery industry and freeing it of corruption.

USA's tax incentive policy to support the arts through private investment and endowments and to ensure that all town planning incorporates the needs of its society through compulsory inclusion of spaces for theatres, museums, libraries, bars and eateries have helped foster the idea of philanthropy and provide a much needed boost for a poorly funded sector.

Technology, Innovation and the Arts

Technology has to be harnessed and seen as a platform to allow for the democratic dissemination of information and knowledge. Traditional musicians, storytellers and puppeteers should be entrusted with the task of teaching their art form in state and private school education programmes using technology to reach out to larger numbers.

Mapping of the arts – traditional, classical and contemporary – will create an incredible variety of wealth generated locally. The arts engender innovation by encouraging and empowering people to think out of the box. MIT Media Lab is an example of this. Each tech group includes the best minds, artists and others to develop and explore new ideas.

In 1999, the Simonyi Professor for the Public Understanding of Science and Professor of Mathematics at the University of Oxford, Marcus Du Sautoy, conducted an experiment which he then shared in a presentation at JLF Belfast. In this, he loaded all of J.K. Rowling's Harry Potter series onto his computer and asked his AI assistant to write a new book. The AI tool managed one paragraph before it began stringing together words, producing disastrous results.

Five years is a long time in technology, and AI has improved vastly and has, in recent times, been able to churn out visual art, poetry and non-fiction, as well as peer-reviewed scientific papers, of commendable quality. It's only a matter of time before it masters the art of writing fiction.

Yann LeCun and Geoffrey Hinton, the fathers of open AI, disagree with the possible future progression of AI. While Hinton feels that AI can and has begun making cognitive decisions, and this will endanger human life as we know it, LeCun feels AI is only at the threshold of major discovery that will help mankind in innumerable ways.

Will AI have a lived experience and be able to feel empathy, hate, anger, love, betrayal, ego and all the human sentiments in full play? If so, we may well be in for trouble, especially if the world depends on them for more and more cognitive decision-making. Can you compute instinct, can you factor in the DNA for genius, the impact of a deeply disturbed individual and the ability to express? Will AI be able to construe innocence? If so, the ghost writers of the past may well be the AI assistants of the future!

Should AI be controlled by innovators of government diktat, what if AI turns rogue? Are there policies that need to be put into place to nudge inventors in a particular direction? AI today is everywhere, from our phones and homes, to the missiles and bombs raining down across the world, to every process that modern society knows, from health to the environment.

Conclusion

In recent years, there has been an awakening and a moderate show of interest in the sector. Industry bodies like Federation of Indian Chambers of Commerce & Industry (FICCI) and Confederation of Indian Industry (CII) have set up silos exploring the space. Nine years after FICCI first hosted a summit in association with the Ministry of Culture and UNESCO, as well as other partners, it was a landmark occasion to hear PM Modi speak about the importance of this in his speech delivered at the UNESCO conference in Delhi in 2024.

FICCI, along with many organizations including the Event and Experiential Management Association (EEMA), British Council India, UNESCO, Art X, Avid Learning, etc. and like-minded partners have tracked the sector's growth as well as challenges and published a series of white papers and reports through COVID, 'Tracking the Temperature'. White papers by FICCI Cultural and Creative Sectors, round tables with state governments, central ministries and quarterly summits with practitioners and impacted communities have thrown up a slew of recommendations which need policy intervention. These include:

Governmental Leadership:

- Create a secretary-level coordination committee with key ministries that cover the sector.
- National mapping and monitoring empowered body that tracks the growth and development of the creative and cultural sector.
- Develop policies that prioritize culture as a driver of social and economic development, leveraging technology to achieve these goals.

Promoting Cultural Districts and Neighbourhood-Based Celebrations:

- Work with local governments to designate and promote cultural and creative districts within cities, where art, music and cultural events can thrive.

Facilitating Public–Private Partnerships:

- Provide clear tax benefits and CSR directives to further this partnership.
- Encourage joint ventures to develop and maintain tourism infrastructure, including transportation, accommodation and entertainment facilities.
- Offer incentives and tax benefits to businesses investing in tourism-related projects that align with cultural preservation and promotion goals.

Integrating Digital and Physical Platforms:

- Develop virtual reality (VR) and augmented reality (AR) experiences that complement physical exhibits and allow remote visitors to access cultural content.
- Collaborate with technology companies and start-ups to create user-friendly apps and websites for accessing cultural information and events.

Creating a 360-Degree Approach to Cultural Infrastructure:

- Develop and protect spaces where culture is created and support culture that is at risk, and communicate and value the enhancement of cultural assets.
- Formulate a productive network with developers, land owners, architects and the artistic community to ensure the longevity of cultural spaces.

Increasing Investment in Arts Education:

- Allocate resources to establish and maintain arts education programmes at schools and universities and provide scholarships and grants to students pursuing degrees in creative fields to reduce financial barriers.
- Partner with cultural organizations to offer workshops and mentorship programmes for aspiring artists and creators.

Research and Development:

- Enhancing teacher training programmes to suit the evolving landscape of education.

- Invest in pedagogical streams as the fundamental plinth on which education rests.
- Design assessments in a formative and summative manner to enable creative, critical and innovative thinking in students.

Creation of Fiscal Policies Suitable and Specific to Arts and Culture:

- Lobby for tax incentives and deductions that encourage private businesses to invest in arts and culture, including tax breaks for donations to cultural organizations, sponsorship of cultural events or investments in cultural infrastructure.
- Encourage the creation of cultural endowments or trusts that can provide long-term financial stability to cultural institutions and artists.
- Development of sustainable funding models, promoting revenue-sharing agreements with cultural venues or the establishment of cultural investment trusts.

Exploring Innovative Digital Integration:

- Collaborate with tech firms and start-ups to develop cutting-edge solutions for cultural preservation, virtual exhibits and interactive learning.
- Advocate for the integration of cultural discussions into political discourse, leveraging technological platforms.
- Encourage the use of AI, machine learning and big data to analyse cultural data and identify trends and insights.
- Safeguards for the creators of culture with particular reference to those who have marginal voices.
- Address the digital divide to enable equitable access to online culture and cultural experiences, thereby expanding the demand

for culture.

- Research on the most widely used and preferred digital technologies in the cultural sector to be examined and shared in a larger ecosystem.
- Draft digital strategies in consultation with relevant stakeholders of the creative sector.
- Technological interventions that pave the network pathways for global cultural collaboration.

7

How Indian Philanthropy Needs to Evolve for Higher Return on Investment

ASHISH DHAWAN, PRAVEEN KHANGHTA, SWAGATO GANGULY

India – a land of widespread poverty and illiteracy in 1947 – has undoubtedly transformed since then, with faster poverty reduction since the 1991 reforms. Life expectancy has doubled in the last 75 years – from 35 in 1950 to 71 now. While literacy at the time of the 1951 census was around 18 per cent, today almost all Indian children in the 6–14 years age group attend school.

However, learning poverty remains a significant challenge. Incremental progress is occurring, but more needs to happen. India produced 4.2 per cent of global GDP in 1950, a ratio that has slipped to 3.4 per cent now, even as it harbours 18 per cent of the world's population.[10] To rise to its incredible potential, what India needs is rapid growth and inclusive development.

To what extent is Indian philanthropy oriented towards these goals? In FY 2024, an amount of ₹1,31,000 crore found its way towards philanthropic projects in India. Of this amount, roughly

30 per cent came from retail sources, 18 per cent from foreign foundations, 25 per cent from corporate social responsibility (CSR) funds and 26 per cent from philanthropy practised by high and ultra-high net-worth individuals (HNIs and UHNIs).[11]

Retail giving is unable to take a long-term view as it is highly unorganized, as well as oriented towards immediate community needs and religious giving. Foreign philanthropy is expected to stagnate as India advances and the former moves on to more vulnerable geographies.

Philanthropy to Pursue Long-Term Goals: A Big Shift Needed

That leaves CSR and HNI/UHNI funding to pursue long-term goals. Moreover, even as the prevailing mental model of philanthropic action is a linear one of providing direct services to local communities, the patient and flexible capital that CSR and HNI/UHNIs are capable of providing can move the needle towards riskier, non-linear and exponential, 'big bet' projects that tackle India's toughest development challenges and aspire to solve them on a population scale.

Such an approach to philanthropy – which has been dubbed the 'Big Shift' or a 'systems change' approach – will necessarily involve the government, for a number of reasons. First, the government has the power of taxation, and its resources are always an order of magnitude larger than anything private philanthropy can deploy. Thus, private philanthropy's expenditure of ₹1,31,000 crore in FY 2024 was dwarfed by public spending in the social sector the same year: ₹24 lakh crore.[12]

Second, it is governments at the central, state and local levels that make the rules and have the mandate to work for all people.

For solutions to work at a population scale, there is no alternative to working with the government. As Rakesh Rajani and Tim Hanstad have argued: 'The well-being of people and planet is largely determined by how government systems are organized and operate.'[13]

Therefore, to catalyse large-scale change, the relevant question to ask is not why work with the government but how.

Road to The Convergence Foundation

The journey leading to the creation of The Convergence Foundation (TCF) began with philanthropic 'big bets' on education as a transformative force – the founding of Ashoka University in 2010 and the Central Square Foundation (CSF) in 2012. Taken together, they focused on both ends of the educational spectrum. While Ashoka University took its mission to be a world-class research university in the liberal arts and sciences on Indian soil – which attracted the brightest and the best – CSF took upon itself the task of improving learning in Indian schools from the earliest stages.

As Ashoka University and CSF matured, a portfolio of organizations working on diverse, yet important areas such as improving leadership capacity in the social sector, reducing air pollution, improving the effectiveness of government expenditure and inspiring other philanthropists to give with purpose were seed-funded. Almost a decade of experience and learning in philanthropy prepared the ground for the establishment of TCF in April 2021.

TCF believes that for a developing country like India, economic growth is the most powerful engine for improving people's lives. There is much research demonstrating that growth in mean incomes is a primary driver of reductions in poverty; no country has achieved a high level of GDP per capita and simultaneously maintained low levels of human welfare, and conversely, no country has achieved high levels of basic human needs at low levels of GDP per capita.[14] As countries transition from low GDP per capita to high middle income, economic growth helps to address basic human needs such as education, sanitation, water, nutrition and more.

India's experience also validates this theory. Between 1950 and 1980, India grew modestly at 3.8 per cent (adjusted for the 2 per cent population growth, GDP per capita rose even more slowly). However, economic reforms elevated annual growth rates of 6 per cent in the 1990s and 8 per cent in the 2000s. During this period, India was able to lift millions of people out of poverty due to a mutually reinforcing effect: people's incomes rose, and high growth led to increases in government revenue, which dramatically boosted spending on social programmes in education, food and rural livelihoods.

Three Pillars of the Convergence Foundation's Approach

Nevertheless, India – with a GDP per capita of around $2,900 as per current IMF estimates – still has a long way to go. In approaching its goal of fostering rapid and sustained economic growth, TCF's work has three mutually reinforcing pillars.

Pillar 1: Accelerating Economic Growth

This comprises areas that can have an immediate impact on catalysing growth and jobs: boosting exports of goods and services, fostering an attractive investment climate, developing cities and industrial regions as growth engines, developing tourism and making India a top science and technology innovator.

Pillar 2: Enhancing Human Capital

This looks at people as the most valuable resource; investing in them can be the most significant contributor to long-term growth. It embraces education at all levels: early childhood education to employability and skilling; economically empowering women; and promoting India as a Global Talent Hub.

Pillar 3:Advancing Development Enablers

This focuses on creating an ecosystem for rapid development by strengthening state capacity to perform its core functions of delivering public services to all Indians, training high-quality leaders for the social sector and enhancing strategic philanthropy to effect population-scale improvements.

Building pioneering institutions lies at the heart of TCF's approach. Institutions enable people to work together to solve complex problems and can drive outcomes at scale over long periods. We believe this represents one of the highest returns on investment and effort for philanthropy. Moreover, there is a large funding gap here as flexible, patient, early-stage funding for risky system change ideas is still uncommon in India.

Realizing a Developed India by 2047: How Philanthropy Can Help

We believe India can become a developed and prosperous nation by the hundredth year of its Independence; all our institutions are inspired by and work towards this goal. We want to be the preferred home to some of the best technical, entrepreneurial and managerial talent solving complex problems at scale. While we seed fund institutions, our biggest value-add is the hands-on support we provide right from recruiting the team to helping shape organizational strategy. We believe in having a clear north-star metric for success. This metric should be meaningful, achievable and lead to a population-level change. We measure ourselves on two simple parameters: the real-world impact we make and the quality of institutions we build.

TCF is determined to move the needle towards more systems giving. What would be the ingredients of a systems approach? It involves testing new ideas and approaches to solving society's toughest problems, piloting new programmes and modifying them so that they become amenable to being adopted by the government and scaled up significantly. It also involves creating an ecosystem for the dissemination of knowledge, building partnerships and connections and providing a platform for learning. The end goal of such philanthropy is shaping and supporting organizations that will be relevant for decades, leading to the creation of sustainable institutions for the public good.

Which level of government – centre, state, local – should TCF and partner organizations engage with to achieve the most catalytic impacts? This will vary from organization to organization and issue to issue; in practice, they have worked at all three levels. However, given India's size and diversity, a great deal can be achieved by working with state governments, which should therefore be a key area of focus.

As development economist Karthik Muralidharan has argued, states are primarily responsible for public service delivery, such as in the areas of education, health and law enforcement. They control budgets and personnel for these areas; even when the centre funds programmes, it is the states that implement them. State governments also have a major role in formulating laws and policies that govern investment and job creation, such as labour and land acquisition laws, and the provision of various permits. It is extremely important, therefore, to work institutionally with state governments.[15]

How Convergence Foundation Network Organizations Work with State Governments

As an example of such work, the Foundation for Economic Development (FED), a TCF network organization, has worked closely with the Uttar Pradesh government to draft the Nodal Investment Region for Manufacturing (Construction) Area (NIRMAN) Bill, a lynchpin of the ambitious 'Mission 1 Trillion' aiming to lift UP's economy to the trillion-dollar mark. Prosperiti, another TCF network organization, works on state-led reforms in land use, labour, building, transport, trading and utilities that will complement and take forward the centre-led economic reforms of 1991, which pushed India onto a path of higher growth and poverty alleviation.

The Centre for Effective Governance in States (CEGIS) works on the premise that most things citizens care for are in the hands of state governments, but not enough attention has been paid to this level of governance, and even the larger states lack rigorous analytical support for development outcomes. It does work at central and local levels too, but sees its primary mission as supporting state governments in delivering development outcomes at scale and in the most cost-effective way possible.

Joys and Sorrows of High-Risk, High-Return Social Sector Investments

Any portfolio of investments needs to have a high-return, high-risk component. Non-profits and funders who adopt a systems approach to working with the government to bring in this element to social sector investment. The direct-service-to-community local model may be relatively easy to execute, while the systems approach may involve dealing with too many variables that are hard to control. Those variables include the difficulties of anticipating the longer term as well as the vicissitudes of working with the government. But if one can persist with this approach, which takes on society's toughest problems and addresses root causes rather than symptoms, the return on investment can be enormous.

It is worth keeping in mind that the government is not a monolithic entity. Many senior and junior personnel, as well as departments, are capable as well as committed to delivering better services for citizens, and it is certainly possible to work with them. Even if the process will seldom be simple, success here will be the biggest force multiplier for one's efforts and philanthropic giving.

To achieve this, it is necessary to meet government agencies halfway or even more – as Rajani and Hanstad put it, it is essential to have a 'low-ego, low-logo' approach.[16] One must be laser-focused on intended outcomes and pay less attention to attribution or the allocation of credit. One must not only suggest approaches but also be willing to learn – how does the government perceive a problem, and what are the incentives and challenges within the government system? Is there a coalition of shared interests one can team up with? Are there political considerations that open up a window of opportunity, such as an impending crisis or a coming election?

CSRs, HNIs and family philanthropies are in a unique position to deploy the kind of patient capital needed to generate exponential gains. Such capital will typically be flexible and long-term, with periodic dialogues on how the investment is going and adaptations if necessary.

An example of exponential gains arising out of a systems approach to philanthropy is CSF's successful advocacy and support for foundational literacy and numeracy (FLN), which has since been integrated into the Union Government's National Initiative for Proficiency in Reading with Understanding and Numeracy (NIPUN) Bharat Mission. The importance of FLN for future educational and livelihood outcomes arises from the insight that if children do not achieve the first milestone of literacy and numeracy by class three, they will be severely handicapped in their ability to engage in higher-level learning, and ultimately, for their success in life.

FLN eventually became a movement across the country, and over 15 states have launched FLN missions and programmes. Its widespread adoption has meant that India has finally moved the needle on what used to be an occasion for despair: the release of the Annual Status of Education Reports (ASER), which indicated high learning poverty. The latest ASER (Rural) Report indicates progress – class three literacy and numeracy levels in rural government schools have gone up to 23.4 per cent and 27.6 per cent respectively, their highest ever levels. Some states that have pursued FLN vigorously have achieved even faster progress.[17] Of course, there is still a long way to go. But at least we know what areas to work on and scale up funding to achieve further success.

Tata Institutions Shaped Indian Modernity: TCF Institutions Aspire to Shape Developed India

That millions more children can now read and solve basic math problems is a testament to the exponential returns on investment that strategic, targeted, systems-oriented philanthropy can achieve. TCF, in collaboration with India Impact Sherpas, has compiled a report on successful social sector organizations that have adopted the systems change approach and achieved large-scale impact in India, profiling 20 of the leading ones.[18]

TCF's belief in the power of building institutions is reinforced by the example of the world's greatest philanthropists. They have made it their hallmark because building great institutions unleashes entrepreneurial energy, has a lasting social, economic and scientific benefit for society and provides the highest leverage on initial funding.

The efforts of Jamsetji Tata and his heirs like JRD Tata resulted, for instance, in a slew of institutions that have gone into the making of modern India: among them, the Indian Institute of Science, the Tata Institute of Fundamental Research, the Tata Institute for Social Sciences, the Tata Memorial Centre for cancer care and the National Centre for the Performing Arts.

TCF is seeding a growing number of organizations, 21 to date. It aspires to shape all of them into institutions that change the course of India's destiny within the sectors that they operate in – tackling India's most complex development problems in a strategic, catalytic manner. Just as Tata institutions shaped Indian modernity, TCF institutions hope to shape the developed India of the twenty-first century.

8

Developed by 2047: Flawed Narratives and Reality

LAVEESH BHANDARI

When Prime Minister Narendra Modi stated that India should aim at achieving developed country status by the hundredth anniversary of Independence or Vikasit@2047, he gave a clearly defined vision for the country. Of course, since society has assigned to economists the task of defining developed country status, a precise benchmark related to per capita income levels and consequently growth rates required to achieve it has been put forth.

For many involved in thinking about such matters, the target seems fairly out of reach. And among such circles, even within the government, I find the concept of viksit being used more as a formality, something that needs to be done to satisfy appearances, like ticking a box on a checklist. But I will argue otherwise. Viksit@2047 is a tough challenge, but it is not unachievable and well within the realm of the possible.

The greatest obstacle to India achieving developed country status is not a shortage of capital, skills or even institutional and political–

economic challenges, but rather the flawed narratives that erode our confidence in the Indian economy. By extension, such narratives also tend to play down the immense potential of individual efforts; instead, they tend to call for greater government effort or greater effort by the international community. As a consequence, such narratives delude us into taking the wrong kind of actions, where we need to depend more on bureaucracies, be they in India or globally.

The second major obstacle to achieving high growth is focusing on what is not possible or difficult and missing out on what is more easily achievable. I will lay out a range of things that need to be done. If, for some reason, some of these desirable policies cannot be implemented, it is not the end of the world. There are other areas where gains can be achieved.

The Income Target

India's per capita gross national income (GNI) for the year 2023 was $2,481 as per data from the World Bank. Going forward, if the World Bank does not change the per capita GNI criteria for high-income countries ($14,005) and the exchange rates are constant, then India's PCI needs to grow at a little under 7.5 per cent annually over the next 24 years for it to achieve high-income status, which translates to overall economic growth at greater than 8.5 per cent annually over the same period. With changes in exchange rates and superior information, these estimates keep on changing, but overall, the growth requirements are in the high single digits, but less than 10 per cent and lower than what China achieved in the past.

The Challenges

Why do people believe that the 8.5 per cent annual growth is a difficult target? There are many reasons, but let me take up three key ones. First, political–economic and institutional considerations reduce policy flexibility and responsiveness to changing circumstances. Recall the 2020 Agri bills? Important bills from the perspective of agricultural transformation had to be withdrawn completely because a few gainers did not see beyond their narrow interests, and the political and economic forces could not control those opposed to the bills.

But the problem is not only about new laws. India is unable to improve its primary and secondary education systems despite knowing for the last many decades that it is not delivering in terms of quality of education. There are issues related to the centre–state division of powers, which creates fuzziness related to who will be accountable and who has the power to take tough decisions.

Another challenge that falls under the same category of institutional challenges is that of judicial delays. There are many adverse human, social and economic impacts of delays in case resolution, and all stakeholders in the government and judiciary are well aware of the problem. However, governments tend to under-allocate funds for more judges, courts and infrastructure. Moreover, they also overburden the judiciary with excess litigation.

The judiciary also has been unable to rectify itself in giving multiple adjournments, unnecessary hearings, etc. And then there are the processes, such as unfamiliar judges, changing roster, registrar-related constraints, etc. All of them work together to create a situation where contract enforcement, answerability, accountability, etc., are severely compromised.

The second class of challenges are related to geo-economic conditions, which are not as sanguine anymore, nor are they likely to be anytime soon. The primary reason is related to limited faith in the trading mechanisms related to the World Trade Organization (WTO). While many countries in the past may have been going by the book, they were not following the spirit behind the WTO and putting in many barriers to the free movement of goods.

That was the era when the US was the predominant power, and the WTO spirit did not work fully then. Note that the US does not have the same level of predominance anymore. And therefore, it is highly unlikely that the US electorate can ever have faith in such a multilateral trading system giving it a fair deal. Consequently, the US will focus on bilateral trade henceforth, irrespective of who the President is.

The third challenge is related to our own low savings and investment rates. For some reason, not very well understood, Indian households now save a lower share of their income than they did two decades back. Moreover, despite many government efforts, global investors are staying away from investing large amounts in India in terms of foreign direct investment (FDI). There is also the strange reluctance of Indian firms to invest domestically. Nevertheless, given these limitations in savings and investment will also be curtailed. And so, the sensible people believe, even growth will be impacted.

Myths and False Narratives

The above are challenges that will no doubt slow down growth, but what are much more dangerous and insidious are flawed narratives that take away agency from a country.

As an undergraduate economics student at Delhi University in the 1980s, I recall being told why India would not be able to have significant foreign exchange earnings, and therefore, the criticality of import substitution to conserve foreign exchange was taken as a given. What the highly regarded economists calling for such policies did not see was that while they were publishing very well-researched papers in economic journals such as the *Economic and Political Weekly*, a few youth in Bangalore were supplying low-level niche IT services to the Western world.

What they also did not see was that a bunch of entrepreneurs were opening software development classes across Tier 1 and 2 towns of India. Eventually, these same private operators were able to supply the human capital to the firms selling IT services to the West. Together, they contributed immensely to India's IT boom of the 1990s, which led to massive forex earnings for India. The moral of this story is that when we leave the markets alone, they figure out spontaneously how to close the gaps; we don't need ministries, departments and experts (and yes, even economists telling us what we need to do!)

Take another example, I first came across the concept of the 'poverty trap' in the 1980s, though the term gained prominence in the early 1970s. The term means that when we have low incomes, the associated low savings and low financial, human and social capital prevent us from investing enough. Therefore, low incomes persist. In other words, the poverty trap pithily captures the point that poverty sustains itself. It's a powerful narrative that lasted for about half a century until the 2014 publication of one of the more important economic papers titled 'Do Poverty Traps Exist? Assessing the Evidence' by two World Bank economists, Aart Kraay and David McKenzie, in the *Journal of Economic Perspectives*.[19]

The authors showed that there was no evidence to back up the claim of poverty traps either at the individual or the country level. That is, they noted that there is no evidence that poverty perpetuates itself. I don't know Aart Kraay or David McKenzie, but if I meet them, I will salute them. Why? Because they busted a false narrative that told poor countries, 'Your condition is such that you will remain poor.'

Of course, I don't make the claim that it is easy to get out of poverty. The point I make is that poverty is not a trap; it is a challenge. The term 'challenge' is typically used in the context of overcoming it, but 'trap' is used in the context of inability to get out of it. The former is empowering; the latter is diminishing.

Another such flawed concept gave rise to the perpetuation of the 'Hindu rate of growth is 3.5 per cent' myth, an abhorrent narrative that took away hope of doing better.[20] It is believed that the economist Raj Krishna first coined it; my guess is he would have come up with it in a lighter vein. More as an aside than a central tenet of an argument explaining India's slow growth. But the damage was done, across the country, students in schools and colleges were exposed to this concept, who knows how many ended up believing it, but I can assure the reader, the Hindu rate of growth was not taken in a lighter vein among many quarters.

Thankfully, Manmohan Singh and Narasimha Rao did not fall for it, or we would still be struggling with industrial licensing norms and small-scale reservations. The reforms of 1991 freed many markets from government intervention, leading to a new growth path. As was the case with the IT training institutes, the markets came to the rescue here as well. Post the 1991 reforms, the high economic growth path enabled India to get out of the poverty trap and the Hindu rate of growth narrative.

And this is where I make my key point. These narratives are not merely stories; they are not simply flawed beliefs that make drawing room conversations interesting. Once out there in the open, they have a life of their own, they insidiously enter the mind-spaces of key decision-makers and from there into hard policies.

But unfortunately, the World Bank did not persist with such myth-busting post the Kraay–McKenzie 2014 study; rather, it went over to the dark side within a decade. The World Development Report (WDR) of 2024 focused on the 'Middle Income Trap'.[21] This particular term refers to a situation where growing economies stagnate at middle-income levels as their costs rise, but commensurate productivity improvements have not yet occurred to compensate for them.

But just as the concepts of poverty trap, skill deficit and Hindu rate of growth took on a larger than intended meaning, so did the middle-income trap. The WDR identifies many salient measures that India needs to undertake, such as investment in research and development (R&D), skills, trade openness, etc. So there was no need to introduce the concept of a 'trap' to push such policies.

Government documents now refer to the middle-income trap not as an artificial construct but as a given that the government must work hard against. Unfortunately, we see policy efforts being used to focus on skills, R&D and production incentives, when the key issues remain land, labour and institutional challenges. The WDR was likely not responsible for this, but the prioritization matters.

Where Are the Opportunities?

At every instance, we must ask ourselves this question: how important is it for the government to intervene? Recall India's IT sector growth story; there was little government effort apart from that involved in building communications infrastructure. On the other hand, there is the green and white revolution story, where the government was intimately involved in removing coordination hurdles between many different stakeholders.

In a previous section, I have also mentioned that institutional/political economic issues, low savings-investment and geo-economic factors pose a challenge that India would do well to address. But these are not easy to do. What if they persist? Can India become viksit despite that? The answer is yes, though a qualified one.

While the global trade climate appears to be worsening, that in services is growing and will continue to grow. A very large and growing number of such services can be supplied through a digital interface, and that is leading to the persistence of outsourcing in India. What started as IT outsourcing spread into business process outsourcing (BPO) and is now expanding in the form of global capability centres (GCCs).

Moreover, given the age demographics and rapidly falling fertility rates across South-east and East Asia, the demand for Indian workers will only increase across Europe, the Americas and Asia. The rise of the long-term temporary work visa pioneered by the Gulf countries is likely to grow unabated, and with a far wider geographical spread.

What this means is that many occupations where physical presence is required would be sourcing labour from India. Not just IT professionals, but expect demand for a whole new set of service providers, including construction workers, nurses, beauticians, yoga instructors, security guards, etc., to source from India. The Indian government needs to do little apart from providing limited supportive policies, including working with countries to ease up on such temporary work visas that do not lead to permanent migration.

In other words, while India may or may not benefit from extensive trade in manufactured items like China and Korea did, it will benefit immensely from trade in services. The supply of services, both digitally and through physical movement of workers, is where the greatest opportunities exist. Moreover, such foreign exchange-oriented services, when seen in tandem with continued growth in the domestic service sector, indicate that India may not need as much capital as China did to grow as rapidly. Furthermore, a large number of workers abroad, especially those who work temporarily, prefer to save in India. In other words, their incomes contribute relatively more to domestic savings, further reducing the savings challenge that India is facing.

Finally, we come to the political–economic and institutional bottlenecks such as those in education, urban governance, agriculture reform, etc. The fact is that such reforms will help spread the benefits of growth and new opportunities to a much larger group of people. And therefore, they must continue to be the focus of reform.

But growth is not solely dependent on them. Many new opportunities are now emanating in the digital, biotech, agritech, fintech, gen-tech, etc., spaces. India has been among the most proactive countries in embracing digital platforms, and that has paid great dividends both domestically and globally. The reason it could do this is that these new opportunities circumvented many of the bottlenecks we have just outlined.

The lobbies and pressure groups are also not present or powerful enough in these new areas to be able to hold up the entry of these new technologies. This has given the space to both private sector stakeholders and public sector technocrats to bring about innovative new rollouts. In other words, many of the new technologies will be able to circumvent or work around many of the hurdles, just as the IT sector did in the past.

9

The Missing Seat at the Table: Engaging India's Youth in Policymaking – An Imperative for Viksit Bharat

APARAJITA BHARTI

The Digital Personal Data Protection Act was passed in August 2023, six years after the Supreme Court gave its landmark Right to Privacy verdict. Multiple drafts of the bill were presented and discussed in these intervening years. One of the most contentious issues in each version was how consent for children and young adults should be collected. While the contract law in India stipulates that citizens need parental/guardian consent to enter into contracts before the age of 18, the question was, can the same principle be applied to the virtual realm? In a country where digital access and literacy remain uneven, and often young people are the ones who usher their families onto the internet, how do we protect them online? While this debate was raging, there were countless roundtables, discussions and opinion pieces arguing for both sides – keeping the same age threshold for online consent (i.e., 18) or making a case for lowering it.

As this debate unfolded, as someone who runs a public policy advisory firm, The Quantum Hub (TQH), working with tech firms on one hand and the youth (through the Young Leaders for Active Citizenship [YLAC]) on the other, I was most intrigued by how less did one group engage with this issue – that is the young people themselves. They were scarcely consulted, surveyed or involved. As a young woman myself, it wasn't lost on me either that a strict parental consent requirement would play out differently for adolescent girls as compared to boys. And while this issue has been settled in favour of 18 for now, there is still much to figure out about how this parental consent is collected and what it would mean for millions of young people in India and their access to the internet.

This is just one example of a significant policy proposal that would impact young people's lives. Every year, there are countless such proposals – from regulating coaching centres to skilling policies, reproductive treatments to marriage rights. Yet, as a country, we have to institutionalize ways to ensure young people's representation and voice in policymaking. Often, it is an afterthought, if not completely ignored. We must fix this. If public policy in India today does not take into account the changing aspirations of a young India, we risk losing out on the future and our goal of Viksit Bharat. The institutions that we build and the decisions that we take today will determine India's fate in 2047, and we need to take into account the opinions of those who will be firmly in the driving seat.

However, even as I make this case, I must address the anxiety that comes with it. Societies change and evolve best when young people's energy is met with the wisdom of the older generations. By creating a seat at the table for the youth, we not only have the opportunity to bring new ideas and perspectives to policymaking, but also to ensure the continuity of good ideas. Intergenerational dialogue ensures the transfer of wisdom and the history of how we arrived at those ideals in the first place. And along with that comes the appreciation of what is worth preserving. Simply put, we don't need to replace anyone at the policymaking table; we just need a bigger and more inclusive one. Young people need to be at it – loud and visible!

And with this, I present my case for involving youth in the public policy process:

1. The Demographic Dividend

India is home to the world's largest youth cohort. India's median age is just 28.[22] Over 65 per cent of our population is under the age of 35, and more than 40 per cent is under 25.[23] The Government of India defines youth as people between the ages of 15 and 29.[24] Internationally, organizations define youth broadly between the ages of 15 and 35. No matter what the definition, the current decade marks a critical window – by 2047, a sizable proportion of the population will have transitioned into the workforce and leadership roles, radically reshaping India's social, political and economic fabric. Juxtapose this against an increasingly ageing world, and there is no doubt that we have an unparalleled advantage and an opportunity.

2. Current State of Youth Engagement in Policy

There have been multiple attempts to update the National Youth Policy of 2014. The most recent draft opened for public consultations in 2021.[25] The draft had a chapter on 'Building Leadership Skills: Youth as Leaders of Change'. The chapter contained several ideas to facilitate this, and they have come to fruition, including involving young people in India's G20 presidency through Youth20, an official forum for the youth from all member nations, and celebrating the National Youth Parliament Festival. These are in addition to older institutions like the National Service Scheme (NSS) and Nehru Yuva Kendra Sangathan (NYKS). The NSS was launched in 1969 to develop students' personality and character through voluntary community service; it primarily works through clubs in universities and colleges. In the Union Budget 2025, it was allocated ₹450 crore. NYKS has been in operation since 1972, works through local youth clubs and mahila mandals, and it was allocated around ₹423 crore. Interestingly, the budget allocations to both these schemes have increased significantly as a percentage in the last five years.[26] However, given the scale of our country, these investments, in an absolute sense, remain paltry.

There are also fellowships now by various state governments (depending on the ruling parties), where promising young people get to work closely with policymakers (elected representatives or bureaucracy). Through these fellowships, young people support their work and receive early exposure to policymaking in action. Further, not-for-profit institutions also run initiatives like the Legislative Assistant to Member of Parliament (LAMP) fellowship that help young people make inroads into public policy. Organizations such as the one I run, the Young Leaders for Active Citizenship, further create and implement experiential learning programmes that help young people get foundational learning in social change and policymaking as a process. However, despite these public and private efforts, youth voices in core policy spaces – such as legislative processes, government advisory bodies and national consultations – remain limited and often symbolic.

3. Barriers to Youth Participation in Policymaking

The architecture of Indian policymaking – centralized, hierarchical and tightly gatekept – means access to policymaking spaces is mediated by informal networks, bureaucratic hurdles and seniority-based norms. Often, young people are also cast as just recipients of guidance rather than as capable contributors. Youth dissent and activism are often stigmatized. In many families and communities, strong hierarchies and an emphasis on deference to elders also shape attitudes towards civic engagement.

Further, the term 'youth' is not a monolith. The relationship between the state and citizens is also dependent on a variety of other factors. For instance, while young people with relative privilege may be better resourced to engage with the state, they may have less incentive to do so due to their lack of dependence on it. On the other hand, those in rural areas may want to engage more with the state due to the direct impact on their lives. However, disparities in internet access and digital literacy may prevent them from doing so effectively.

Other forms of intersectional identities lead to exclusions. A Lokniti-CSDS survey found that 15 per cent of Dalit, 11 per cent of Adivasi and 10 per cent of Muslim youth reported caste-based discrimination, with the numbers rising to 18 per cent among Dalit graduates. Youth interest in politics was 31 percentage points higher among college-educated respondents (56 per cent) compared to non-literate youth (25 per cent). Gender, class and geography also mediate access: 42 per cent of young women expressed political interest versus 55 per cent of young men, and only 26 per cent of youth from poor households did so, compared to 37 per cent of upper-class youth. Accessibility adds another layer – only 48.5 per cent of state government buildings had been made accessible to persons with disabilities as of 2023, far short of national targets.[27]

This uneven access to civic life impacts the ability and motivation of young people to contribute effectively to the policymaking process. Therefore, it is imperative to institutionalize platforms that allow young people to participate meaningfully in policymaking rather than leaving their involvement to chance.

4. Global Examples of Structured Youth Participation in Policymaking

There are some models that India can draw inspiration from to shape its efforts. For instance, according to the Finnish Youth Act, municipalities are obligated to consult youth councils when drafting policy proposals affecting young people. The Act requires that the youth councils assess the impact of the measures taken by the government on young people and the services and activities intended for them. They are also obligated to 'carry out evidence-based assessments of young people's growth and living conditions and generate up-to-date information'.[28] This data is intended to inform the government's initiatives for young people.

Scotland's Youth Parliament, launched in 1999 and composed entirely of elected young people aged between 14 and 25, acts as a shadow Parliament to provide policy recommendations directly to the government. Many other countries, including Canada and Rwanda, have institutionalized regular youth consultations at national and provincial levels, embedding young voices in public consultations and advisory bodies.

In addition to these engagement models, investments need to be made in improving the quality of civic education across the country.

Even though 'civics', as it is colloquially referred to, is a mandatory subject till class 10 in Indian school boards as a part of the broader social sciences, there are rare initiatives to upskill and invest in civic educators. Other school boards, now becoming popular among India's well-to-do, in fact, seldom touch upon India's democratic history – a lost opportunity to engage young Indian citizens. In some European countries, such as France, Finland, Estonia and Greece, the subject is compulsory and is taught separately at each level of general education (primary, lower secondary and upper secondary). In most Organisation for Economic Co-operation and Development (OECD) countries, there is a thriving philanthropy ecosystem that supports civil society to periodically survey and measure young people's civic engagement as well as invest in civic education. The relatively nascent domestic philanthropy ecosystem in India and restrictions on foreign funding and CSR spending further limit the scale of such interventions here.

5. Let's Fix This: No Time to Waste!

We must act now to give young people the voice they (we?) rightfully deserve. The following interventions can help solve this:

a) **Mandatory Pre-Legislative Consultations:** The Indian Constitution, unfortunately, does not outline a pre-legislative process. However, over the years, through a maze of precedents, necessity, good intentions and common sense, we arrived at a pre-legislative policy in 2014. While not mandatory to be followed, it advises the government to publish draft bills, along with supporting documents like justifications and financial implications, on the relevant ministry's website. A minimum 30-day period is advised for stakeholders to provide feedback. There is a need to mandate youth consultations as a part of this process, especially for those proposals that impact young people significantly, such as education, employment, health, technology, personal laws and the environment.

b) **Fellowships/Internships and Work Opportunities:** There is a need to expand and institutionalize fellowship and internship opportunities in government ministries, legislatures and research bodies, ensuring equitable access regardless of region, language or economic background. While many of these have been launched in the past few years, they are often shelved with changing political equations and require funding support from philanthropy instead of being government-funded. While many ministries and departments at both the centre and the state also hire young professionals, their tenures are often short and unstructured due to a lack of clear career pathways.

c) **Advisory Councils:** Establish statutory youth advisory councils with representation from diverse socio-economic, regional and gendered backgrounds, tasked with providing direct input to policymakers. These are especially important at the local government level. Young people's engagement in improving their immediate living conditions is the surest way to foster them as engaged citizens in the future. Institute a minimum representation for young people in national commissions, consultative bodies and local governance forums.

d) **Digital/Civic Engagement Tools:** India's robust digital ecosystem provides opportunities for scalable engagement. Efforts such as the MyGov platform are tapping into this opportunity. Such platforms and engagement channels can also be created for young people to engage at the local level. Platforms enabling crowd-sourced policy input, such as participatory budgeting tools and AI-powered feedback mechanisms, can supplement traditional forms of engagement. However, the flip side of digital tools is the ability to deal with the volume of inputs. The feedback loops need to be strong for young people to build trust in these platforms.

e) **Strengthen Data Systems around Young People:** The government should periodically survey young people to understand their changing preferences, catch early trends around education and employment and barriers they face. This can help policymakers make informed decisions around subjects that concern young people. Further, a Youth Policy Participation Index could also be created to measure inclusion across institutions, ministries and geographies. More regular, independent audits of youth engagement policies, such as NYKS and NSS, can provide for course correction.

f) **Partner with Civil Society:** Civil society plays an important role in youth mobilization and can ensure the continuity of efforts. It is also more nimble in adapting to new trends. The government should empower and partner with civil society to co-create civic engagement programmes. Furthermore, by creating space in CSR law, it can nudge philanthropic funding in this direction. Partnering with civil society organizations can also entail empowering youth to frame, prototype and test solutions to public problems through hackathons and policy labs.

6. Conclusion

Young people need to be shaped as co-creators and champions of a shared national future. This requires humility and openness, proactive engagement from young people themselves and a willingness to experiment with new participatory processes. The consequences of inaction are grave – disenchantment, civic apathy or worse, misguided policy decisions – but the rewards are transformative: a robust, innovative, buoyant and genuinely democratic India leading on the world stage in 2047. It is only by ensuring a seat at the table for India's young people that the table itself can be made fit for the future.

Economy

10

Evolution of Policy Paradigms: Transitions and Continuity

A.K. BHATTACHARYA

The critical role of policy in paving the path of a country's development has been rarely questioned. Indeed, the correlation between policy and development has been recognized almost as a truism to the point that any debate on this subject has become distinctly passé.

This, however, can potentially lead to an unfortunate fallout for governance. The role of policy for ensuring development could be taken for granted, resulting in inadequate attention to the need for crafting relevant and effective policy to ensure development. Policymakers could even overlook the fact that realizing development goals needs active support from policy.

In India, the debate over securing the country's steady development is yet to reach such a state of complacency and negligence for policy. However, there have been phases in India's post-reforms development journey when experts have argued that growth and development can be reasonably assured even without doing anything because of its demographic advantages and the large size of its market.

In casual conversations, economists have often contended that given the young working-age profile of India's population and the relatively low workers' participation rate, particularly among women, and the huge market size requiring sustained investment, economic growth will continue to see a northwards movement even without any policy push. The natural momentum of a young developing economy, with a relatively low base of economic activity, will take care of an annual growth rate of about 5 per cent.

But even such forecasts for India's economic growth, reeking of complacency and imprudence as they do, come with a caveat. They suggest that a growth rate of a certain level should be achievable in the normal course, only when policymakers do not harm the inherent potential of the Indian economy. Ironically, such a caveat underlines, although indirectly, the importance of policy in ensuring growth. Just as good policy can hasten the pace of economic activity, bad policy can derail growth.

The Past as a Pointer to the Future

This backdrop must be kept in mind while studying the evolution of India's policy paradigm since the country gained Independence from British rule. For the benefit of this assessment, the policy evolution in India has been segmented under five broad periods.

The first phase is the longest period of marked volatility in economic policymaking in India – from 1947 to 1980, when barring a short interregnum of a year and a half, the Union government was headed by Jawaharlal Nehru and his daughter, Indira Gandhi. Nehru's economic policymaking saw the establishment of a socialistic pattern of development, where state-owned enterprises were groomed to attain the 'commanding heights of the economy' with the help of an Industrial Policy Resolution in 1956. The rise of industrial policy meant not just nationalization of a few key enterprises like the Imperial Bank of India, Air India and the life insurance industry. It also led to the growth of public sector enterprises, the imposition of import controls and the launch of a planned model of development through five-year plans.

Barring a short phase of about 19 months, when Lal Bahadur Shastri became the prime minister and tried unsuccessfully to introduce more market-friendly economic policies by liberalizing industrial and trade controls, the march of a statist model of economic development remained unhindered till the late 1970s.

Indeed, Indira Gandhi, who succeeded Shastri, doubled down on the path her father had mandated. She nationalized many more private-sector entities in industries such as coal, textiles and general insurance, apart from enforcing many more restrictive laws on industrial licensing to ostensibly curb the concentration of economic power and reduce market dominance. Laws on foreign exchange and import controls were also made more stringent to the point that freedom for enterprises was seriously undermined.

This was followed by an attack on the democratic institutions and rights of Indians by Indira Gandhi, when she declared an internal Emergency in 1975. Fortunately, India reclaimed its democracy about a year and a half later. The governments that followed, led for the first time by a coalition of non-Congress political parties, adopted a confused approach to economic policymaking. Unsurprisingly, they presided over a steady decline in economic growth till Indira Gandhi bounced back to New Delhi in 1980.

The nature of the impact of such statist economic policies for the most part in these three decades and three years after India's Independence was underwhelming, to say the least, for its growth and development. Of course, India built heavy industries, irrigation projects and set up many public sector enterprises. But the scope of these efforts was limited to promoting a state-led economic development model. Simply ignored were the areas of agriculture, primary education, health and basic infrastructure like roads, housing and water.

It was no surprise that average annual economic growth in the 1950s was a little less than 4 per cent. Even in the 1960s, this growth rate was stuck at 4 per cent and worsened to less than 3 per cent in the 1970s. Exports of goods and services were in low single digits as a percentage of the GDP right through this period, never crossing the 7 per cent mark. What became too obvious to be ignored was the correlation between an inward-looking economic policy approach with tight controls on industrial activities and sub-optimal levels of economic growth.

The return of Indira Gandhi in 1980 also marked the early signs of the government focusing on the need for economic policy liberalization, although in slow doses and at a halting pace. Indira Gandhi's term was cut short by her tragic assassination in 1984, but slow doses of economic reforms kept the growth engine revving up at a slightly higher pace. Her son, Rajiv Gandhi, succeeded her as prime minister and promised to usher in policy reforms after an unprecedented electoral victory later that year. However, the focus on reforms got a little muted as the Rajiv Gandhi government was mired in political controversies over bribes.

On the economic policy front, industrial policy and fiscal policy reforms were introduced, but the pace of their implementation was slow. Instead, the government went in for external borrowing to fund its development plans. By the time the 1980s came to an end, the Indian economy was in deep trouble – an unprecedented rise in fiscal indiscipline made worse by an adverse balance of payments. Despite that, however, the Indian economy's annual average economic growth during the 1980s rose smartly to over 5.6 per cent, even though exports of merchandise goods and services hovered between 6 and 7 per cent of the GDP during this decade. This was yet another indication of how economic policymaking could make a positive difference to growth and development, even though the focus on reforms got a little diluted because of political events.

The Role of Crisis in Policymaking

The 1990s began with an unprecedented economic crisis, with India's foreign exchange reserves dipping to a level barely enough to meet its import needs for a week and its fiscal deficit exceeding 8 per cent of GDP. But a minority government, led by a reform-friendly prime minister, P.V. Narasimha Rao, and his finance minister, Manmohan Singh, one of India's finest technocrats, unleashed a series of reforms that from 1991 to 1995 made fundamental changes to the country's major economic laws and systems that governed industrial, trade, exchange rate, fiscal, capital markets and financial sector policies.

Political developments did threaten to derail those reforms, but the pace of those policy changes remained largely unaffected. Even the three coalition governments led by H.D. Deve Gowda, Inder Kumar Gujral (both representing the United Front) and Atal Bihari Vajpayee of the Bharatiya Janata Party (BJP) from 1995 to 2004 did not dilute the focus on economic reforms. Despite many setbacks on account of crises arising out of stock market manipulations and the Asian financial meltdown, a significant reduction in tariffs, privatization, subsidies rationalization and fiscal consolidation were among the major policy initiatives seen during this period. The outcomes could be easily gauged from the way the Indian economy performed during this decade. The annual average GDP growth during the 1990s was close to 6 per cent, and the share of merchandise goods and services exports in GDP rose from 7 per cent in 1990 to over 13 per cent in 2000.

When All Boats Rise on the Back of Reforms

The general elections of 2004 led to the installation of another coalition government led by Manmohan Singh, which lasted for 10 years. While the broad principles of economic reforms were followed during the tenure of Singh, a new rights-based governance model was introduced by conferring on Indian citizens the legal right to information, rural jobs, education and food. However, apart from entering into a civil nuclear deal with the United States that promised gains both on energy and strategic fronts, there was no pronounced attempt at pushing ahead with the much-needed second-generation economic reforms. But the effects of the reforms initiated in the previous decade and a half were still showing in the performance of the Indian economy. The buoyant global economy also helped. Average annual economic growth in the noughties exceeded the 6 per cent mark, and exports of merchandise goods and services jumped from 13 per cent in 2000 to 22 per cent in 2010.

The last few years of the 10-year regime of Singh were bogged down by a slowdown in policymaking and imprudent taxation moves like the retrospective enforcement of tax laws on the acquisition of domestic companies by overseas entities, better known as the Vodafone tax. This was further complicated by charges of corruption in the government's decisions to allocate spectrum to telecom firms and coal blocks to mining companies, accord environmental clearances to projects after inordinate delays and to award projects under controversial circumstances for the Commonwealth Games that India held in 2010. These developments were a big blow to governance processes in India.

A Mixed Picture on Policy and Growth

Not surprisingly, economic growth had begun to decelerate from over 8 per cent in 2010–11 to a little over 5 per cent in 2012–13, thanks also to the US Federal Reserve threatening to wind down its bond purchases programme. A change of political guard in 2014 took place after the general elections. A new majority government led by Narendra Modi of the BJP raised hopes of a new momentum in economic policymaking to revive growth. Promises of reversing the retrospective taxation law and a gradual reduction in corporation tax rates were among the factors responsible for a slow but steady revival of economic growth from about 6.4 per cent in the last year of the Singh regime to 7–8 per cent in the first three years of the Modi government.

Note that this recovery in India's economic performance was not accidental. In those three years, the Modi government took a series of reformist steps to boost growth. A new regulatory structure for an orderly and smooth development of the real estate sector, a new law for resolution of insolvency and bankruptcy cases, a new monetary policy regime for inflation management and a big push for strengthening digital infrastructure, specifically for facilitating digital payments, were among the economic policy initiatives that went a long way in oiling the wheels of the Indian economy. The strong connection between policy reforms and economic growth was once again established beyond doubt.

But a policy misadventure in November 2016 pulled down that growth rate. Demonetization of over 86 per cent of currency in circulation was ostensibly aimed at unleashing a massive crackdown on unaccounted money. In effect, however, that move caused a huge disruption to the economy, dealing a serious blow to the unorganized sector and the small-scale business units. On top of that was the launch of the much-delayed indirect tax reform in July 2017 in the form of a goods and services tax or GST for the entire country. However, its design was a little flawed, and in the first couple of years after its launch, the GST rates were raised, and the number of rates was increased instead of being brought down or rationalized.

Economic growth in these three years came tumbling down by more than half, from 8.3 per cent in 2016–17 to 6.8 per cent in 2017–18, 6.45 per cent in 2018–19 and 3.87 per cent in 2019–20. And with the increase in import duties on a wide range of goods, India's exports, whose import intensity was quite high, suffered as they also failed to take advantage of plugging into global value chains (GVCs), which had become critical for sustaining exports. From a high of 25 per cent in 2013, exports of merchandise goods and services fell to just about 19 per cent of GDP by 2019.

A bigger crisis followed. The COVID pandemic devastated the economy, with GDP contracting by close to 6 per cent in 2020–21. The Modi government unveiled a robust package of financial support, including a substantial increase in capital expenditure to shore up the infrastructure sector. The Union government's capex rose from 1.7 per cent of GDP in the pre-COVID year of 2019–20 to 3.2 per cent of GDP in 2024–25. The principles of fiscal consolidation, however, were followed as the fiscal deficit of the Centre was gradually brought down from 9.2 per cent of GDP in

2020–21 to 4.8 per cent in 2024–25. Such an approach had a limited impact on government finances and helped the Indian economy bounce back with a fast recovery. India's average annual GDP growth in the five years after COVID (from 2020–21 to 2024–25) was 5.44 per cent, a reasonable performance given the challenges the economy faced. However, exports made only a marginal recovery to just about 22 per cent of GDP.

The broad message from the trajectory of India's economic reforms over the last seven and a half decades is unmistakably clear. Economic crises and political instability do enhance prospects of reforms and focused policymaking to revive growth. But an equally important ingredient for ensuring sustainable growth is the creation of an environment that allows policymakers to debate, discuss and experiment with policy reforms. Without that key element in policymaking, even the best intentions of reforms fail to achieve the desired results.

Dealing with Uncertainties

But any discussion on the future trajectory of policy reforms must take place in the context of the current economic and political situation that prevails in the world. The outlook for the Indian economy from a policy perspective is not too rosy. The challenges for growth are rising by the day. GDP growth in 2024–25 decelerated to 6.5 per cent, compared with 9.2 per cent in 2023–24. Economic growth in 2025–26 is projected to stay at 6.5 per cent or within a range of 6.3 per cent to 6.8 per cent, according to different official estimates. The newly appointed chairman of the Prime Minister's Economic Advisory Council, Prof. S. Mahendra Dev, believes that despite global uncertainties, these growth projections are feasible.

Indeed, global uncertainties have clouded the prospects of India's economic growth in quite an unprecedented way. The Asian financial crisis, the Y2K disruption for tech companies, the North Atlantic financial meltdown, the Taper Tantrum triggered by the US Federal Reserve and the COVID pandemic had all impacted the Indian economy's growth in varying ways. But the global uncertainties that India faces now are caused largely by geopolitical tensions resulting in military conflicts in different parts of the world, affecting both international trade and fossil fuel prices.

Complicating such uncertainties could be the US President Donald Trump and his disruptive trade policies. It has already signalled the demise of the multilateral trade order, which was ushered in with the setting up of the World Trade Organization (WTO) in the last decade of the last century, laying down the norms for a rule-based non-discretionary system that guaranteed a most-favoured-nation treatment for all member countries.

Even though no attempts have been made to revive that WTO-mandated multilateral trade order, Trump's threats of retaliatory tariffs have had one positive outcome. It has pushed India to resume its trade negotiations with different countries. A free trade agreement has already been concluded with the United Kingdom; another one with the European Union should be concluded before the end of 2025; and, most importantly, a bilateral trade agreement with the United States could also be concluded soon, although Trump's decision to levy a 25 per cent tariff on imports from India and imposing an additional 25 per cent duty to penalize India for buying oil from Russia have created major complications in Indo–US economic relations.

In a way, the Trump-induced uncertainty for India could well be an opportunity. Of course, the Indian government should continue to battle for the retention of the WTO-mandated multilateral trade order. However, if Trump's disruption can help India seal a few trade agreements with major countries, including the US, and extend that principle to join international trading arrangements like the Comprehensive and Progressive Agreement for Trans-Pacific Partnership (CPTPP), India's exports would be a net beneficiary.

During the Modi government's first term, India came close to joining the Regional Comprehensive Economic Partnership (RCEP), the world's largest trading bloc accounting for 30 per cent of the world's total population, global GDP and worldwide trade. The arrangement came into force from January 2022 and comprised 15 countries of the Asia Pacific region, including 10 South-east Asian countries, China, Japan, South Korea, Australia and New Zealand. India took a last-minute decision to pull out of RCEP for its fear that China would have easier access to the Indian markets, flooding its products at the cost of India's vulnerable sections of small and medium-scale industry.

The irony is that even though India did not join RCEP, imports from China have grown, even though at a slower pace at a compound annual growth rate of over 6 per cent in the three years since the launch of the regional trading arrangement from $94.57 billion in 2021–22 to $113.45 billion in 2024–25. If Trump's threats of retaliatory tariffs goad India into signing more trade agreements with different countries like the US and the EU, in addition to joining trading blocs like CPTPP (in which China is yet to become a member), the gains for the Indian economy would be substantial.

Once again, a crisis of sorts could potentially help India usher in growth-enhancing reforms of its trade policies. Instead of raising tariffs, it would be obliged to bring them down to create better linkages with GVCs. The twin crises induced by a precarious balance of payments and an unsustainable fiscal situation in early 1991 had forced the Narasimha Rao government to push through major economic reforms that laid the foundation for an over 6 per cent annual growth for the next decade or two. Perhaps the trade reforms, induced by the ongoing uncertainties created by the Trump administration in the US, would give a similar push to India's economic policymaking and enhance its growth prospects.

Reviving Abandoned Reforms

However, there is no gainsaying that despite the crisis of uncertainties offering an opportunity for reforms, there are many other policy areas in India that need to be fixed if the goals of speeding up growth and development are to be realized. Needless to add that such reforms brook no delay. A good start will be to revisit some of the reforms that the Modi government had initiated but had to back down for a variety of reasons, including political resistance.

Early in its first term, the Modi government had promulgated an ordinance to reform land acquisition laws to facilitate the setting up of job-creating industrial projects, after ensuring adequate compensation for land losers. But this had to be rolled back in the face of stiff political resistance, not just from the opposition parties but also from its political base. Almost a decade has passed by, but there has been no visible effort at reviving the land reform legislation. There have been reports, though, which suggest that various state governments have introduced easier land acquisition rules in their respective jurisdictions.

Almost similar has been the fate of another key factor-market reform. Stuck in disputes and differences of opinion with trade unions and a few state governments are the notifications meant to enforce the four Parliament-ratified labour codes on occupational safety, health and working conditions, wages, industrial relations and social security, which would have subsumed in them the 44 central labour laws along with their 1,200 sections. There are no clear timelines by when these four labour codes will be enforced across the country. Here also, suggestions have been made on how different states have already modified their respective labour laws.

Agriculture that employs over 40 per cent of India's labour force is also in dire need of reforms. Three specific agricultural laws were passed by India's Parliament in 2020 to allow, among other things, corporate farming, relaxed norms for storage of harvested crops and more freedom for farmers to sell their produce in the marketplace instead of being tied down to local outlets only. However, these laws (the Farmers' Produce Trade and Commerce [Promotion and Facilitation] Act, the Essential Commodities [Amendment] Act and the Farmers [Empowerment and Protection] Agreement on Price Assurance and Farm Services Act) had to be repealed under political pressure, primarily from powerful sections of farmers from the Punjab and western Uttar Pradesh. Again, the Union government in the last few years, since the repeal of these laws, has not succeeded in restoring them to the statute book. Instead, the buck seems to have been passed to the states once again.

But all these critical reforms are responsibilities of the Union government so that the whole country can enjoy their benefits. Investors do not look at the specific policies and rules that prevail in different states before making up their minds on their investment plans. The assurance of the Centre backing these policies with their reformed laws is critically important to ignite the industry's animal spirits, especially at a time when its investment rate needs to improve.

Minding the Political Economy

The list of economic reforms that need to be implemented to ensure growth can be longer. But focusing on that alone will not be enough. The political economy aspects of policymaking and reforms to boost growth will be equally important, if not more. Three political economy issues need to be accorded the topmost priority.

First, consensus building is critical and needed even more when the government in power enjoys relative political stability. The criticality of consensus-building is higher when there is no immediate economic or political crisis staring the government in the face. Consensus building on the need to bring about policy reforms is to be ensured not just through consultation and discussion with political leaders from the opposition parties, but also with the political masses as well as leaders of the ruling party. The latter is even more important as leaders from within the ruling party can play a vital role in creating an environment conducive to a smooth implementation of reforms. The learning from the stalled land acquisition law under the Modi government was that those reforms were challenged not just by the opposition parties but, more importantly, by some forces within the ruling party. That lesson cannot be ignored.

Second, a successful execution of reformist policymaking is also dependent on well-trained and empowered civil servants. Unfortunately, not enough attention has been paid to this aspect of policy reforms. The big-bang reforms of the 1990s were greatly facilitated by a group of reform-friendly civil servants and technocrats hand-picked by the finance minister, Manmohan Singh. During those years, civil servants and technocrats were as keen and supportive of reforms as their finance ministers –

Manmohan Singh, Palaniappan Chidambaram and Yashwant Sinha.

Since then, however, the burden of reforms has been largely carried by the top political leadership or the finance ministers in charge. A time has come for the government to focus on training and retraining the bureaucracy to make them effective instruments of economic policymaking. There is no dearth of ideas on how to retrain the civil servants, as several official committees, including the celebrated administrative reform commissions, have outlined what needs to be done to make the steel frame more accountable and effective. But the biggest stumbling block to civil service reforms has been the civil servants themselves. A way forward would be for the political leadership to take the lead in this vital area.

Also, the strength and vitality of regulatory apparatuses need attention. The fine distinction between regulatory responsibilities and policymaking powers has been a casualty of late as a result of the regulatory capture effected by civil servants, perhaps at the behest and with the connivance of the political leadership. Governments are expected to frame policies with the help of civil servants, and independent regulators are expected to monitor and enforce the rule of law and policy.

In the recent past, however, civil servants after their retirement are often used by the political executive to play the role of regulators. This has often created an avoidable conflict of interest, undermining the integrity and independence of regulators. For effective policymaking to ensure growth, regulatory independence is of utmost importance, and these jobs cannot be the preserve of only retired bureaucrats. The fact is all the three finance-sector regulators in 2025 were secretaries in the Union finance ministry in 2024 or 2025 and had been involved in policymaking in the government before they became regulators. This would suggest that there is a dearth of private-sector talent that could regulate the financial sector. This is certainly not the reality. A single misadventure, as seen in the recent appointment of a chairperson of the markets regulatory body, cannot result in the abandonment of a well-established and globally followed principle. Casting aside that development, the government should revive the idea of considering experts from the private sector with proper safeguards for appointment as regulators.

And third, there is a need for building an environment for open debate and discussion on the pros and cons of reformist policymaking. Such a debate should also be focused on examining the need for making reforms inclusive by reducing their possible adverse impact on different sections of people. The government of the day, therefore, must actively engage with NGOs and think tanks, both government-sponsored and those in the private sector, media organizations and academic institutions to generate a healthy and open debate on the pattern of economic growth and development that should be planned and what steps should be undertaken. In many ways, such debates can help address the weaknesses and shortcomings of any policy that is under the government's consideration.

The Way Forward

A quick look at the fundamentals of the Indian economy reveals that it offers a viable platform for sustaining growth to make India a developed economy. Its demographic profile is both its strength and a potential weakness. Over 68 per cent of India's population is in the working-age group, or between 15 and 64 years. The median age is 28 years.

A recent report by SBI Research (an outfit of the State Bank of India, which is India's largest commercial bank) pointed out that India's dependency ratio is estimated at 35 per cent. In other words, 35 per cent of India's working-age population (those between 14 and 64 years) are dependants, or are aged below 14 years and over the age of 65 years. This, according to the SBI Research report, is a dependency level comparable to what prevailed in China, South Korea and Thailand when these countries experienced high growth. To make sure that India can take full advantage of its demographic advantage, it will be necessary to have a more detailed understanding of the composition of the working-age population. The sooner that exercise is completed, the better it will be for India to exploit its demographic dividend, before that opportunity goes to waste due to the natural process of ageing. The upcoming census, details of which should be available by 2027, will be hugely useful in that context.

China can be an example from which India could draw some lessons. Its dependency ratio was below 40 per cent between 2005 and 2015, a period during which its poverty rate dropped from over 30 per cent to about 6 per cent and its per capita income from $1,500 to $8,000. Along with massive investment in infrastructure creation and strengthening of its vocational training facilities, China also saw during this period its exports-led manufacturing sector rise to a level of 30 per cent of its GDP.

India has been rapidly increasing investments in infrastructure in the last few years, but its manufacturing accounts for about 15–16 per cent of GDP. Merchandise goods exports continue to languish at about 22 per cent of GDP, and only a tenth of India's total workforce is formal, with access to vocational training for workers remaining very low.

Given the uncertainties about global trade in the post-Trump world, India's policy challenges for boosting exports will, therefore, remain formidable. But a continued rise in infrastructure investment and a boost to manufacturing, backed by measures to enhance vocational training facilities to ensure a higher level of formalization among the workforce, are achievable policy goals.

India's latest numbers on economic growth show private consumption expenditure making a marginal recovery with a growth rate of 7.2 per cent in 2024–25, up from 5.6 per cent in 2023–24. There are worrying signs evident in income and wealth inequalities, requiring the incentive structure and the taxation system to encourage a greater dispersal of income and wealth distribution. In capital formation, the government continues to play the lead role, but it will be necessary for the private sector to contribute to higher investments. For achieving that goal, a policy package will be of the utmost necessity. Once again, the role of policy reforms will turn out to be a crucial instrument in furthering the cause of India's economic growth.

11

It's a Matter of Policy

AMITABH KANT

In today's constantly changing world, where global challenges like climate change, technological disruption and economic uncertainty threaten to reshape societies, the power of public policy has never been more critical. Good policies are the backbone of stable, inclusive growth and guide nations through complex transitions, ensuring no one is left behind. Under Prime Minister Narendra Modi's leadership, India has taken bold, transformative steps that demonstrate how strategic policy initiatives can be game changers. The launch of Startup India and Make in India has propelled India into the global innovation map, creating millions of jobs and catalysing a vibrant entrepreneurial ecosystem. The Digital India movement has expanded access to services and increased transparency, enabling millions of citizens to participate more actively in the economy. Meanwhile, ambitious climate initiatives like the Green Hydrogen Mission and National Solar Mission are positioning India as a leader in sustainable energy.

Through the course of my career, I have been privileged to contribute to this vital field, and reflecting on this journey, I feel a deep sense of gratitude for the opportunities and challenges that have shaped my life.

From my earliest days in the Indian Administrative Service, starting with the Kerala cadre in 1980, I realized that public policy is a vital engine that drives growth, prosperity and transformation in scales both big and small. My career has been dedicated to harnessing this power to bring predictability, transparency and progress wherever I have served.

Kerala, known for its significant investments in health, education and nutrition, is an evergreen example of how social sectors are the levers on which achieving lasting progress is built. My time there taught me that effective governance requires a deep understanding of people's aspirations and challenges and the ability to inspire collaboration with communities and stakeholders.

My first posting in Tellicherry (Thalassery) in the early 1980s was the start of this learning. Facing immediate challenges like a congested town and an overpowering fish market, I learned the importance of decisive action and the power of community support. Relocating the market and widening roads, though tough, showed me that good work is both achievable and appreciated. People respond to outreach – more than anything, they want to be heard, considered and cared for by their governments – and this was made possible through administrative and infrastructural improvements, but also through the understanding that people are incredibly creative, community-oriented and cultured. The Tellicherry carnival was perhaps one of my greatest achievements in bringing people together.

Moving to Matsyafed, the Kerala State Co-operative Federation for Fisheries Development, presented me with a unique opportunity to make a meaningful impact on the lives of traditional fisherfolk.

The central challenge was the oppressive control of middlemen who left fishermen with only a fraction of their catch's market price. My policy response was to introduce 'beach-level' auctions to connect supply directly with demand and open bank accounts for fishermen to ensure direct payments. This financial model, where 50 per cent went towards direct payment and 50 per cent towards loan repayment, was incredibly effective and would form the basis of many of my future endeavours. We also facilitated access to modern boats and nets through loans and addressed transportation issues for fisherwomen. Through all this, I was also an outsider from North India, but one who had taken the time to learn Malayalam. Truly understanding the people you serve is the bedrock of good policymaking. Without trust, the best policies cannot be effectively implemented.

By 1992, I was the district collector of Calicut, and came face to face with a city seemingly 'frozen in time'. Calicut was made almost entirely of narrow streets with a lack of public spaces. My vision was to transform it into a modern city. This required using policy powers decisively, such as removing encroachments at Mananchira Maidan to create a vital green space. Widening 26 roads and pushing the Calicut bypass project involved significant challenges, including legal battles, but the support from the community and media, combined with a highly literate society, made sure that we prevailed.

Perhaps the most significant policy initiative in Calicut was the transformation and expansion of the airport. Facing funding constraints, we proposed a novel approach: raising resources directly from the Malayali community working in the Gulf. Establishing the Malabar International Airport Development Society, a Special Purpose Vehicle (SPV) and introducing a User Development Fee were pioneering policy decisions that enabled us to fund the runway expansion. Calicut airport became the first in India built on a public participation model, inspiring future projects like the Cochin and Kannur airports. This demonstrated that policy can leverage community resources for large-scale infrastructural development that looks decades ahead, serving the region's diaspora for years to come.

Beyond infrastructure, I used innovative policy for cultural development, transforming a dilapidated library into a world-class facility funded by commercial rentals on the lower floor. Organizing the Malabar Mahotsav further enriched the city's cultural landscape. During a moment of national tension following the Babri Masjid demolition, I employed a unique policy response: inviting artists, led by M.F. Husain, to create a massive painting on communal harmony in a public space, showcasing how cultural initiatives fostered by policy can help maintain peace and unity.

Later, as tourism secretary in Kerala, I took on what many considered a less-than-desirable posting. Kerala was not a known tourist destination globally. My mission quickly became to elevate Kerala into a global brand – God's Own Country – by taking the destination up the value chain through public–private partnerships. We rebranded traditional art forms, Ayurveda and cuisine, and introduced innovative eco-tourism projects like training former poachers as guides and developing 'tree huts'. This policy-driven approach, supported by effective marketing, led to global recognition, with the *National Geographic Traveller* listing Kerala as a must-see destination. This experience laid the groundwork for the national 'Incredible India' campaign.

As the joint secretary, Ministry of Tourism, I faced the challenge of promoting Indian tourism amid the global crisis following the 9/11 attacks. This adversity prompted the ambitious decision to launch the 'Incredible India' campaign. Recognizing the need for quality over mere cost-cutting, I pushed for a quality-cum-cost-based (QCB) model for selecting creative agencies – a policy shift that enabled partnership with top firms. The campaign, despite initial scepticism, proved immensely successful, significantly increasing tourist traffic. The 'Atithi Devo Bhava' campaign further demonstrated the power of policy in empowering stakeholders like taxi drivers and guides, instilling civic pride and enhancing India's reputation as a welcoming destination.

My tenure in the Department for Promotion of Industry and Internal Trade (DIPP) saw the launch of transformative national policies like Make in India, Start Up India and Ease of Doing Business. These initiatives were designed to simplify regulations, liberalize FDI and boost manufacturing, fundamentally reshaping India's economic landscape and catapulting it into a global powerhouse. A key component of this shift has been the Production Linked Incentive (PLI) scheme, which incentivizes manufacturing in sectors like electronics, pharmaceuticals and more, encouraging large-scale investment and innovation. Startup India, in particular, continues to be a policy masterstroke in encouraging a dynamic entrepreneurial ecosystem and creating jobs.

As the CEO of NITI Aayog, I spearheaded the Aspirational Districts Programme (ADP), a landmark initiative aimed at uplifting India's most backward districts. Inspired by my learnings from Kerala, the ADP leveraged data-driven policies, the 3C's of convergence, collaboration and competition, real-time monitoring and technology to drive radical transformations in education, healthcare and nutrition standards, which are critical for India to achieve developed nation status. The programme's success, recognized globally by the United Nations Development Programme (UNDP), exemplifies the transformative power of targeted, evidence-based policy intervention and a competitive spirit among implementing units. We also championed forward-looking policies in sunrise sectors like Green Hydrogen and Advanced Chemistry Cell Batteries, initiatives essential for India's transition to cleaner energy and sustainable development decades into the future. Initiatives like the National Asset Monetisation Pipeline and indices for competitive federalism further showcased how policy can unlock resources and drive performance across states.

At NITI Aayog, I also spearheaded the asset monetization programmes and policies for the Government of India and conceptualized the $81-billion National Asset Monetisation Pipeline. This significant initiative was designed to accelerate India's transition to cleaner energy and support infrastructure development, and it exceeded its target in the first year.

Serving as India's G20 Sherpa has been the most challenging and compelling experience in my career, requiring high-level policy engagement on a global stage. With a clear mandate to represent the interests of the Global South and push for an ambitious agenda, we successfully navigated geopolitical conflicts to achieve a 100 per cent consensus on critical issues in the New Delhi Leaders' Declaration. This included championing significant policy outcomes like the inclusion of the African Union in the G20 and pushing for ambitious climate finance reforms, demonstrating how policy can shape global cooperation. This was made possible by partnering with a dynamic team of young officers who brought fresh, dynamic perspectives to the table.

My journey from the heart of Kerala to the centre of Indian bureaucracy has driven home one fundamental truth: policy is the most potent tool for transformative change. It is about daring to look decades ahead, envisioning what the country could and should be and crafting frameworks that bring predictability, transparency and sustainable progress. I have always believed that policy should drive positive disruption and innovation, whether through beach-level auctions for fishermen, public participation in airport development or global consensus on climate finance. The challenges I encountered, far from being deterrents, have been opportunities for reinvention and strengthening policy design and implementation.

To the youth of India, I say this: the civil services and the realm of public policy offer an incomparable opportunity to make a real difference in people's lives and shape the destiny of our nation. If you are driven by a desire to do good, are enterprising in your approach and are committed to quality and innovation, you will find immense support and the chance to contribute to India's growth story.

The lessons I have learnt confirm that effective governance relies on truly understanding people's needs and contexts, and then using that awareness to build bridges between the government and citizenry.

Today, more than ever, the world needs policies that are visionary while also being firmly rooted in empathy and inclusivity – policies that listen to the voices of the marginalized, harness local knowledge and promote genuine participation. It is through this deep connection with the people we serve that governments can develop solutions that are sustainable, impactful and resilient in the face of today's unprecedented global challenges.

12

A Ringside View of Policymaking: From State and Centre to Global

CHANDRAJIT BANERJEE

Introduction

India's policies for economic growth and development are crafted at multiple levels, including the central and state governments, regulators, institutions and district authorities. Non-economic policies, such as those for societal development, environmental issues, R&D and many more, bear strong implications for the economic framework as well. The impact of governmental and institutional policies on businesses is not just significant, but it could be a defining differentiator for their growth and progress. With businesses as the key driver of employment, incomes and overall economic development, India's policies have proactively worked at building a facilitative and welcoming entrepreneurship climate that ignites innovation, catalyses investments and boosts local economies and global integration.

As a key stakeholder in policy development, the Confederation of Indian Industry (CII) has been deeply and strongly engaged with policymakers on creating and shaping policies that conform to changing global and Indian trends to benefit Indian industry, which in turn feeds into the larger national progress journey. The defining objective of Viksit Bharat by 2047, when the nation completes 100 years of Independence, is a clarion call that inspires industry to accelerate its growth, thereby creating jobs and enhancing prosperity. According to CII's estimates, India enjoys the intrinsic potential of reaching an economic size of $35–38 trillion by 2047, with a compound annual growth rate of 8–8.9 per cent.

Achieving this target for Viksit Bharat or a developed nation requires a concerted effort from all stakeholders. As an important player in national policy development since 1895, CII has built a wealth of deep insights and key lessons from its engagement with the central government, state governments, regulators and policy institutions over the decades. Initiated in Kolkata, the forerunners of CII saw success in advocating for a greater role for India-based businesses during colonial times, and with its move to New Delhi as a national engineering industry body in 1974, it was closely involved in manufacturing policies at a time of industrial licensing. Led by industry stalwarts, CII evolved into a national industry organization coinciding with the advent of India's economic reforms process in 1991.

As an ardent champion of liberalization, CII offered continuous solutions and ideas on reform policies to the central government to calibrate and balance evolving policy frameworks in a manner that would enable Indian businesses to align with the transformational changes. CII's recommendations on tariffs, investments, taxation and sectoral policies positioned it as an advocate for open markets on the one hand, and as a supporter of industry's competitiveness on the other. Building close relations with policymakers over the years, the organization offered analytical and data-based reports that served as a rationale for its recommendations. With its grassroots industry insights and bottom-up approach to developing its policy stance on major economic areas, CII's policy suggestions found favour with the central government across multiple areas of industrial and international trade and investment policies during the liberalization period.

Recent Policy Advocacy

As the Indian economy has expanded, CII's engagement covers all sectors of the economy, including manufacturing, services, social sectors such as education and healthcare, infrastructure, energy, agriculture and allied sectors, sustainability, technology and so on. Let me give a few examples of areas with which we have been closely associated.

Manufacturing Policy: The National Manufacturing Policy of 2011 was derived greatly from consultations with CII. The confederation outlined many of the elements that were required to be part of a comprehensive and overarching manufacturing policy – competitiveness, micro, small and medium enterprises (MSMEs), quality and standards, technology and ease of doing business – for the government's consideration. Most of these found their place in the policy. Taking this forward, the CII was closely engaged with the launch of Make in India at the Hannover Messe in 2015 in the presence of Prime Minister Narendra Modi and then German Chancellor Angela Merkel. Across manufacturing sectors, CII's inputs have found place in policies for capital goods, electronics, MSME, food processing and others. We were part of the Steering Committee for Advancing Local Value-Add and Exports

(SCALE) government-industry dialogues that brought together concerned officials with industry leaders for developing policies for key manufacturing sectors.

Ease of Doing Business: CII's constant advocacy on facilitative processes and procedures resulted in greater attention being accorded to ease of doing business. The government undertook the initiative of the Business Reform Action Plan (BRAP) with the states and defined the parameters that would rank states on their progress in developing a facilitative business climate. CII played an important part in highlighting the need for simplified administrative processes and procedures, time-bound and deemed approvals, self-certification, transparency and digitalization. Recognizing CII's leadership in this area, a CII–DPIIT task force has been set up that meets regularly to resolve specific issues and consider policy suggestions from industry. Ease of doing business is a cross-cutting area that requires convergence of multiple ministries and departments, state governments, regulatory authorities and organizations, from the district level to the port authorities, customs and taxation departments, environmental regulators and so on. The CII convenes different players and synergizes their perspectives to develop holistic solutions to hurdles in doing business.

Decriminalization: On decriminalization, CII worked with industry and legal experts to identify specific business laws that the government could consider for removing from criminal statutes. This is an ongoing process, and so far, our research has helped contribute to the Vivad-se-Vishwas scheme of the government and the decriminalization of hundreds of business laws.

Budget Inputs: Our inputs on taxation and GST, presented in detail each year during the preparation of the Union budget and taken forward through interactions with the Ministry of Finance, are regularly reflected in the final documents. As an example from Budget 2025–26, CII had requested high priority to labour-intensive manufacturing sectors and infrastructure status for tourism facilities, which found place in the announcements.

Fixed-Term Employment: In some areas, we have worked over the years with the relevant ministries to craft a conducive policy for industrial growth and employment creation. The issue of fixed-term employment was led by a CII task force that initially raised the importance of such a policy that would help Indian industry to align with global manufacturing trends and requirements. Following a general awareness among policymakers that this issue required attention, CII engaged both with the government as well as trade unions to craft a policy that would be acceptable to all stakeholders. This process took several years to finalize and build the buy-in among employers, employees and the government. Finally, the policy was introduced, meeting the expectations of all sides.

These are just a few examples of CII interventions which have been viewed favourably by the government while framing policies.

Engaging with State Governments

CII has greatly intensified its policy advocacy with the state governments through its state-level councils. Each state has a CII council headed by a chairperson and including various committees and working groups. These develop ideas for the state's progress and offer solutions while identifying issues to be resolved.

State governments are prioritizing the ease of doing business, attracting investments and generating employment, and CII is supporting these efforts through constant interaction with their representatives and providing new ideas and industry inputs. Through our extensive network in the states, we have also learnt best practices and have suggested successful policies of one state to other states to adapt.

For example, CII has been a partner to various states in their investment summit events, commencing with the Vibrant Gujarat series. It is encouraging to witness a changing mindset among states in recent times, aligning with the spirit of cooperative and competitive federalism.

Over the years, CII has worked with most states on developing their industrial policies, sectoral policies and investment policies. We have provided reports and studies to the state governments with recommendations to encourage greater business engagement. CII has also bolstered their external engagement by leveraging its global networks for actions at the state level and organizing interactions with overseas industry.

Whether it is export policies, budget recommendations or district-level administrative procedures, CII engages closely with the states. This proved to be vital during the COVID-19 period when businesses were challenged to operate in lockdown conditions. Drawing upon the inputs from firms at the grassroots, CII detailed the hurdles on the ground to the district and state authorities, thereby clearing the way for businesses to function and keep vital supply chains running.

Global Engagement

One of CII's core activities is to reinforce Indian industry's overseas engagement. This involves not only taking business delegations to other countries to meet with their governments and businesses but also setting out pathways for trade and investment with them. Going beyond trade, CII has also stepped up international cooperation in areas such as skill development and labour mobility, technology and innovation and sustainability and climate change, as well as healthcare, renewable energy, sustainable mobility and other areas of priority for the Indian government and industry.

CII shapes international cooperation policies through its robust participation in strategic and Track-2 dialogues. It is also the lead industry body for several bilateral CEOs forums set up by the Indian government for dialogue between the government and industry of the two countries. These forums help in devising new areas for cooperation and provide roadmaps for accelerating economic engagement, while also highlighting issues that both countries can address to expand trade and investment.

Through its deep research, CII identifies sectors of cooperation between India and other countries and makes recommendations on how these can be catalysed. Our bilateral reports identify the potential exports from India to partner nations at a granular level in terms of Harmonized System (HS) codes and also outline the hurdles faced by Indian companies in the respective overseas markets. This enables the Indian government to take up issues with the partner nations for tariff and non-tariff barriers and processes and procedures.

A key new area of cooperation is emerging and critical technologies. CII has been working with the Indian and US national security advisers on the India–US Initiative on Critical and Emerging Technologies (iCET), which brings together industry leaders from both countries to elaborate on cooperation mechanisms for specific technologies such as AI and quantum. Such dialogues on technology cooperation have also been instituted with other countries and blocs, and CII is often an integral part of the discussions to strengthen and deepen industry partnerships.

The CII Playbook

The government proactively seeks industry views and ideas when developing policies and takes them into account in their implementation. Through long years of extensive and successful policy advocacy, CII has developed an adaptable model of supporting policymaking in the country. While this is not explicitly defined, CII deploys a certain methodology and terms of engagement with the overarching goal of building trust that helps in expanding the industry's role in policymaking.

First, consistent interaction with the government and other policymaking bodies is central to building the relationship. CII office-bearers take time out to consult with the government and seek views of ministers and officials continuously. Policymakers are key interlocutors in CII platforms to guide industry and learn from their ideas.

Two, CII's policy inputs come directly from industry members and represent real-time issues and solutions. This is done through industry councils and committees in a wide range of areas. The suggestions carry credibility because they are granular in approach and reflect real-life issues. CII sources ideas cooperatively and collectively and takes up issues that affect the industry.

Three, the industry discussions and policy suggestions are supported and backed up by research, data and analysis. The analysis factors into account larger issues and coordination between policies. For example, often policies relating to import duties and domestic manufacturing can be at odds with each other. CII takes into account diverse views as well as data inferences while presenting its recommendations, and these constitute a common policy stance from industry.

Four, in general, CII has moved away from policies relating to subsidies and incentives, and we focus more on ease of doing business. This is appreciated by the policymakers and adds to CII's credibility.

Five, the policies that CII takes up relate to sectors and issues and are not for specific firms or enterprises. If a company suggests a certain policy, CII delves into the suggestion in detail to make sure it would apply for the good of the entire industry and would not be inimical to other sectors.

This approach helps CII's recommendations carry a certain weight, which is seriously considered by policymakers when looking at different angles to a policy. Through its outreach, CII also enables the success of a particular policy by supporting its implementation. A key example is when the Goods and Services Tax (GST) was introduced in 2017. CII worked with the Ministry of Finance for organizing workshops in many industrial centres in the country to develop a better understanding of the new indirect tax regime. Similarly, the government has entered into several free trade agreements, and CII has been hosting awareness and information sessions across the country to apprise industry members of the benefits and how to leverage the policy.

Key Lessons

Participatory policymaking is known to be the most effective in implementation and meeting the envisaged goals. From our long experience of working with stakeholders on formulating policies, certain lessons can be gleaned.

First, it is important to work with policymakers through a partnership approach. The government is to be viewed as a facilitator of entrepreneurship, and industry needs to work in alignment with its objectives for national growth. This is best done with both sides as partners in a common endeavour.

Two, intrinsic to this effort is the issue of building trust between the governments and stakeholders. Policy advocacy should be seen to be considerate, authentic, fair and accountable. Clear value and ethical leadership add wings to the formation of possible policies for governments and institutions to consider. Stronger relationships and engagement are central to the lasting impact of policy development through consultations and partnerships.

Three, CII works with all political parties that are in government in a non-partisan approach. Political parties are aware of this, and in case of a change in leadership in a state, CII work, in general, continues uninterrupted.

Four, CII has consistently taken up issues that matter to industry. Many policy recommendations have been carried on over several years, which only emphasize their importance to growth and entrepreneurship development.

Five, as most of CII's suggestions derive from intra-industry consultations, they are viewed as credible and synergistic. CII presents its ideas to the government after these have been debated and discussed at length by its members, and these are seen as cohesive policy actions with buy-in from industry.

Six, CII has created a strong institutional framework for supporting the competitiveness of Indian industry through 12 centres of excellence as well as several other centres. These centres provide capacity building, assessments and consultancy services to enterprises through a range of programmes of interest to industry.

CII has been a pioneer in areas such as quality management, green buildings, sustainability, manufacturing excellence, MSME development, water management and logistics, among others. Led by industry members, the specialized work of the centres enables firms to align with evolving policy frameworks and changing globalization scenarios. The centres support CII's policy advocacy through action on the ground and therefore add to its developmental role.

Conclusion

The participation of interest groups in public policy, be it from any stakeholder, needs caution and care. It should be impartial, non-partisan and for the overall benefit of the particular field. It should be exercised with responsibility and understanding of the larger picture. The credibility of the interest group is important, and the trust needs to be carefully built with policymakers through a range of different modalities.

Over the years, CII has had many successes in contributing the industry perspective to policymaking. There have also been instances where the government of the day has not agreed to CII's views, but this has not stopped us from advocating the interests of the overall economy. In the future too, CII will continue to play a vital, positive and constructive role in converging industry recommendations for the consideration of the government and policymakers and contribute to the collective objective of nation-building.

13

India's Policy Priority: Promoting Private Enterprise

RAJIV KUMAR

After 35 years of post-liberalization rapid and inclusive economic growth, India is today poised at the cusp of a real breakthrough in its development trajectory. The past 11 years, with Prime Minister Modi leading the massive development effort, have seen the economy double in size from $1.98 trillion in 2014 to $3.9 trillion in 2024. This has been achieved despite the COVID-19 shock and marked uncertainty, rising protectionism in the global economic situation. These negative features have been exacerbated with the weaponization of global trade and finance and the rising intensity of armed conflicts. To have achieved an average annual economic growth rate over the last 11 years of about 6.5 per cent in these relatively adverse global circumstances is universally applauded. India's inexorable rise to be among the three largest economies by 2030 is now accepted and acclaimed by the global community.

What is perhaps even more impressive is that India has achieved this growth along with improving the welfare levels of those at the bottom of the pyramid. Antyodaya, or taking care of those at the end of the queue, has been effectively adopted as the operating principle of economic and social policymaking. This is strongly reflected in the sharp decline in the levels of multidimensional poverty, which has declined from 29.17 per cent in 2013–14 to 11.28 per cent in 2022–23. More importantly, perhaps, there has been a significant reduction in the incidence of absolute degrading poverty. According to the latest estimates from the World Bank, the percentage of the population living below $3.65 per day (raised from $2.60 used in the earlier estimates) has declined from 61.8 per cent in 2011–12 to 28.1 per cent in 2022–23. India's economic growth has not only been rapid and sustained but also inclusive.

The inclusive nature of India's economic growth is under-represented by these income measurements of absolute poverty. It does not fully reflect the improvement in the welfare levels of those at the bottom of the pyramid that have resulted from the multiple schemes of direct benefits transfer (DBT) from the government. Among these, the Jan-Dhan Yojana, Aadhaar and Mobile (JAM) trinity has acquired an iconic status among benefits transfer schemes. With the opening of more than 450 million new, zero balance bank accounts, of which more than 70 per cent are in female names and the near universal coverage of Aadhaar cards and mobile phones, JAM has facilitated the transfer of more than 323 schemes to direct digital transfer. This reflects an 11-fold rise in schemes under the DBT regime over 2014, when only 28 were included. The estimated savings in revenues, which were earlier leaked within the system, are about ₹3.48 lakh crore between 2014 to 2024. But JAM is but one of the innovative programmes directed at the poor households. Extending health insurance to 500 million persons; providing cash subsidy for lower income housing;

benefiting nearly 100 million households with gas stoves; ensuring food security by transferring subsidized foodgrains to nearly 800 million people; all these schemes and several others have improved the lot of the absolute poor households in ways that are certainly not captured in the income estimates of absolute poverty.

One of the strongest and yet under-recognized benefits accrues to the poorer sections of the population from the rapid development of the physical infrastructure. All components of physical infrastructure, like highways, rural roads, railways, airports, ports, electricity generation and distribution have witnessed unprecedented expansion over the last decade. Apart from generating the much-needed direct employment, the marked rise in public capital expenditure also benefits the poor by improving their access to urban opportunities and also contributes to a tangible rise in productivity.

Overall, therefore, it will be fair to conclude that the Indian economic growth over the last three and a half decades and especially in the most recent 11 years, has been one of the high points of the global economic scene. The size of the Indian economy in 1991 was $ 270 billion. In 2024–25, it had reached $3.9 trillion, having risen 14 times over this period. Correspondingly, per capita incomes have grown from $326 in 1991 to $2,900 in 2024, a nine-fold increase. Between 2014 and 2024, the Indian economy more than doubled in size. This performance becomes even more laudable as it was achieved during the last decade, which has been characterized by growing uncertainties, continued disruption of global supply chains and rising fragmentation of the world economy.

While congratulations are certainly in order, the success over the past decades still does not warrant any complacency. The country is faced with enormous challenges as it tries to complete its transition to an upper-middle-income economy by 2035 and then progress onwards to becoming Viksit Bharat by the time we celebrate the centenary of our Independence in 2047. This requires that we raise our average economic growth rate from a creditable 6.5 per cent at present realized over the past three and a half decades to above 8 per cent per annum. Can this be done? The answer is an emphatic yes, given the country's enviable pool of entrepreneurs and human talent and its diverse and plentiful set of natural resources.

It must also be attained because otherwise India faces the unsavoury prospect of being permanently caught, like the majority of Latin American economies, in the middle-income trap with unacceptable levels of inequality. Our demographic dividend, which implies a rising share of the working population in the total population, is set to start declining by 2045. After that, given the declining fertility rates, higher longevity and rising population of senior citizens, we will witness the reversal of our demographic advantage. India has a 20-year window in which it must make a spurt to break through the middle-income trap. It is virtually now or never for realizing our aspiration of becoming a Viksit Bharat.

But there is another equally, if not more compelling, challenge facing the country. India is perhaps the only country in world economic history which will be required to grow its economy at exponential rates and at the same time reduce its carbon footprint. In other words, a steady rise in per capita incomes will have to come along with declining levels of per capita carbon emissions. Like all advanced economies, which are members of the rich economies club of the OECD, we *cannot* choose to ignore the goal of reducing our per capita emissions and focus only and only on economic growth. It can perhaps be persuasively argued that weak economic growth and persistence of degrading poverty inflict the strongest ecological damage. Based on this traditional understanding, the argument stands that we should go for growth and treat it as the dominant objective in the trade-off between economics and ecology. In my view, this is a fallacious argument.

Suffice it, at this stage, to make two observations. First, both domestic public opinion and the global ecosystem will exert enormous pressure against this visualization of an economy-ecology trade-off with a preference for growth. India will not be able to withstand this rising pressure, especially in light of our global commitment to achieve 'net-zero' status by 2070, made by the prime minister in Glasgow. Second, India faces the dual calamitous reality of melting glaciers and rising sea levels. These two negative environmental trends have made it imperative that we need an innovative policy response that makes growth and ecological security complementary rather than conflicting. That it can be done successfully is now plentifully evident in evolving alternative development paradigms in agriculture, urbanization, transportation and the accelerating transition to green energy, whose costs have become equal to fossil fuel energy. By successfully tackling the simultaneous twin challenges of economic growth and ecological security, India will emerge as an exemplar for the entire Global South.

The necessary condition for tackling this enormous historical challenge is to firmly and urgently jettison the mental state and operational stance of 'business as usual' that includes the imitation of foreign development models, and be drowned in the ocean of intellectual subterfuge which surrounds them. This isomorphic limitation in our policy thinking must be overcome. Therefore, we should, after nearly eight decades of being besotted with these models and being subservient to imported ideas, now recognize that these are not relevant for our ground realities. We have to devise our development pathway that not only responds to our evolving ecosystem but is also in sync with our traditions and ethical values. It will, for example, be much easier to persuade Indians to adopt the 3Rs (refuse, reuse and recycle) lifestyle given our long-standing ethos of preserving and even worshipping nature. Thus, a development framework that posits ecology and growth as complementary and not as a trade-off will be easier to design and execute than most of us imagine.

The second essential condition is to reimagine and redesign the private–public partnership such that it becomes the basis for unleashing the immense creative potential of India's historically and globally acclaimed private enterprise and individual capabilities. This would require a fundamental change in the governance model that we inherited from the colonial period and with which we have persisted, with only some marginal changes incrementally undertaken over the past seven decades. The colonial administration was consciously designed and perfected over decades as an instrument of control and regulation. The administrators perceived the population over whom they *governed* with mistrust and not in sync with the objectives of the 'ruling dispensation'.

This was a natural outcome of the colonial dispensation, whose goal was to maximize the extraction of all available surplus from India and transfer it to the colonial beneficiaries. Quite unsurprisingly, over two centuries of colonial exploitation left India racked with famines, widespread abject poverty, dismal health and education levels and denuded forests. All this devastation is summed up in the shocking statistics that India's share in global GDP was 18.5 per cent when India was formally brought under British monarchy in 1850, and it plummeted to less than 3 per cent by the time the colonizers left India in 1947. However, the peaceful transfer of power left intact the administration infrastructure in independent India. Let's remember that our colonial masters had designed perhaps one of the most efficient systems of surplus extraction and suppression of popular sentiment. The incongruity of such an administrative system with an independent democratic India cannot be overstated.

This inherited administrative structure, largely left unchanged from its colonial legacy, has resulted in a massive infusion of regulatory cholesterol in the governance mechanism. It effectively stultifies and kills all private initiative and enterprise. The post-colonial state views the private sector with suspicion and mistrust. It also views it as a source of rent seeking, which is maximized by subjecting the private sector to increasing regulatory and compliance burdens. On the other hand, the private sector, perhaps because of the ground realities in which it has to survive, views the government machinery either as a major impediment on account of the extensive regulatory and compliance burden or as an unrelenting rent seeker. In both cases, the optimal survival strategy for the private sector is to either remain below the regulatory radar, which implies remaining small or to appease the administrative machinery in all its multiple dimensions and at all levels of the government. Remaining below the radar has resulted in the well-recognized problem of the missing middle in the Indian industry and is the reason for SMEs always remaining small and not organically evolving to a larger scale. It also explains why so very few Indian companies have gained global scale and competitiveness.

Industry–government relations have changed only marginally over the past decades. They remain like the 'regulator–regulatee' relations despite the liberalization efforts, which started in 1991 under the Narasimha Rao government. According to Prime Minister Modi himself, private enterprise has to contend with more than 60,000 regulatory and compliance requirements for its routine operations.

The time taken for starting a business and also to close it in India, while it has come down over the past ten years, remains woefully longer in our competing economies like Thailand, Singapore and China. Even the insolvency and bankruptcy process that has started with so much promise has now almost completely unravelled due to executive capacity weakness and judicial overreach.

An extensive network of regulators, licensing authorities, compliance officers and prosecution agencies is now firmly entrenched to ensure that private enterprise toes the line and operates well within these regulatory and compliance boundaries. Thus, it is an existential requirement for private firms and entrepreneurs to remain on the 'right side' of this enforcement mechanism.

Remaining on the right side of the government and its regulations, which can change even retrospectively, has resulted in four distinguishable behavioural responses from private enterprise. First, it is to strictly conform to all regulatory and compliance requirements, even if these add substantially to operating costs and cause extensive delays. The expected result is that a great majority of these firms, even if they have the inherent capability to become globally competitive, are unsuccessful in penetrating global markets and remain confined to the domestic market.

The second type of corporate behaviour is to cut regulatory corners, dodge compliance requirements and take recourse to meeting the rent-seeking demands of the regulatory authorities. This is a form of 'state appeasement' which is prevalent at all levels of the government and virtually across all sectors of the economy, bar perhaps the software and Information Technology Enabled Services (ITES) sector. The very large majority of Indian firms have adopted this set of practices in which they constantly face the risk of retroactive retribution and grave unpredictability. This again hampers the growth ambitions of the affected corporations.

The third form of corporate response is to try and influence government policy either through 'behind the door interactions' with regulators and policy makers or through indirect lobbying through industry and commerce associations. However, unlike the US, lobbying of public agencies and government entities is not considered a legitimate activity in India. Consequently, the predominant form of lobbying prevalent in the country is through collective representation of industry interests through industry and commerce associations, which exist at the national, regional and sectoral levels. There is a huge plethora of such associations which represent sector, sub-sector and even component manufacturing interests. Most, if not all, of these industry representative bodies have either been co-opted by their respective ministries or departments or worse still, have become subservient to them. An impact evaluation of the effectiveness of these bodies in serving the interests of their member private enterprises will yield some interesting and insightful revelations.

The fourth response, affordable only for a handful of the large Sensex 500 corporates, is to successfully get informal access to the inner track of policymaking. These corporations boast of large 'government relations' departments populated by some of the most talented and dynamic individuals. Some of them are drawn from the highest echelons of superannuated and, on occasions, younger officers who have taken voluntary retirement. This represents perhaps a very constructive, albeit exclusionary, nexus between private enterprise and the government at many different levels. It enables rapid expansion and, over time, huge diversification of business for corporations with well-functioning government relations departments. Plenty of anecdotal evidence for this phenomenon can be found over the decades and in current times as well. The question is often asked about the very low level of R&D expenditure by the Indian private firms. It is less than 0.2 per cent of GDP! I hypothesize that this is rational corporate behaviour as large private firms find it far more and consistently profitable to spend on sustaining and improving government relations than the expected returns on R&D outlays. This must change if India is to tackle the challenges facing it today.

A final type of response will become the most debilitating of all if it gathers momentum in the coming days, as it is threatening to do. This is for the younger generations of entrepreneurial families simply exiting India and choosing to operate from other, more corporate-friendly ecosystems. This phenomenon is now increasingly visible and needs to be taken into cognizance by policymakers. An ostrich-like approach of denying that the young rich are exiting or claiming that this is just a trickle from a vast pool of available entrepreneurial talent will both be counterproductive.

The way forward is to first and foremost recognize that it is the Indian private enterprise that has, for millennia, taken India ahead to the point of establishing the Indian footprint from Rome to Jakarta, long before Western countries could even conceive of global trade and high levels of human welfare. It was not without reason that Alexander of Macedonia, Columbus from Spain and Vasco da Gama from Portugal came looking for the economy with the golden footprint. This success and affluence of the Indian people were built solely by the amazing industry and initiatives of the private enterprise, duly supported by the ruling dispensation. Somnath, Konarak, Angkor Wat and the Prambanan temples in Yogyakarta are living testimony to the global success of India's private enterprise.

It is now imperative that a similar ecosystem that prevailed in the earlier centuries is once again put in place if India has to achieve its aspirations of once again regaining the same share in world GDP commensurate with its share in the total world population. This ecosystem will recognize the primacy of Indian private enterprise as the main dynamo of economic growth that is both ecologically sustainable and socially inclusive. The Indian private sector has been, for millennia, sensitive to the environment, a sentiment which is enshrined in its worship of nature. Private enterprise has also been socially responsive, as shown by the very long and rich tradition of voluntary philanthropy. Therefore, we should now be moving with as much speed as possible towards an ecosystem in which the government and its of regulators and compliance officers see themselves as promoters of private enterprise and accountable to it. This new form of private–public partnership is the necessary condition for India to find the innovative policy answers to the humongous challenges it faces today in a world characterized by several simultaneous challenges.

PAFI can play a significant role in reversing the regulatory tide and nudging the government towards becoming a promoter of private enterprise. For success in this important endeavour, it will have to persist with its commendable practice of not seeking government financial support for its activities. It will do well to create a coalition with think tanks across various sectors to come up with innovative policy initiatives that will allow private enterprise to break new ground, convince the policymakers and convert the apparent policy trade-offs (as in climate change versus rapid agricultural growth) into policy complementarities.

PAFI and domestic think tanks, which are focused not only on idea generation but also on the implementation of these new ideas, can together construct the platform to which government agencies are also invited. The three prominent stakeholders can then together push forward the policy frontiers based on mutual trust and transparent accountability. Such a platform, operating within the framework of a vibrant democracy and an active civil society, will ensure that India attains its aspirational objective of becoming a high-income economy when it celebrates the centenary of its Independence and is well on the path of becoming a 'net-zero' society.

14

Policy in Transition: Navigating the Past, Present and Future of Public Affairs in India

CHETAN KRISHNASWAMY

As India accelerates its economic and technological progress, its regulatory frameworks are adapting to balance innovation with long-term national priorities. With the country projected to become the world's third-largest economy, this rise is accompanied by a quiet yet profound shift in policymaking. Once confined to closed-door deliberations and dense government files, policymaking has become more inclusive and participatory. Governance, previously seen as distant and opaque, now reflects greater engagement. Nowadays, it is increasingly common to see start-up founders, academia, civil society leaders and policymakers working together, exchanging ideas and shaping regulations that are both forward-looking and grounded in real-world contexts.

This transition in the policy space is neither superficial nor temporary. For those of us who have worked in public policy for decades, the progression has been steady and unmistakable. Having spent nearly 30 years at the intersection of public policy, technology and governance – first as a journalist and later as a policy professional with some of the world's most influential technology companies – I have had the privilege of witnessing the policy landscape evolve from multiple perspectives. A world once dominated by compliance and clearances has grown into a strategic arena where policy not only enables business but actively shapes its trajectory.

Expanding the Circle: The Growing Openness in Policymaking in India

In the earlier years, the role of a corporate public policy professional was quite different from what it is today. Many of them, often retired bureaucrats, focused largely on public procurement tenders and permissions. Their role majorly involved knowing which doors to knock on, which files to follow up on and which officials might be sympathetic to their cause. A policy professional's job was to work within the system's opacity, where information asymmetry was power. Success often relied more on who you knew and how well you could navigate the system and less on understanding the nuances of an issue.

While the system is not yet completely transparent, and understanding key players still matters, today, subject expertise has become essential. As India moved towards liberalization and adopted digital technologies, policymaking began to slowly shift. Influence was no longer tied solely to connections – deep knowledge, relevant experience and the ability to offer meaningful insights grew equally, if not more, important.

The broader political and economic context played a big role in this transformation. During the 1990s, the reality of coalition governments often resulted in slow progress and compromise. However, with liberalization came economic competition and the need for more agile and responsive governance. Indian companies had to compete not just locally, but with the best in the world. This demanded more open and adaptive institutions. Over time, new actors began participating in shaping policy. Professionals from the private sector were brought into ministries through lateral entries. Consulting firms were invited to help design public programmes. Organizations like NITI Aayog established platforms that encouraged collaboration between government, industry and civil society.

I remember being in policy meetings in the early 2000s where the idea of public consultation was still seen as a formality, something done to check a box rather than to genuinely listen. That is no longer the case. Today, consultation is expected and encouraged. Ministries now routinely publish draft policies and invite public comment. Stakeholders who were once on the margins – private companies, start-ups, advocacy groups, academics – are now regular participants in these conversations.

A good example of this evolution is the policy formulation process of the Digital Personal Data Protection Rules in 2025. Not very long ago, such an important regulation would likely have been written behind closed doors, with minimal external input. This time, however, the process unfolded in full public view. Over 200 stakeholders submitted their feedback, and their suggestions were reflected across multiple versions of the draft. The outcome carried the imprint of many voices. In parallel, the Joint Parliamentary Committee on the Personal Data Protection Bill, working closely with the Ministry of Electronics and Information Technology, held over 78 meetings across 184 hours, carefully gathering and weighing a wide range of perspectives from across the ecosystem.

Another change has been in the way regulators approach innovation. Take the idea of regulatory sandboxes. Inspired, in part, by global practices from the European Union and the United States, India has embraced the model as well. The Reserve Bank of India led the way, and soon after, both the Securities and Exchange Board of India (SEBI) and the Insurance Regulatory and Development Authority of India (IRDAI) followed. These sandboxes provide a safe space for experimentation, allowing new ideas to be tested in a controlled manner, with active oversight from the regulators.

More broadly, the culture of engagement has become more structured. Institutions like the Telecom Regulatory Authority of India, the Ministry of Commerce and Industry, Ministry of Electronics and Information Technology, to name a few, now regularly issue discussion papers, hold open consultations and seek stakeholder input as a standard practice.

In fact, the prime minister's meetings with corporate leaders now draw as much attention as bilateral discussions with other heads of state. This reflects a growing recognition that businesses are not just participants in the economy but active contributors to national policy discourse.

Naturally, not every part of the process is perfect. There are still frictions. Power is not distributed evenly, and some consultations can feel more performative than genuinely participatory. However, taken together, these changes point to a clear shift: policymaking in India is steadily becoming more iterative and truly reflective of the diverse voices that shape the country's democratic fabric.

Building for Scale: The Role of Innovation in Shaping Inclusive Policymaking

India's journey towards inclusive policymaking was not a coincidence. It was a deliberate response to a unique moment in the country's development. With liberalization, India saw the arrival of leading multinational companies, bringing with them global standards and competitive expectations. At the same time, a young demographic and rapid urbanization created an urgent need for systems that could serve over a billion people. In such a context, building for scale was not optional – it was essential. However, rather than proceed in small, cautious steps, India chose bold leaps.

Nowhere is this more visible than in the country's Digital Public Infrastructure (DPI). Unlike many other economies that developed gradually, India leapfrogged legacy systems altogether. Take mobile phones: while countries like the United States and the United Kingdom spent decades building landline networks, India almost skipped that phase and witnessed a rapid and widespread adoption of mobile technology. This mobile-first approach laid the foundation for transformative platforms like Aadhaar, Unified Payments Interface (UPI) and DigiLocker – public goods designed not for profit but for public use at unprecedented scale.

Aadhaar gave more than a billion Indians a secure digital identity, enabling targeted welfare delivery and easier access to services. UPI revolutionized payments, turning smartphones into wallets and processing over 17 billion real-time transactions in April 2025 alone. DigiLocker digitized essential records – like academic certificates and licenses – for millions of citizens.

This forward-thinking approach is also evident in India's rapid technological rollout. The country now boasts the fastest 5G expansion in the world, with coverage in over 99 per cent of districts. The launch of the Bharat 6G Vision in 2023 further reinforced India's ambition to lead in future technologies. These are not isolated successes – they reflect a policy mindset focused on long-term, system-wide impact.

None of this would have been possible without a strong legal framework. The Information Technology Act of 2000 laid the groundwork, validating electronic transactions and offering a safe harbour to intermediaries. At a time when regulation often lagged behind innovation, the Act provided clarity and room to experiment – making it clear that speed would not be penalized, so long as accountability was maintained. Even today, that legal clarity remains a vital enabler of India's digital journey.

But as the country's digital capacity has grown, its regulatory environment is becoming increasingly complex. National security concerns have started to shape policy more strongly, leading to demands for data localization, tighter cybersecurity regulations and enhanced government control over critical infrastructure. This shift mirrors India's broader effort to assert digital sovereignty amid a constantly changing geopolitical climate.

In today's interconnected world, multinational companies operating in India find themselves playing a dual role: both market players and informal ambassadors. Balancing the interests of their home countries with the regulatory expectations of India requires diplomacy, agility and foresight. Public policy is no longer an afterthought – it is front and centre.

Large global companies now engage early, embedding public policy into their core operations from the outset. A major US-based electric vehicle manufacturer hired its India policy head even before selling a single car. In 2024, one of the world's leading AI company's first hire in the country was a government relations lead, as it prepared to engage with India's emerging AI regulations. These moves underline a key truth: in India, success increasingly depends not just on the strength of your technology, but on how well you navigate the policy environment.

The Rise of the Ecosystem: Public Policy Comes into the Boardroom

As India's regulatory framework and geopolitical landscape grow in complexity, public policy has become a central pillar in shaping how businesses operate, compete and grow. In boardrooms today, I see conversations that go far beyond compliance or approvals. Executives now ask: 'Where is policy headed?'; 'Which government programmes should we align with?'; 'Who do we need to work with to make this happen?' This marks a significant departure from just a few years ago, when the focus was largely limited to taxes or tariffs. Whether it's building a climate roadmap that supports India's Paris Agreement goals or setting up internal rules for AI that match India's new tech laws, companies are now thinking about policy early – and often – as part of their core strategy.

One of the key reasons for the government and the industry coming together for iterative policymaking is how much industry associations have matured. Many now operate through focused groups that handle specific areas like AI, hydrogen, digital payments and data privacy, etc. These dedicated teams make it easier to provide informed and structured input to the government.

When early drafts of India's AI rules raised concerns about how they might slow down research, industry associations quickly brought companies together and passed on their feedback in a clear, constructive way. The government listened – and revised the rules to strike a better balance between safety and innovation. This kind of real-time, two-way engagement shows how India's policy environment is becoming more responsive and solutions-driven.

The growing willingness to collaborate between the government and the private sector is no longer confined to policymaking alone, but extends to policy implementation and the delivery of key national priorities. This partnership is evident in initiatives that were rare even a decade ago. For instance, NCERT textbooks are now distributed through e-commerce enterprises, significantly broadening access to quality education and tackling piracy concerns. Similarly, these entities, along with logistics companies, are working with Indian Railways and India Post to enhance last-mile delivery, helping these traditional platforms become more competitive in a rapidly changing market.

These efforts are not isolated experiments, but clear demonstrations of how the government's unparalleled scale and reach, combined with the private sector's agility and technological expertise, can effectively address real-world challenges. I witnessed this capability to handle challenges first-hand during the COVID-19 pandemic, when the organization I work for partnered with the government to develop the CoWIN platform – an ambitious digital infrastructure that enabled the vaccination of 1.4 billion people. It was a powerful example of how technology, grounded in public trust and designed for scale, can respond to a national emergency.

As partnerships between government and private companies deepen, the demand for skilled policy professionals is rising sharply, projected to grow by over 20 per cent annually in the next five years. The range of subjects public policy now covers, including AI, cybersecurity, climate change and worker protection, has broadened significantly. Boutique consulting firms, legal experts and think tanks are playing an increasingly vital role in helping companies interpret evolving regulations and turn them into practical, actionable strategies.

Together, these changes show how public policy in India is no longer a background concern – it's become a key part of how businesses succeed.

Envisioning the Next 30 Years

Thirty years ago, the idea of multistakeholder policymaking in India seemed unlikely. Today, it's the norm. Looking ahead, the scope of public policy will only expand as technology advances, social priorities evolve and new challenges emerge. Public policy won't just be about keeping up with emerging technologies like AI or quantum computing; it will surface new riddles about where, how and for whom innovation works.

Questions that once sat on the fringes – like how teenagers engage with social media or how gender inclusive new technologies are – will increasingly shape mainstream policy debates. One will need to understand how a policy might play out not just in principle, but on the ground – in a warehouse, in the distribution network, in a local classroom.

Two areas of particular interest to me are AI and data analytics. We are already seeing AI tools being used to analyse vast amounts of public feedback, map sentiment and simulate the socioeconomic impact of draft regulations. AI is also accelerating research, helping policy professionals work faster and with more precision.

Similarly, the ability to work with data is becoming critical. As business decisions grow more nuanced, policy professionals need to be as comfortable interpreting balance sheets and operational metrics as they are reading a government circular. Understanding where policy intersects with business outcomes – such as profitability, supply chain resilience or customer impact – has become essential. The ability to combine data-driven insights with policy understanding strengthens credibility and sharpens advocacy.

Even as technological tools evolve, the bedrock of effective public policy remains profoundly human. While algorithms excel at data analysis, they cannot forge the trust that defines lasting policy success. Often, the most impactful policy conversations happen in person, in local languages rather than a fancy white paper.

The ability to read a room, understand unspoken political dynamics and navigate complex stakeholder relationships comes from years of practical experience and multidimensional thinking. While technology can enhance our capabilities, core elements like understanding long-term societal impact, cultural sensitivities and maintaining the delicate balance between profit and purpose will continue to require human judgement, empathy and authentic relationship-building.

As global dynamics shift and regulators grow more assertive, the most valuable skill in public policy will be seeing around corners. I think of it as skilled crystal ball gazing: reading signals early and helping businesses navigate what's coming next – not just reacting to today's headlines. It means understanding not only how a company runs today, but what it might become tomorrow.

This is what makes public policy so compelling – and why I remain both optimistic and deeply curious about what lies ahead. It's no longer just about interpreting rules; it's about shaping the future with foresight, knowing that each decision defines the opportunities of tomorrow.

15

Policy to Boost Trade in the Current Environment

T.S. VISHWANATH AND ADHIRAJ GUPTA

The global trade environment today is paradoxical – on the one hand, highly interconnected and, on the other, increasingly fragmented by protectionist measures. After decades of tariff cuts and liberalization, new barriers are rising. The World Bank notes that 'growing protectionism, trade tensions and geopolitical challenges are raising concerns about the future of globalization'. Nevertheless, global trade remains substantial ($33 trillion in 2024) despite recovering from pandemic shocks. Paradoxically, value chains are rebounding even as some economies talk of 'de-globalization' through various measures to calibrate the flow of cheaper imports. In this unsettled context, India's leadership has set a goal of a Viksit Bharat 2047 – a developed, resilient economy by its centenary.

Achieving this will require deft navigation of the global order: taking advantage of new openings while guarding against the headwinds of protectionism, high standards and geopolitical upheaval. Despite multiple conflicts and supply shocks the world faced recently, India's exports still hit a record $825 billion in FY 2024–25, implying the need to build on that resilience even as rules evolve. This chapter captures the shifting international trade landscape and India's response, highlighting its emerging trade doctrine, competitive strengths, structural challenges and a strategic roadmap to 2047.

The Fractured Global Arena

Divergent trends shape today's trade world. The pandemic and significant power tensions have spurred firms to rethink over-dependence on any one source. Many companies, especially in technology and manufacturing, are exploring a 'China Plus One' strategy – retaining China in their supply chains but shifting parts of production to India, the Association of Southeast Asian Nations (ASEAN) and other hubs. At the same time, the World Bank notes that GVCs remain central to trade – indeed, GVC content of trade grew to 52 per cent in 2022 from ~48 per cent in 2015 – underscoring that supply networks are reconfiguring, not disappearing. However, supply-chain shifts are one facet of a more turbulent economy. Geopolitics is casting a long shadow. The US–China rivalry has spawned new tariffs, export controls and reshoring. The US CHIPS Act, stringent tech export curbs and scrutiny of foreign investment in critical sectors all push for the 'reshoring' of strategic industries. Europe, too, has become a rule-making force: its Green Deal, carbon border tax (CBAM) and strict digital and sustainability standards impose new non-tariff barriers on exporters. For instance, an analysis finds that the EU now takes ~27 per cent of India's aluminium and 38 per cent of its steel exports, which could face hefty carbon levies under CBAM. Meanwhile, regulatory regimes on chemicals, traceability, forced labour and plastic waste proliferate globally. Today's exporters must navigate a thicket of such standards beyond just tariff lines.

Into this mix comes the steady erosion of multilateral trade governance. The WTO, once the lodestar of rules-based trade, is visibly weakened. Its dispute settlement Appellate Body has been non-functional since late 2019 – 'paralysing the dispute resolution system' for appeals. Countries increasingly settle trade frictions bilaterally or via newer clubs rather than through WTO panels. Negotiations at the WTO ministerial yield only modest progress: the recent 2024 Ministerial (Abu Dhabi) achieved no new global deal on farm subsidies or digital trade. However, India won assurances of policy space for its farmers and fishermen. In short, the multilateral trading system is under strain from shifting power balances and new policy priorities, even as the need for cooperation – to keep markets open and predictable – remains high.

India's Trade Doctrine: Policy Evolution and Strategic Shifts

In response to this dynamic world, India has quietly remade its trade policy. The new Foreign Trade Policy 2023–28 (FTP 2023) moves towards a WTO-friendly 'remission' model, where embedded taxes on exports are refunded (e.g., via the Remission of Duties and Taxes on Exported Products [RoDTEP] scheme) rather than cash incentives. This 'incentive to remission' shift is designed to improve compliance and fiscal sustainability. The FTP also doubles down on digitization and de-bureaucratization: it envisions single-window clearance, e-certificates, online filing and an end-to-end digital interface for exporters. To spur exports beyond the big metros, it launched 'District as Export Hub' plans: each district will identify local potential sectors, join exporters with buyers and improve state-level support. The Commerce Ministry has also set up a Trade Facilitation Forum and launched projects to streamline Certificates of Origin for Free Trade Agreement (FTA) compliances, alongside new Export Facilitation Centres to handhold MSMEs overseas. The message is clear: India is upgrading its export machinery to match global best practices.

Sectoral strategy is sharpening, too. Traditional strengths – textiles, gems, auto parts, pharmaceuticals – are being complemented by focus industries. The government's PLI (Production-Linked Incentive) schemes now cover a dozen sectors, and early results are encouraging: PLI-approved projects have already drawn ₹1.61 lakh crore of investment, generated ₹14 lakh crore in output and supported over 1.5 lakh jobs. Crucially, high-tech exports have surged; PLI electronics and pharma helped India cross ₹5.31 lakh crore ($62 billion) in related exports. In parallel, India is scouting FTAs as part of a larger geo-economic approach. In recent years, India signed new trade deals with the UAE (Comprehensive Economic Partnership Agreement [CEPA], 2022); Australia (Economic Crime [Transparency and Enforcement] Act, 2022); European Free Trade Association (2023); and now the UK (2025). These pacts are intentionally made with advanced, transparent markets to leverage India's massive demand. For example, the UAE FTA significantly cut tariffs on Indian textiles, opening big markets. Negotiations are underway with Chile, Peru, the EU and even the US for a limited bilateral pact by late 2025. India's trade doctrine has shifted from passive integration towards proactive management: diversifying markets and products, streamlining processes and ensuring that trade agreements serve economic and strategic goals.

Engines of Opportunity: India's Competitive Levers

Despite headwinds, India has strong trade growth levers. Its service sector remains world-class. India now accounts for about 10.2 per cent of global telecommunications, computer and information services exports, making it the second-largest IT-enabled and BPO services supplier. Other business services (engineering, R&D, consulting) also have a world share of about 7–8 per cent. With a booming digital economy, India is positioning itself as a hub for start-ups and global capability centres. The result is a services export boom: in FY 2024–25, India's service exports jumped to about $383.5 billion (up ~12.5 per cent over the previous year). IT and software continue to lead, but non-traditional services like digital healthcare, fintech, animation and remote professional work are adding momentum. India's youthful, English-speaking talent pool – roughly 50 per cent of STEM graduates globally – underpins this strength.

In manufacturing, India is also turning domestic potential into an exportable reality. The Make in India push, backed by the PLI incentives, is building new capacity for computers, mobiles, medical devices, auto components, industrial electronics and more. For example, led by PLI, India's electronics sector has flipped from a net importer to a net exporter of mobile phones. In pharmaceuticals, India is already the world's third-largest producer by volume and exports about half its output, benefiting from ongoing biotech R&D and generics leadership. Newer industries also beckon: government initiatives target aerospace parts, defence manufacturing and semiconductors (IDM/IC factories), viewing them as future GVC niches. Private investment is following – global brands from Apple to Foxconn and Volkswagen are expanding Indian production –

suggesting India could become a meaningful export platform for once-imported goods.

Green tech is an emerging horizon. India is ramping up solar, wind, battery and EV manufacturing under its National Green Hydrogen and renewable missions. Installed renewable capacity already tops 223 gigawatt (GW) (a fast-growing 108 GW solar plus 51 GW wind), and plans are afoot for 500 GW by 2030. More strategically, India aspires to be a major exporter of green hydrogen by 2030. The government's Green Hydrogen Mission has earmarked $2.4 billion of incentives to reach 5 million tonnes annually by 2030. If achieved, this could catalyse new industries (electrolysers, fuel cells, green steel and ammonia) and open trade flows to Europe and East Asia (already planning hydrogen imports). Crucially, India is also securing supplies of critical minerals needed for these technologies. For example, the proposed India–Chile Comprehensive Economic Partnership Agreement (CEPA) will expand precisely to access Chile's vast lithium and copper reserves, essential for EV batteries and renewable grids. Such 'commodities-for-technology' trade pacts could underpin a green-industrial boom.

Finally, India's large and young population is itself an asset. With a median age of ~28 and two-thirds of Indians in the workforce today, the domestic market is growing. Household consumption has already driven 60 per cent of India's GDP, up from 55 per cent a decade ago, even as real incomes rise. This vast market allows exporters to achieve economies of scale before selling abroad. In practice, India's middle-class and rural consumers create demand for electronics, automobiles, consumer goods and services that encourage domestic production (e.g., India is now a leading auto producer with ambitious EV targets). In short, India's demographic dividend and buying power form a stable foundation: companies can

'Make in India for the World' with confidence that home demand will help sustain scale.

Confronting the Headwinds: Structural and External Challenges

India's promise comes with challenges that cannot be glossed over. Chief among them are infrastructure bottlenecks. India's logistics performance still trails many peers. Although it has climbed steadily – the World Bank ranked India thirty-eighth (out of 150) in its 2023 Logistics Performance Index – gaps remain in port efficiency, rail-road connectivity and customs clearance. Initiatives like the PM GatiShakti plan and Sagarmala port modernization seek to build multimodal corridors and 35 upcoming multimodal logistics parks, but progress is gradual. Export competitiveness requires faster moves: congested ports and last-mile delivery costs continue to dull India's edge.

Another concern is integrating small businesses into global chains. Indian MSMEs account for nearly half of manufacturing output, but many lack the quality, scale or finance to export. They struggle with meeting complex standards, negotiating finance at competitive rates or absorbing tech upgrades. Without targeted support, many exporters remain clustered among big conglomerates. The government's new MSME export e-portals and financing schemes help, but accelerating MSME compliance is an ongoing need for India to broaden its export base beyond a few dozen marquee firms. Non-tariff barriers constitute another structural headwind, both externally and at home.

Globally, countries are deploying more product standards and regulations. India's Economic Survey cites that Technical Barriers to Trade (TBTs) now affect 31.6 per cent of product lines (covering ~67 per cent of global trade), with another 19.3 per cent of lines subject to export measures. Indian exporters frequently encounter foreign sanitary rules, labelling norms and carbon or digital taxes that can block or add shipment costs. Conversely, India has introduced numerous import restrictions under the 'Atma Nirbhar' push. In 2023–24, the government issued over 700 Quality Control Orders (QCOs) on imports, aiming to keep out substandard products. While intended to improve local quality, critics warn that QCOs also raise input costs for domestic firms that rely on imported parts.

Mandatory quality checks or rising compliance can disrupt just-in-time supply lines. For example, requiring stringent certification on machinery imports might protect local producers, but it inadvertently slows down Indian companies trying to build exportable goods. India must, therefore, calibrate these measures carefully: they can promote 'Make in India' quality standards, but if overused, they risk alienating trading partners or raising production costs.

Human capital is a final concern. India's workforce is young, but education and skills often lag. Many workers lack vocational training or the digital skills that GVC-led firms demand. The Economic Survey notes that sustaining service export growth will hinge on continual skill development and training. Similarly, manufacturing firms often cite labour productivity and ease of hiring (especially in unorganized sectors) as limiting expansion. Addressing this requires more schools or technical institutes, flexible vocational policies and lifetime learning programmes so that workers can move fluidly between industries. Bridging the skill gap is critical: without it, India may miss out on higher-value segments in electronics assembly, biotech manufacturing or advanced engineering, leaving too much value in addition to others.

A Strategic Roadmap to 2047

Looking ahead, India's trade strategy must be multidimensional to be future-ready. Digitization of trade processes should be accelerated: fully implementing electronic clearances, blockchain-based customs and AI-driven risk management can cut transaction costs. The government's nascent Single Window, Goods and Services Network (GSTN), e-invoicing and the Common Digital Platform for Certificates of Origin are steps in the right direction. Further, extending digital trade agreements (DTAs) or mutual recognition for e-documents with partners (as seen in the Regional Comprehensive Economic Partnership [RCEP] countries) could streamline cross-border e-commerce and data flows. At the international level, India should shape global digital and fintech rules (including promoting interoperable standards for digital payments and data protection) so that its firms can scale platforms abroad.

Regarding manufacturing, India will benefit from doubling down on select GVC niches. The successes in mobile phones and pharmaceuticals suggest similar opportunities in other segments. For example, electronics assemblies (beyond mobiles, such as laptops and EV chargers) are ripe for expansion, given India's skilled workforce and low labour cost. In chemicals, India already has a foothold in Active Pharmaceutical Ingredients (APIs); clustering more API and speciality chemical production could lift Indian pharmaceutical exports further. The green tech sector is also strategic: India should invest in 'green exports' like solar modules, wind turbine blades, EV batteries and electrolysers, where it has learning advantages. Encouraging R&D in clean tech (through tax credits or incubators) and strengthening patent protection can help 'design in India'. For example, a robust Intellectual Property

Rights regime (building on the 2016 IPR Policy) would attract global companies to research and patent new products in India – an evolution from manufacturing to captivating talent and innovation.

India must align its trade policy with its broader foreign and security strategy. This means negotiating agreements that are not just commercially liberal but also geopolitically complementary. On this note, India is already moving in this direction. While one track pursues a limited trade deal with the US and an FTA with the EU, another track deepens ties with East and West Asia through trade and infrastructure (such as the I2U2 Quad and expanded Asia–Africa corridors). Trade policy must remain coherent with national security – for example, screening foreign investment in strategic sectors even as export restrictions are eased – so that India's industries grow without compromising technological autonomy.

Finally, resilience, inclusivity and ESG must become core planning pillars. Trade resilience implies not only diversification of markets but also 'self-reliance' in inputs for critical industries. This could mean expanding local testing or backup supply chains for essentials (medical supplies, food grains) while keeping markets open enough to stabilize prices. Inclusivity means ensuring that trade benefits accrue across society: programmes to upskill informal sector workers, support rural exporters and spread manufacturing bases beyond big cities. ESG compliance is no longer optional either. India should embed environmental and labour standards into its policies (e.g., India's Producer Responsibility standards and labour law reforms) so its exporters are not penalized abroad. Initiatives like the Business Responsibility and Sustainability Reporting (BRSR) requirements for large firms and the Green Hydrogen Certification scheme signal India's intent to meet global norms. Over time, exporters who demonstrate social and environmental compliance will gain market access and long-term partnerships in Europe, Japan and North America, turning a challenge into an advantage.

Conclusion

India stands at a crucial juncture. Globalization and protectionism shape today's trade environment, but smart policy can tilt the balance. By judiciously combining openness with strategic safeguards, India can use trade as a powerful engine for growth. It must remain outward-looking to attract investment and new markets while ensuring domestic industries and farmers are not left vulnerable. Despite myriad headwinds, the record exports of FY 2025 show the resilience built in recent years. Looking ahead, proactive reforms (digital trade, infrastructure, skills), targeted incentives (PLI, green missions) and well-chosen trade partnerships will be key. If India plays its cards right, it can transform the current turbulence into an opportunity window, making trade a pillar of its Viksit Bharat 2047 vision.

16

Reforms in the Financial Market Regulation in India

AJAY TYAGI

The financial sector is the backbone of the economy in any country and needs to be managed well with the required expertise and calibre. The financial markets are the heart and soul of the financial sector.

The financial markets, driven by 'greed and fear', are inherently susceptible to market failures because of asymmetry of information with the different market participants at any given time, and therefore need to be regulated. The need for having independent regulators for regulating the financial markets is well recognized world over.

This essay examines various issues relating to the financial sector regulators in India, namely, the need for autonomy and independence, clarity in roles, selection procedure, regulation-making and accountability.

Autonomy and Independence

Given its statutory role, a regulator has to be an autonomous institution, in letter and spirit, functioning as per law. Regulatory capture would be the worst thing that could happen to such an institution.

Talking of autonomy, to begin with and among other things, having 'financial independence' is a sine qua non for a regulator. It should have its revenue stream, not dependent on budgetary support, freedom to decide capital and revenue expenditure, as well as the terms and conditions of employment of its personnel.

The regulator–government relationship is an evergreen subject of debate the world over, even in developed economies. While undoubtedly, the government is an important stakeholder, it has to realize that a regulator, created by the government itself, has a statutory mandate to fulfil.

Consider the case in India. The government is a major player in the Indian financial markets. The government is the largest borrower in the bond market. Many even hold the view that their huge market borrowings crowd out the potential debt raising by the private sector from the markets. The government owns a large number of banks, NBFCs and insurance companies. Many public sector undertakings (PSUs) have their equities listed in the stock market. The government-owned entities compete with the privately owned entities in almost all sectors. In a free market economy, not only should all the regulated entities have a level playing field, but they should also be perceived to be similarly treated by the regulators.

The need for the regulators to work independently and at arm's length from the government is thus obvious. In fact, there is no point in setting up statutory regulators if they were to function as departments or attached offices of the government.

Notably, the International Monetary Fund–World Bank study on India's financial system, based on the report of the Financial Sector Assessment Program (FSAP) Mission, which visited India in 2024, points out the need to make regulators more independent.

Clarity in Roles

The enactment setting up a regulator should have a clear purpose, explicitly stating the objective, role, powers and functions of the regulator. The regulator should stick to the statutory mandate and eschew the tendency to take on additional functions.

In India, the Reserve Bank of India (RBI) is undoubtedly the most conflicted financial sector regulator. This is on account of the provisions under the RBI Act, which prescribe conflicting roles, due to various functions and activities assumed by the regulator and the government diktat.

RBI decides the monetary policy of the country – a well-recognized function, as is the case with the similarly placed central banks across the world. But then it is also the debt manager for raising debt for the central government and state governments. The conflict is obvious – while the debt raising function demands raising debt at the lowest possible interest rates at any given time, the inflation targeting mandate under the monetary policy role may not support this. The need for setting up a separate debt management framework has been examined umpteen times in the government, and appropriate solutions have been suggested. However, the vested interests have stifled these proposals.

A regulator can't itself be a market participant. But in the case of the RBI, it is worse – it even owns market infrastructure institutions. RBI owns an exchange, namely, the Negotiated Dealing System-Order Matching (NDS-OM) and a clearing corporation, namely the Clearing Corporation of India (CCIL), to facilitate trading and settlement of government securities (G-Secs). While the latter has been set up under the Payment and Settlement Act – a law enforced by the RBI – NDS-OM has no legal backing. Why should the RBI set up these institutions? The question to be asked is why shouldn't G-Secs be treated like any other securities, and their trading and settlement happen in stock exchanges and clearing corporations regulated by the securities market regulator?

Take the case of National Payments Corporation of India (NPCI), which owns UPI with a virtual monopoly in the payment system in India. Although RBI doesn't hold any equity in NPCI (various banks do), the central bank is effectively the owner, operator and regulator of UPI. While this model might have been helpful in giving the idea its initial push and establishing the system, a regulator with an interest in a regulated entity is undesirable. RBI came out with a policy in 2019 for licensing so-called new umbrella entities (NUEs), envisaged as UPI competitors and invited expressions of interest from eligible parties. But it didn't see the light of day.

An important function that the RBI handles is the regulation of banks. The Indian financial sector is bank-dominated, and a failing bank could lead to overall financial stability issues. RBI provides comfort to the banks as their lender of last resort.

That said, the RBI's overreach in micromanaging the functioning of all banks is a cause of worry. RBI approves the appointment, tenure and remuneration of the chairpersons, managing directors (MDs) and board directors (both executive and non-executive) of all the private sector banks. At times, the RBI also send its representatives on bank boards as additional directors for different periods. While the RBI taking on this role in respect of a few systemically important banks is understandable, doing so for all the banks, irrespective of their size, implies not only spreading out their regulatory resources too thin, but also raises a serious moral hazard issue. Among other consequences, this is likely to lead to an increased forbearance tendency on the part of the regulator. As a result, the regulator may find it difficult to extricate itself from certain possible awkward situations. In the process, it may even risk its credibility. The RBI needs to review this policy.

Another problem with the banks, though not of the RBI's creation, is the dual regulatory oversight mechanism of public sector banks. The government approves the appointment and terms and conditions of the chairpersons, MDs and directors of these banks as per its procedure. There is no role for the Nomination and Remuneration Committees (NRC) and bank boards in their appointments. In the case of any wrongdoing requiring action against banks' personnel, including their removal, the RBI can only make recommendations to the government.

The public sector banks, set up under statutes, create another problem. They aren't companies under the Companies Act, and seek a differentiated treatment vis-à-vis the banks are incorporated as companies. It may be particularly difficult to consider such requests in the listed space, wherein all listed entities, whether in the private or public sector, have to follow a uniform regulatory regime.

The government ought to have a relook at these issues. The board-level appointments on public sector bank boards should be left to the wisdom and decision of the NRCs and boards. The government-nominated directors on these bank boards could convey the government's views on the matter to the boards. The banks set up under the parliamentary acts should be converted into companies under the Companies Act at the earliest.

Appointment Procedure

The financial sector regulators are selected by the Financial Sector Regulatory Appointments Search Committee (FSRASC), with the approval of the Appointments Committee of Cabinet, headed by the prime minister.

Getting the right people to fill the regulatory jobs can prove to be a challenging task. Financial markets in an emerging economy like India are ever evolving and getting more and more complex, with newer products and increasing use of technology. The regulator has to keep itself abreast with the changes and adapt quickly. It cannot be seen as behind the curve vis-à-vis the market participants. More importantly, the regulator has to have the trust of all the stakeholders. Considering the sensitiveness and criticality of financial markets, the financial sector regulators' reputation has to be beyond suspicion by the strictest standards – Caesar's wife plus credentials.

Recent events have sparked a media debate on whether such appointees should come from the government or the private sector. There are no straight answers to this question. Ideally, a regulatory board should have the right mix of professionals from the government and private sector. The private sector professionals, who have been practitioners in the market, are expected to have a better understanding of the fine operating nuances and nitty-gritty of the markets. Their insights could definitely enrich the regulator's working and decision-making. The people from the government, in addition to having worked in the finance sector, have decades of experience in government service. They are well-versed in the milieu in which a public office typically works, the broader policy issues, and may find it relatively easier to deal with and coordinate with the other related agencies.

The possibility of 'conflict of interest' is the biggest issue to safeguard against while considering eligible candidates. Working in a public office is very different from that in the private sector. It has a distinct work culture and ethos. The incumbent is in public gaze, and is expected to conduct himself/herself impeccably. While a civil servant, used to following well-documented conduct rules, is used to all this, the private sector persons may need to go through a quick learning process. They need to be cognizant of the constraints of working in a public office, and should analyse all pros and cons before taking the plunge. Needless to say, the code of conduct for the members of all the financial sector regulatory boards needs to be fortified.

As for the selection of candidates from the government, the common public perception that these jobs are sinecures for the retired officials has to be strongly negated. The government should identify and offer appointments to suitable candidates, with the requisite knowledge and expertise and impeccable reputation, well ahead of their superannuation. Autonomous regulatory bodies with substantial and well-defined roles would definitely attract the right people ready to leave their government jobs to take up these roles.

Regulation Making

The laws governing the financial sector regulators give a lot of flexibility, and rightly so, to the regulators for subordinate legislation. Everything can't be hard-coded in the parliamentary laws, and the regulators ought to have the flexibility to frame regulations to meet the market requirements from time to time. That said, considering that it's a parliamentary delegation for law-making to a body, the regulators have to be responsible, demonstrate maturity and be careful in making the regulations.

The statutes should broadly state the standard operating procedure for regulation-making. The procedure should be to bring the concerned subject matter before the regulatory board, along with a draft consultation paper; to put the approved consultation paper in the public domain for adequate time for stakeholders' views; to bring back to the regulatory board a summarization of the public views and the proposals thereupon along with reasoning; and finally obtain board approval of the draft regulation. All this may sound like a tedious procedure, but it is a must to ensure transparency and sturdiness of a regulation. Many times, the regulators tend to avoid this process and instead issue 'circulars' and other forms of communications on policy matters. This must be avoided unless there is an exigency, and there are valid reasons to believe that the matter can't wait. Even in such cases, the circular(s) on policy issues should be converted into regulation(s) at the earliest after following the due process.

Considering the dynamic nature of the market, the regulations need to be constantly reviewed, their relevance and impact assessed and appropriate corrective actions taken. Making a regulation is an art – a fine balance between the requisite regulatory oversight and ease of doing business. A flexible approach and stakeholder consultation hold the key.

Accountability

The accountability of regulators is a serious issue requiring careful consideration. After all, the regulators cannot be given a free pass in the name of regulatory independence.

Let us first examine the legal provisions in some existing statutes that may be relevant for ensuring oversight of regulators' work. These include the powers of the central government to make rules, issue directions to regulator and even supersede them in certain situations; the requirement for regulators to submit an annual report to the government, which is subsequently laid before Parliament; the provision for laying regulations before Parliament; and the establishment of an appellate body to hear appeals against the quasi-judicial orders passed by regulators.

These provisions only serve a limited purpose. The government's rule-making is restricted to administrative issues, and rightly so; issuing directions could be perceived as a violation of the arm's length working principle; instances of a regulatory board being superseded are virtually unheard of; annual reports don't have a standard format and any critical analysis of regulators' functioning; and there are no instances of regulations laid before Parliament being modified. There is no prescribed appellate mechanism against the executive orders passed by the RBI.

The desirable approach for ensuring regulators' accountability would be to have direct parliamentary oversight through parliamentary committees over their functioning. The parliamentary standing committee of the Ministry of Finance should be given this role. The committee should be strengthened by providing well-qualified supporting staff and streamlining the processes. The committee could call a regulator twice a year to review its functioning and also hear from stakeholders and experts. Regulators should be obligated to file an action-taken report on the committee's observations, within a defined timeframe. The committee may then finalize its report, which should be placed before the Parliament, and later in the public domain.

In fact, as the system matures, the concerned parliamentary committee may also be entrusted with the authority to confirm the appointment of regulators.

Conclusion

As the Indian financial markets grow in size and complexity and increasingly integrate with the global markets, they would need to be regulated by best-in-class regulations, by competent, professional and well-equipped autonomous regulators. The government needs to nurture these institutions for the betterment of the economy and stakeholders' interests. The government–regulator relationship should be handled carefully and with maturity.

17

Unlocking India's Economic Potential: Women's Workforce Participation as a Critical Driver of Viksit Bharat

POOJA SHARMA GOYAL

Presently, 196 million employable women remain out of India's workforce. That is equivalent to the population of Brazil, the sixth most populous country in the world. Imagine the unlocking of opportunities that is waiting to happen; imagine the talent that is waiting to be unleashed.

Over the last few decades, we have made remarkable progress in preventing female infanticide and foeticide, improving maternal health and increasing enrolment of girls in schools and colleges. The gross enrolment ratios of girls in the country are inching toward 50 per cent. Yet women's workforce participation in the economy continues to be poor. Even though the Female Labour Force Participation Rate (FLFPR) in India has gone up from 27 per cent in 2022 to 41.3 per cent in 2024, women's participation in the formal economy continues to be static at 18 per cent over the last five years. Women continue to be pushed into the informal economy due to significant barriers on the demand side.

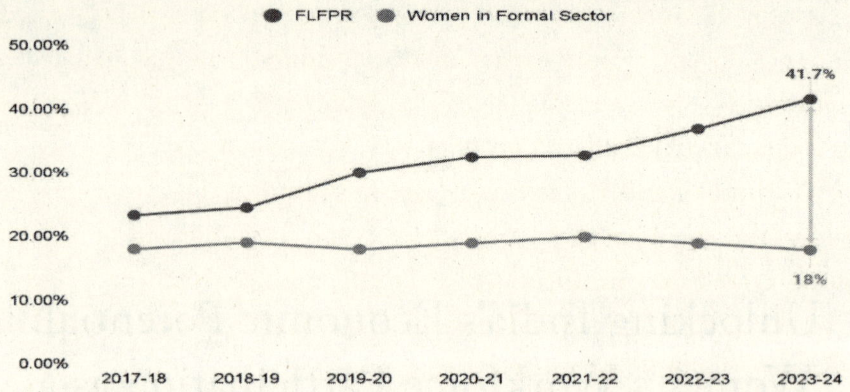

Source: Women's Formal Employment Tracker for FY 2023–2024 by Udaiti Foundation

In most countries, economic growth and female workforce participation tend to rise together: higher GDP creates more job opportunities, and more women enter the labour force. But India's experience has diverged from this trend. Despite steady growth in income and educational attainment, women's participation in the

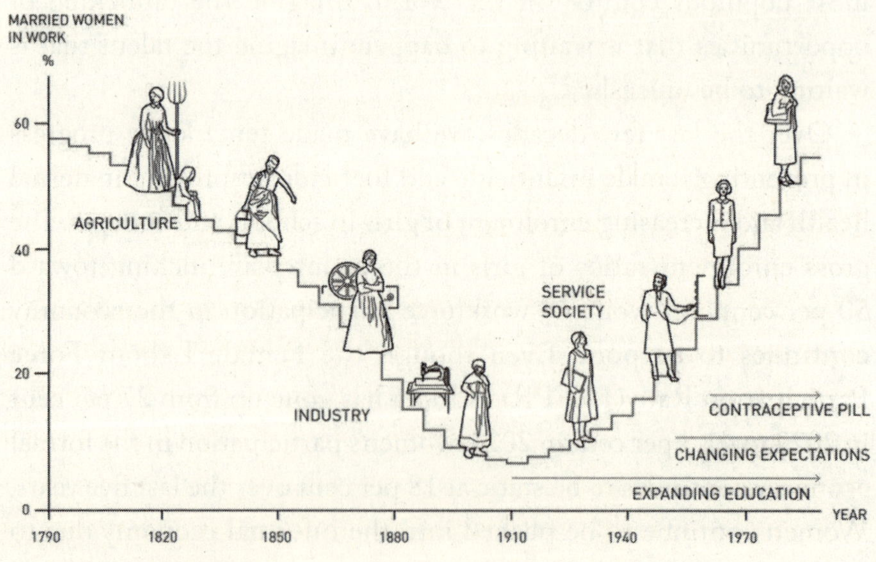

Source: Nobel Prize Website

economy has not kept pace. This is one of the great paradoxes in India today and points to deeper structural barriers that need to be addressed if we are to realize the full potential of our demographic and gender dividend and grow to be Viksit Bharat by 2047.

As things stand, the Periodic Labour Force Survey data show that India is at the cusp of the U-shaped curve for female employment, popularized by the Economics Nobel winner, Claudia Goldin. Simply put, as India's income grows, more women should be entering the workforce – triggering a virtuous cycle of development.

The Kudumbashree model in Kerala promotes the formal care economy through its K4Care initiative, where trained women provide paid elder-care, child-care and patient support services. Over 500 women have been trained under this programme, which aims to offer affordable, community-based care while creating dignified livelihood opportunities for women. Source: SV Rajesh, 'Looking for Quality Caregivers for Elderly at Home? Kudumbashree Can Help', *On Manorama*, 20 October 2024, http://onmanorama.com/lifestyle/health/2024/10/20/kudumbashree-k4care-for-senior-citizens-service-details.html.

Bold Bets for a More Inclusive Economy

Over the past decade, India has been laying the groundwork for a more inclusive economy, one that increasingly recognizes women as central to its growth story. This shift hasn't been sudden, but it has been steady. Across public spending, global positioning, financial infrastructure and grassroots programming, the country has taken meaningful steps that are beginning to create the right conditions for women's economic participation to grow.

Today, 8.9 per cent of the Union Budget is gender-tagged, placing India among the global leaders in gender-responsive budgeting. This reflects a deeper recognition that economic growth can't be engineered in isolation from women's participation. Women aren't a separate constituency to be catered to; they are half the engine we're relying on to move the economy forward.

This commitment has also played out on the world stage. In 2023, during India's G20 presidency, Prime Minister Modi's articulation of 'women-led development' was a reframing of the national narrative. For the first time, 'Nari Shakti' was positioned as the architect of development, signifying that India's growth story would be incomplete without women in the mix. The message resonated widely as a powerful symbol, but more so, as a principle that is now being embedded into how we think about economic design. Within government machinery as well, intent is now translating into targets. The Ministry of Labour and Employment has set an ambitious goal: to raise India's FLFPR to 70 per cent by 2047. This long-term vision aligns closely with the Viksit Bharat agenda, and it places women's economic participation at the heart of our development strategy.

A strong foundation has been laid, and now we must translate intent into sustained impact through a systems-level approach. A key challenge that is often cited as a barrier holding women back from the workplace is the patriarchal mindset and gender norms. There, we have an opportunity to learn from other comparable economies. Countries across South and South-east Asia share similar patriarchal contexts; they have, however, managed to significantly raise female labour force participation by intentionally shaping economic policies that generate demand for women's work. Their experience offers valuable lessons for India as it moves from groundwork to full-scale implementation.

Global Lessons: Building Women's Economic Power through Policy

Most of South and South-east Asia share patriarchal social norms. Yet, many of these countries have found ways to pull women into their growth stories by deliberately designing economic strategies that create jobs for women.

Across Asia, countries are demonstrating that intentional public policy can powerfully increase women's participation in the workforce. Vietnam, Bangladesh, South Korea and Malaysia are clear examples. In Vietnam, women make up nearly 80 per cent of the footwear industry workforce.[29]

In Bangladesh, women constitute 60 per cent of the ready-made garments sector, and in Malaysia, they form the majority of workers in the electronics industry.[30] These sectors not only provide large-scale employment but are also key drivers of export earnings and national growth. Effective, gender-inclusive policies in these comparable economies fall into three broad buckets.

1. Gender Mainstreaming as a Governance Priority

Malaysia and Vietnam have adopted gender mainstreaming as a clear policy goal. Malaysia's gender mainstreaming framework ensures that gender perspectives are integrated into national planning, policy design and budgeting. This includes building institutional capacity and strengthening data systems that track gender gaps.[31]

Vietnam's gender mainstreaming policy supports women's economic participation by making gender equality a core part of national laws and planning. The Gender Equality Law, Labour Code and the Constitution prohibit discrimination and protect equal rights in work and public life. Government ministries are required to include gender goals in their sector plans, backed by dedicated budgets and regular monitoring. This approach helps ensure that women's access to jobs, skills and leadership roles is a part of everyday governance, not treated as a separate issue.[32]

2. Supporting Childcare and Return-to-Work Transitions

Several countries have implemented innovative childcare policies that directly support women's workforce participation through strategic government intervention. These policies demonstrate a crucial understanding: investing in childcare creates a powerful multiplier effect. First, it enables women to pursue formal employment by removing a key barrier to workforce participation. Second, it generates significant employment within the care economy itself, creating jobs for crèche workers, pre-school teachers and support staff who are mostly women. This creates a virtuous cycle where childcare investment both facilitates women's participation across sectors while opening new employment opportunities, particularly for women in the care economy.

Vietnam's Early Childhood Education Development Policies provide monthly allowances for preschool children of workers in industrial zones, directly addressing the childcare burden that often prevents women from maintaining stable employment.[33] Malaysia takes a comprehensive approach, offering returning mothers personal income tax exemptions for up to 12 months while encouraging employers to provide on-site childcare facilities.[34] South Korea's Nuri Initiative provides free daycare for children aged three and four.

3. Employer Benefits and Incentives

In Malaysia, policies aim to level the playing field for hiring women by addressing the additional costs and barriers employers often cite. Companies hiring women returning from a career break benefit from double tax deductions for training and childcare-related expenses. Employers also receive additional deductions for providing childcare allowances and setting up on-site centres.[35] By making it financially attractive to support women's return to work, these measures reduce the perceived hiring risk and help companies tap into a wider, experienced talent pool.

Across these countries, policy and employer action work hand-in-hand to remove barriers and unlock women's economic potential. India now has the opportunity to adapt these lessons to its own context and lead with a bold, gender-responsive agenda.

Addressing Demand-Side Barriers to Women's Employment

India's next phase of transformation hinges on re-imagining three critical enablers on the demand side: inclusive design, enabling infrastructure and catalytic policy.

1. Inclusive Design

Too often, economic systems have been built with a 'default male' lens, unintentionally excluding women. Whether it's job roles that assume round-the-clock availability, hiring processes that reward linear career trajectories or policies that overlook caregiving responsibilities, these design choices have ripple effects. Inclusive workforce design requires rethinking everything from how roles are structured and advertised, to how performance is measured, to how flexibility and re-entry are normalized. The goal is not to create 'special provisions' for women but to design systems that reflect the diversity of real lives.

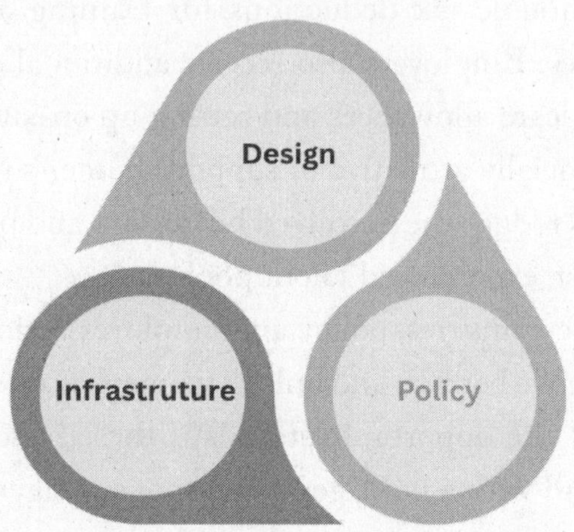

2. Enabling Infrastructure

Physical infrastructure is the backbone that determines whether opportunity is accessible. Safe public transport, washrooms at the workplace, secure housing near job sites and reliable childcare are not 'women's issues'; they are economic enablers. Investing in gender-smart infrastructure, both in urban and rural settings, directly impacts whether women can take up formal work and remain in it. It also creates new jobs, especially in the care economy, for women to step into.

3. Catalytic Policy

Governments play a critical role in shaping markets. Policies that encourage gender-responsive hiring, incentivize return-to-work pathways and mandate disaggregated workforce data can all shift organizational behaviour at scale. From public procurement targets for women-led businesses to tax incentives for companies investing in workplace equity, policy can act as both a carrot and a compass, nudging the economy towards inclusion.

Policy Solutions

Public policy can play a crucial role in creating conditions for women to enter and participate in economic activities from which they have been traditionally excluded.

1. Incentivizing and Reforming Workplace Practices for Inclusive Design

The private sector plays a key role in creating quality jobs. Workspaces need to be redesigned to systematically dismantle demand-side barriers.

- **Redesign Workspaces for Inclusivity**: This involves addressing the lack of flexibility, occupational segregation, unconscious biases in hiring and advancement, unwelcoming monocultures and lack of pathways for return to work after career breaks. Companies should adopt a data-driven approach and intentional design throughout the employee life cycle, implementing steps such as gender-neutral job descriptions, diverse interview panels, bench hiring, unconscious bias training and rewarding diverse referrals.

- **Promote Flexible Work Arrangements**: Options like compressed working weeks, part-time work or flexible start/finish times are critical to retain women, helping them balance work with care responsibilities. Normalizing access to these for both men and women can combat the 'mommy track' stigma. The pandemic has accelerated this adoption, with many Indian companies now offering greater flexibility.
- **Invest in Women's Leadership Development**: Mentoring programmes, sponsorship opportunities and tailored leadership development interventions are crucial to build a robust pipeline of women leaders and support career acceleration. Creating forums for networking and open dialogue also helps build a sense of community among women employees.
- **Introduce Women-Linked Incentives (WLI) Schemes**: Existing Employee-Linked Incentive (ELI) schemes, especially in manufacturing sectors like apparel, textiles, footwear and electronics (where women's representation is high and has potential), can be modified to include additional benefits linked to women's representation. These can include:
  - **Payroll Subsidies**: Providing a greater subsidy for women employees or extending the duration of subsidies, potentially with tiered benefits based on women's representation.
  - **Employees' Provident Fund Organization (EPFO) Reimbursement Subsidy**: Linking subsidies to employer EPFO contributions for women employees for easier implementation has the dual benefit of smoother authentication and fewer payroll processing resources being required.
  - **Capital Investment Support**: Integrating specified gender diversity targets into Capex subsidies, tax benefits or

preferential financing for infrastructure investments, ensuring facilities are built with a diverse workforce in mind.

- **One-Time Hiring Support**: Offering slab-wise subsidies to offset initial hiring costs associated with hiring women, including for senior or highly skilled roles, as exemplified by a three-year subsidy in Tamil Nadu for jobs paying over ₹1 lakh per month with an additional amount for women.

> Udaiti, is working with private sector empoyers to identify and address design-level frictions across the hiring, retention, and advancement journeys of women. Through partnerships in key sectors like pharma, manufacturing, retail, logistics, and flexi-staffing, we help companies examine their job structures, shift workplace norms, and create practical pathways that make women's participation viable at scale. This work helps align business incentives with inclusive talent strategies, ensuring design choices support women's economic engagement.

2. Creating Enabling Infrastructure and Support

Public policy and investments can help create the enabling conditions and infrastructure that make it easier for women to access economic opportunities.

- **Promote the Formal Care Economy**: This is seen as central to unlocking women's equal participation in the workforce. Policies should support the establishment and growth of crèches, daycare facilities and elder-care facilities that employ caregivers and pay fair wages. This approach frees up working-age women from unpaid care work and creates new employment opportunities for caregivers. Examples like Kudumbashree in Kerala and Anganwadi Centres can be strengthened and scaled.

> The Kudumbashree model in Kerala promotes the formal care economy through its K4Care initiative, where trained women provide paid elder-care, child-care and patient support services. Over 500 women have been trained under this programme, which aims to offer affordable, community-based care while creating dignified livelihood opportunities for women. Source: SV Rajesh, 'Looking for quality caregivers for elderly at home? Kudumbashree can help', *On Manorama*, 20 October 2024, http://onmanorama.com/lifestyle/health/2024/10/20/kudumbashree-k4care-for-senior-citizens-service-details.html.

- **Provide Accommodation Close to the Workplace**: For jobs created in large factories and industrial clusters, often on city outskirts, distance becomes a barrier for women. Providing common working facilities, dormitories and working women's hostels near these clusters can reduce travel times and attract a larger pool of workers. The Ministry of Labour and Employment advises MSMEs to facilitate such accommodations, ideally with attached childcare/senior-care facilities. Building residential facilities that cater to all workers and allow families to move in together is also recommended to attract women across all age groups and enhance worker retention.

> The Thozhi Hostels in Tamil Nadu provide safe and affordable accommodation for working women near their workplaces. Built through a public–private partnership, the state provided land and partial funding, while the Tamil Nadu Shelter Fund co-financed construction and guided the process. Private operators, selected through open bidding, manage the hostels to ensure good quality services and upkeep. Source: 'Tamil Nadu Working Women's Hostels – A Home Away from Home', World Bank Group, http://worldbank.org/en/news/feature/2024/09/23/tamil-nadu-working-women-s-hostels-a-home-away-from-home.

- **Invest in Reliable, Safe and Affordable Public Transport**: Women commute differently, often over shorter distances and relying more on public transport or walking. Increased investment in public transport availability, frequency and safety (e.g., round-the-clock transport, hub-and-spoke models) is crucial to ensure women can access jobs far from home or with late/early shifts. While schemes like free bus travel for women have shown positive impacts, greater investment is needed to manage increased ridership and safety.
- **Ensure Provision of Clean and Functional Sanitation Facilities**: The lack of toilets at workplaces, especially in informal settings, poses significant health and safety risks for women, negatively impacting their productivity. Government laws mandate such provisions, but compliance is often poor. Providing clean and functional public toilets in markets and public spaces can also support floating worker cohorts, reducing compliance costs for small firms.

Udaiti is running multiple pilots to explore infrastructure needs for working women. In Odisha, we've initiated a pilot to assess the feasibility of improving Worker Women's Housing (WWH). We're also working with state governments in Uttar Pradesh and Punjab to enable job-linked transport schemes, recognizing that mobility is often a first-order barrier for women in both urban and peri-urban labour markets.

3. Addressing Legal and Regulatory Barriers and Enhancing Compliance

Public policy must ensure a level playing field for both men and women when seeking employment opportunities, and the differential legal barriers holding women back should be actively dismantled.

- **Discriminatory Laws**: As of 2022, there are over 50 Acts and 150 Rules in India that legally restrict women from accessing employment opportunities. These laws often prohibit women from working late at night, or in jobs deemed hazardous, arduous or morally inappropriate (e.g., selling liquor, lifting heavy objects).[36] The goal should be to facilitate safe and humane workspaces for all, rather than imposing paternalistic discrimination that limits women's opportunities to learn high-growth skills and earn potential.
- **Refine Policies with Unintended Consequences**: Some policies, though progressive in intent, can have counterproductive effects. For instance, the Maternity Benefit (Amended) Act, 2017, which extended maternity leave to 26 weeks and required crèches in larger companies, places the financial burden on organizations. This, as an unintended consequence, has led to

subtle discrimination against married women at the hiring stage. Policy adjustments are needed to address such adverse outcomes.

- **Enhance Compliance with Existing Progressive Policies**: India has enacted several progressive laws and policies aimed at promoting gender equity and inclusive growth, but enforcement remains uneven. Strengthening compliance mechanisms across the following areas is essential:
  - **Transparency and Public Disclosure:** Measures like the SEBI's Business Responsibility and Sustainability Reporting (BRSR) for NSE-listed companies are a positive step towards transparency in gender metrics. However, similar reporting should be extended to a larger set of companies beyond just those listed. Increased transparency is crucial to ensure equal pay for equal work. Requiring companies to disclose their gender wage gaps can foster accountability and bridge the gender pay gap.
  - **Workplace Infrastructure and Safety:** While the law mandates the provision of childcare centres in establishments with 50 or more employees, there is limited audit and compliance. Similarly, despite the landmark Sexual Harassment of Women at the Workplace (Prevention, Prohibition and Redressal) Act, 2013 (POSH), its implementation leaves much to be desired. Effective implementation requires using data from reported cases to understand the landscape of violence, identifying non-compliant firms and supplementing with employer-employee surveys to influence safety policies.
- **Implement a Minimum Living Wage**: Beyond the minimum wage, ensuring a minimum living wage for all workers can significantly help women, who are often concentrated in low-paying roles and industries, narrow the gender wage gap and

improve retention. Industries often keep wages low to cut costs, particularly in women-dominated sectors like textiles. Organizations paying living wages also report higher retention.

> To support evidence-based policymaking, Udaiti has developed the WEE Index – a first-of-its-kind tool that enables state governments to track and improve the empowerment. By offering data across 5 key levers and 17 departments, the Index helps identify systemic gaps, allocate resources more effectively and embed WEE goals into mainstream governance.

4. Leveraging Emerging Opportunities

The future presents unique opportunities to further gender equity in the workforce.

- **Leverage Digital Transformation and Build Women's Skills in STEM and Digital Literacy**: Increased penetration of smartphones and internet access, along with the rise of fintech and digital financial services (e.g., Paytm, PhonePe), can empower women with access to educational resources, online training, e-commerce platforms and economic independence, especially in rural areas.
- **Systematically Build Skills for Women in Caregiving and Social Services**: As highly skilled jobs face automation, human-centric roles like palliative care, geriatric care, dementia care and mental health support become more attractive and less replaceable by technology.

In conclusion, a multistakeholder, data-driven approach involving collaboration between the government, private sector, industry bodies and civil society is essential to redesigning workplaces and creating enabling ecosystems for women's increased participation. This will not only contribute to India's economic growth but also foster a more inclusive and equitable society.

As India advances toward its vision of Viksit Bharat, we are uniquely positioned to translate our demographic strength into economic leadership. Women's participation is not just a matter of equity; it is a multiplier for growth, innovation and resilience. The choices we make today in how we design work, infrastructure and policy will determine whether we unlock the full potential of this moment. With coordinated intent across government, industry and civil society, we can build an economy where women's aspirations find pathways, and their contributions shape the next chapter of India's development journey.

Diplomacy

18

A Yogic Foreign Policy for a Fractured World

AJAY BISARIA

Since the end of the Cold War in 1990, the contours of global power have shifted with unsettling speed and complexity. The brief 'unipolar moment' that followed the collapse of the Soviet Union – marked by the unchallenged ascendancy of the United States – was never destined to last. By 2008, global politics had begun to shift, with the rise and fall of major and middle powers in the global system. The rise of China, the resurgence of Russia and the relative decline of American influence ushered in a new phase of geopolitical multipolarity. Yet even this new order has not fully taken shape. Ours is a world suspended between orders – one where old hierarchies have eroded, but no new equilibrium has taken their place.

The fracture runs deeper than geopolitics. Technology, climate change and a shifting global economy have caused upheavals across domains. Each decade of the twenty-first century has been marked by seismic disruption: the terrorist attacks of 9/11, the global financial crisis of 2008, the COVID-19 pandemic and a succession of wars, including the continuing conflict in Ukraine and renewed violence in Gaza. The 2020s have already unfolded as a long and volatile decade: a pandemic in 2020, economic dislocation in 2021, war in Europe in 2022, upheaval in West Asia in 2023, defining elections in 2024 and by 2025, a familiar disruption in the form of a Trumpian return to American politics.

In his 2024 book *New Cold Wars*, David E. Sanger aptly captured the zeitgeist: major powers are once again locked in strategic contestation, reminiscent of Cold War rivalries but now playing out in a far more interconnected and unpredictable world. China and Russia – and a disruptive middle power like Iran – are actively challenging the liberal hegemonic order that the United States built and led in the latter half of the twentieth century. These tensions erupt not only in overt warfare but through proxy battles, economic coercion and cyber confrontation.

The economic order, too, has shifted. The creation of the World Trade Organization in 1995 heralded an era of deep global integration and multilateralism. But this phase of globalization has been undercut by protectionist impulses, trade wars and the strategic reshaping of supply chains. Meanwhile, climate change and pandemic-scale biological risks continue to pose existential threats that global governance seems ill-equipped to handle.

This is, in every sense, a fractured world – disjointed, volatile and increasingly unpredictable. The term captures the sense of systemic breakdown: where the certainties of a bipolar or unipolar world have vanished, and new architectures of cooperation and contest are yet to solidify. The assertive rise of China, the diminishing appetite of the United States for global stewardship and the technological bifurcation of the world into rival ecosystems of data, surveillance and AI have all compounded this fragmentation.

India was impacted by each of these disruptions and by several others closer home: China's aggressive border behaviour, Pakistan's terrorism and upheaval in the sub-continental neighbourhood. But even in this unstable context, India has emerged as a study in pragmatic resilience. Eschewing doctrinaire non-alignment but retaining a strategic autonomy, Indian foreign policy since the 1990s has embraced a supple, multialigned posture. India's instinct is to engage the West through strategic and economic partnerships, preserve long-standing ties with Russia, cautiously manage the relationship with an unruly China, check Pakistan's revisionist violence and assert leadership in the Global South.

India's post-Cold War diplomacy – particularly in the past decade – has reflected a realist recalibration, shaped by the imperatives of national interest and a long-term vision: to secure its strategic environment and fuel its ambition to become a developed economy by 2047. In a fractured and contested world, India's foreign policy will need to be yogic-calm but nimble and flexible, as it seeks not just to respond to crisis, but to navigate complexity with agility and foresight.

Evolving Multipolarity: Shifting Geopolitics and India's Strategic Choices

For India, the redefined global landscape of the 1990s required strategic recalibration. The loss of the USSR as a key partner and a severe balance of payments crisis at home led to economic liberalization, and by the turn of the century, after the country went nuclear, a pivot towards the West, especially the United States. Yet, India maintained strategic autonomy with a cautious stance, balancing its non-aligned heritage with pragmatic engagement in a US-dominated order. By the 2000s, especially after the 2008 global financial crisis, a shift towards multipolarity became evident. China's rise began to challenge US hegemony, while powers like Russia, the EU, Brazil, Turkey and Iran asserted regional influence.

This evolving multipolar world poses a series of complex challenges for India: first, managing its strategic partnership with the US while preserving critical defence and energy ties with Russia. Second, confronting China's assertiveness – reflected in its Indo–Pacific expansionism, strategic alliance with Pakistan and direct clashes with India in areas like Doklam (2017) and Galwan (2020). Third, the erosion of multilateral institutions like the UN, WTO and WHO has limited India's ability to shape outcomes through neutral global platforms. Fourth, the unpredictability of partners – exemplified by Donald Trump's transactional foreign policy – underscores the fragility of bilateral relationships. Fifth, regional instability across South Asia and the Indo–Pacific, including Afghanistan's turmoil, increased Chinese naval activity and shifts in Pakistan's posture on terrorism, complicates India's security calculus.

The shift from a unipolar to a multipolar world has thus intensified India's need for strategic autonomy, robust security, creative diplomacy and agile decision-making.

The Changing Economic Order and India's Developmental Dilemmas

The global economic order has undergone equally profound changes – from the globalization wave of the 1990s to today's fragmented, protectionist environment, which could even be described as de-globalization.

Emerging from a 1991 balance of payments crisis, India embraced liberalization: reducing tariffs, ending the license permit raj, freeing up its currency and attracting foreign investment. This spurred growth but also exposed India to the inequities of the global trading system, especially under WTO rules skewed in favour of the global rich. Key sectors like agriculture and pharmaceuticals were constrained by Trade-Related Aspects of Intellectual Property Rights (TRIPs) and Trade-Related Investment Measures (TRIMs).

The 2008 financial crisis shook the neoliberal consensus, fuelling protectionism and regulatory fragmentation. Shrinking export markets and volatile capital flows created external pressures. India's 2019 withdrawal from the RCEP reflected its caution against exposing domestic markets to cheap imports, especially from China. China's WTO-driven rise hurt Indian manufacturing, widening trade deficits and limiting policy flexibility.

Recent disruptions – COVID-19, the Russia-Ukraine conflict and the US–China trade war – intensified global decoupling. But they also presented an opportunity. India recalibrated its trade policy to focus on resilience and strategic autonomy, seeking to position itself as a China Plus One alternative in global supply chains. This triggered investments in infrastructure, skilled labour and the articulation of a coherent industrial policy. For India to become a manufacturing hub requires not just structural reform,

Make in India and Production-Linked Incentive schemes, but also a sustained commitment to structural reform and major public investment.

On the climate front, India took a leading role in demanding equity and climate justice in global fora, even as it pushed domestic green transitions through solar, EVs, hydrogen and carbon markets. Its consistent advocacy for fair technology transfers and climate finance underscores its broader goal of reforming global economic governance to better reflect the needs of the Global South.

India's core economic policy thus rests on the principle of 'calibrated globalization', combining global engagement with domestic capacity-building, policy flexibility and an assertive leadership role in shaping a more equitable international economic order.

The Evolving Technological Order and India's Policy Dilemmas

Since 1990, the global technological order has been the strongest disruptor, not just for the private sector, but also for nations. Tech disruptions have transformed economies, societies and power structures, presenting India with both opportunities and challenges.

The Third Industrial Revolution, driven by ICT – internet, mobile telephony and software – enabled India's rise as a global IT outsourcing hub through firms like TCS and Infosys. The 1999 telecom boom and Y2K crisis bolstered this position. Yet, India remained reliant on imported hardware and lacked investments in electronics manufacturing and core research.

The Fourth Industrial Revolution (4IR), featuring AI, Big Data, IoT, 5G and quantum computing, has deepened these gaps. India depends heavily on foreign tech, particularly for semiconductors and platforms, while a significant digital divide persists. Despite rising internet access, disparities in digital education, devices and connectivity remain. India has indeed asserted digital sovereignty by developing public platforms like Aadhaar, UPI and CoWIN, and passed the Digital Personal Data Protection Act in 2023. Still, India remains among the most cyber-attacked nations, lacking comprehensive cybersecurity laws. Internationally, it advocates a 'third way' in digital governance – promoting inclusivity over US dominance or Chinese authoritarianism.

Though its start-up ecosystem boasts over 100 unicorns, challenges persist due to low R&D investment, weak academia-industry ties and limited deep-tech innovation. India's challenge will continue to be balancing digital growth with sovereignty and democratic values, encouraging frugal AI innovation to seek breakthrough 'DeepSeek moments' and develop niches for global tech leadership.

Climate Change and Global Health: The New Frontiers of Foreign Policy

Since 1990, non-traditional security threats – especially climate change and global health crises – have increasingly disrupted domestic policy and global governance. For India, with its vast population, ecological sensitivity and developmental ambitions, these challenges are complex and deeply interconnected. Climate change has become an urgent concern, with rising temperatures across the Indo–Gangetic plains and more frequent extreme weather events like floods, droughts, cyclones and heatwaves. These shifts are driving water stress, reduced agricultural productivity, ecological degradation and impacting food and water security, rural livelihoods, migration, urban planning and disaster resilience.

At the same time, India faces growing global pressure to decarbonize, despite its low per capita emissions and the need for economic growth to reduce poverty.

Simultaneously, the COVID-19 pandemic exposed the fragility of global interdependence. In India, the 2020 lockdown halted economic activity and strained millions of migrant workers. The second wave in 2021 brought a humanitarian crisis, with oxygen shortages and overwhelmed healthcare systems. However, the crisis also marked a pivotal moment for India's global health diplomacy, highlighting both vulnerabilities and the potential of its health infrastructure. Together, climate and health emergencies now shape India's national strategy and international engagement, underscoring the need for resilient systems and equitable global cooperation.

India has addressed these non-traditional security threats – both climate change and global health crises – through domestic adaptation, policy innovation and international engagement. To combat climate impacts like floods, droughts and heatwaves, India launched the National Action Plan on Climate Change (NAPCC), featuring eight missions, including the National Solar and Water Missions, to promote clean energy, water efficiency and ecosystem health. It expanded renewable energy, became a global solar leader and co-founded the International Solar Alliance (ISA) in 2015.

At COP26, India pledged net-zero emissions by 2070, balancing development with environmental responsibility. Domestically, it promoted compensatory afforestation (through the National Compensatory Afforestation Fund Management and Planning Authority [CAMPA]) and urban resilience (via the Smart Cities Mission). The National Clean Air Programme (NCAP) targets air pollution reduction in 122 cities.

India's approach reflects a balance between resilience, strategic autonomy and developmental priorities. This balancing act must be sustained, but will become harder as the impacts of global warming intensify.

The Trumpian World of 2025: Disruption on Steroids

The return of Donald Trump to the White House in 2025 has deepened the fractures in an already unsettled global order. His second term signals a revolutionary departure from the US-led, UN-defined 'liberal hegemonism' that shaped post-war multilateralism. In its place stands a worldview defined by transactionalism, protectionism and institutional scepticism.

This new US iconoclasm has profound implications for India, even though it is in the sweet spot of being only a 'friend', not a 'free-riding' treaty ally (like Europe, Japan) or adversary working against US interests (like China). Still, while opportunities have sprung up, the challenges are sharp and evolving quickly.

Traditional US alliances like NATO and the G7 are under strain, and US commitments to global governance are no longer assured. Trump's sporadic overtures to Russia for peace in Ukraine and his mercurial stance on China have increased unpredictability. US behaviour has simultaneously encouraged Chinese assertiveness and cemented the China–Russia axis – an unwelcome development for Indian strategic planners.

In response, India has adopted a strategy of hedging – multivector engagement, deepening ties with the US through mechanisms like the Quad, iCET and defence agreements, while continuing robust military and energy cooperation with Russia. Simultaneously, India is expanding its engagement with Europe, ASEAN and West Asia to broaden its strategic base and is placing greater emphasis on self-reliance in defence and critical technologies to insulate itself from global disruptions.

On the economic front, Trump's return has revived tariff threats, weakened the WTO's dispute settlement mechanism and reinforced an 'America First' re-industrialization policy. These actions reflect a broader move away from free trade and global economic coordination, exacerbating global economic uncertainty and compelling nations like India to recalibrate their trade and investment strategies.

India faces complex challenges amid rising global economic volatility: protectionism, trade wars and supply chain disruptions that hurt India's exports and expose its firms to tariffs and tech controls. But opportunities also arise. India is gearing up to attract investment, and particularly the China Plus One hedge by global corporations. To benefit from new trading realities, India has entered into FTAs with the UAE, Australia and the UK and is negotiating new ones with the EU and the US, while pushing for Global South-centric trade norms via G20, BRICS and SCO. On the tech front, the US–China decoupling is fragmenting digital ecosystems, but could present India with advantages if it leans towards the US AI ecosystem.

In global public goods like climate and health, where Trump's disengagement has left vacuums, India has some space to step up. From leading the International Solar Alliance and the Coalition for Disaster Resilient Infrastructure to championing LiFE (Lifestyle for Environment) and Vaccine Maitri, India is shaping the global commons even as traditional powers retreat.

India Needs a Yogic – Calm but Nimble – Foreign Policy

India's post-Cold War foreign policy evolution is a study in strategic agility. Faced with shifting power equations, economic realignments and non-traditional threats, India has not merely adapted – it has begun to lead. Rather than succumbing to the binaries of the Cold War or the false comfort of rigid alignments or blocs, India has embraced a multialigned strategy – collaborating with competing power centres while maintaining strategic autonomy. It has encouraged issue-based coalitions like the Quad or I2U2, diversified partnerships and responded to disruptions with composure and creativity.

This approach – best described as yogic: simultaneously calm, supple and nimble – has allowed India to sustain its rise in a fractured world. Initiatives like Transforming Relationship Utilizing Strategic Technology (TRUST), the Digital India stack, the G20 presidency and Vaccine Maitri exemplify this posture. India is no longer a rule taker; it is steadily becoming a rule shaper – asserting its voice on trade, climate, technology and development.

The global system is entering a hybrid era, where nineteenth-century realist impulses of hard power and spheres of influence coexist uneasily with twentieth-century ones of the rule of law and interdependence. As institutions falter and transactionalism rises, India's capacity to operate across this spectrum – anchored in autonomy, guided by principle and responsive to change – makes it uniquely placed to act as a bridging power between the West and the Rest.

Looking ahead, India aspires to be a developed economy and a major power by 2047, as well as a leading power of the Global

South. It will be the third-largest economy by 2030, and a global stakeholder that offers solutions, not just critiques. It seeks to bring equilibrium to its periphery and credibility to global fora through a reformed multilateralism.

In this turbulent century, India's foreign policy must remain grounded in its civilizational ethos yet attuned to the churn of geopolitics. The world will continue to fragment and reconfigure – but if India takes some deep breaths to maintain its calm, flexibility and policy agility, it will not just survive this disorder. It will shape what comes after.

19

A Journey beyond Borders: The Story of the Indian Diaspora

DR VIJAY CHAUTHAIWALE

The Indian diaspora is not just a population scattered across continents – it is a living, breathing thread that ties the story of India with the world. Long before the term 'globalization' entered our vocabulary, Indians had already begun to journey far from their homeland, leaving behind not just footprints but lasting legacies.

The story of India's diaspora dates back to the mid-sixteenth century. From trade routes in Punjab to bustling urban centres like Delhi and Bombay, and the culturally vibrant regions of Rajasthan and Gujarat, Indians ventured overseas – travelling by sea and land – to destinations in Central Asia, the Caucasus and Russia. These early travellers, known as Multanis, Shikarpuris and Banias, laid the foundations of the Indian merchant diaspora, becoming integral connectors between their homeland and new lands abroad. They weren't just traders; they were cultural ambassadors, quietly weaving India's spirit into the commercial and cultural fabric of foreign lands.

Centuries later, during the British colonial period, the pattern of migration took on new forms. One of the most poignant chapters in the story of the Indian diaspora is that of the Girmityas – indentured Indian labourers who were transported to far-flung British colonies such as Mauritius, Fiji, Trinidad and Tobago, Guyana and Suriname during the nineteenth and early twentieth centuries. The term 'Girmitya' is derived from the word 'agreement', referring to the contracts these workers signed – often under coercion or misleading promises – for bonded labour in plantations. Uprooted from their homeland, they endured gruelling conditions, social isolation and cultural dislocation. Yet, over generations, the Girmityas and their descendants not only preserved their linguistic, cultural and religious identities but also emerged as integral parts of their host societies. Today, they represent a proud and resilient segment of the global Indian diaspora, embodying both the hardships of colonial displacement and the enduring strength of cultural continuity. Some Indians made brief trips to England and parts of Europe – seeking education, knowledge or opportunity – but rarely with the intent to settle. For them, India was always home. Even when distance separated them from their loved ones, the connection remained unbroken – letters, remittances and memories continued to flow back.

The years following India's Independence marked a new chapter in migration. No longer bound by the legacies of indentured labour or colonial servitude, Indians began venturing abroad as students, professionals and entrepreneurs. Many sought higher education, technical training or new opportunities; some returned home to contribute to the nation's progress, while others stayed on and built new lives in foreign lands.

Unlike many immigrant communities often seen as transient or temporary workers, Indians established themselves steadily across

North America, Europe, the Middle East and South-east Asia. They earned respect through quiet determination and meaningful contributions – helping shape more inclusive, multicultural societies and building bridges between cultures. Wherever they settled, they carried their heritage with pride, maintaining Indian traditions even as they embraced the life and rhythm of their adopted countries.

As the decades passed and borders became less daunting, the Indian diaspora grew – not just in numbers, but in influence. What began as a tale of merchants, students and seekers has evolved into a powerful story of global presence and partnership. Today, the Indian diaspora – spread across more than 100 countries – is one of the largest in the world. But its true strength lies not merely in size; it lies in the unshakable emotional bond that millions of overseas Indians continue to share with their motherland. It is this enduring connection that has quietly transformed into what we now recognize as diaspora diplomacy.

For the diaspora, India is not a faraway land. It is a living presence, a sacred bond, a mother whose warmth reaches across oceans. For years, the connection between India and its diaspora was rooted in nostalgia – letters from home, tin boxes of pickles and sweets, memories carefully carried across borders. But with time, that nostalgia turned into purpose. Today, the Indian diaspora is no longer just looking back; it is helping shape India's future.

The turning point came when India, under the visionary leadership of Prime Minister Shri Narendra Modi, began to see its diaspora not as a group to be managed – but as an extended family to be embraced. Over the years, Indian governments have reached out to Non-Resident Indians (NRIs) and Persons of Indian Origin (PIOs) not just for cultural exchange, but as vital partners in nation-building.

From the glittering gatherings at Madison Square Garden in New York to the powerful diaspora addresses in Sydney, London and Dubai, Narendra Modi turned these moments into more than just speeches – they became homecomings. He did not speak *to* the diaspora; he spoke *with* them, often beginning with. 'Bharat ke mere pyare saathiyon (My dear friends of India...)'. That emotional connect, grounded in shared pride, turned every overseas auditorium into an echo chamber of patriotism.

Prime Minister Modi's relationship with the Indian diaspora is uniquely personal and impactful. His approach stands apart from other global leaders, particularly through landmark events such as 'Howdy Modi' in the United States and 'Marhaba Namo' in the UAE. These gatherings successfully bring together members of the Indian diaspora who are often dispersed and divided by occupation, geography or religious beliefs. Notably, these community-driven events are frequently funded by the local diaspora themselves, emphasizing their deep commitment and pride in their heritage and connection with India. The high-profile presence of global leaders, including former US President Donald Trump, Israeli Prime Minister Benjamin Netanyahu, former UK Prime Minister Boris Johnson and Australian Prime Minister Anthony Albanese, at these events further underscores Modi's global influence. This international recognition has significantly elevated the stature of the Indian diaspora in their resident countries, encouraging local politicians and representatives, such as senators and community leaders, to engage actively with these vibrant gatherings.

India's foreign policy today goes beyond traditional diplomacy and trade – it actively connects with its diaspora, recognizing them as integral to India's global strategy. Under Prime Minister Modi's leadership, this approach has significantly deepened, emphasizing the diaspora as a key component in India's international influence. Concrete steps underline this shift: At the peak of global uncertainty during the COVID-19 crisis, when leaders worldwide grappled with solutions, India initiated the Vande Bharat Mission on 7 May 2020 – one of the largest evacuation operations in history. Aiming to safely repatriate stranded Indian nationals, the mission involved extensive logistical coordination and diplomatic engagement. Over 2,17,000 flights facilitated the safe return of more than 1.83 crore passengers. The Vande Bharat Mission exemplifies India's unwavering commitment to citizen safety, underscoring the nation's resilience, efficiency and empathy in navigating extraordinary global challenges. India also launched Vaccine Maitri, supplying over 162 million vaccine doses to 96 countries, strengthening global solidarity and providing reassurance to overseas Indians.

During global crises, India has consistently acted swiftly. In 2022, Operation Ganga evacuated nearly 25,000 Indian citizens, mostly students, from conflict-hit Ukraine. Operation Devi Shakti similarly assisted more than 800 individuals during the Taliban's takeover of Afghanistan. These missions were more than rescue efforts; they signified a pivotal shift in India's foreign policy – demonstrating that India stands firmly by its citizens, wherever they are.

One of the more understated but meaningful changes in India's diaspora outreach has been the transformation of the Pravasi Bharatiya Samman, the country's highest honour for overseas Indians. Established in 2003, the award was initially seen as largely ceremonial, often recognizing prominent names for their achievements abroad. Under Prime Minister Narendra Modi, however, the award has quietly evolved. In 2016, the government expanded its scope also to recognize contributions made within India by NRIs and PIOs – whether through philanthropy, social impact or grassroots development. The shift reflects a broader change in how India views its diaspora: not just as ambassadors of the country's image, but as active partners in its progress. Today, the award celebrates not only success, but service. The selection process, overseen by a jury chaired by the vice president, has grown more transparent and inclusive – giving the award new credibility as a genuine bridge between India and its global community.

Additionally, the Know India Programme (KIP) has been instrumental in connecting young PIOs with their heritage, offering immersive experiences designed to deepen their understanding of India's rich cultural traditions, diverse history and rapid economic and social progress. Under Prime Minister Narendra Modi's leadership, the programme has experienced significant transformation, evolving into a dynamic platform that deeply engages diaspora youth with their cultural roots. Originally launched in 2003, the KIP has been expanded substantially in terms of scale, frequency and content under Modi's tenure. Today, participants enjoy a more comprehensive itinerary that not only introduces them to India's historical and cultural heritage but also provides first-hand experiences of the nation's rapid economic and technological advancements. Recent editions of KIP have been strategically integrated with major national events like the Pravasi Bharatiya Divas, offering attendees opportunities for meaningful interactions with prominent leaders and decision-makers. Additionally, the adoption of digital platforms and social media for outreach has improved the accessibility and global reach of the programme, reflecting the Modi government's proactive approach to diaspora engagement.

More than anything, Prime Minister Narendra Modi gave the Indian diaspora a voice in the nation's development story. His vision of Jan Bhagidari – people's participation in governance and growth

– was not confined to India's borders, but extended meaningfully to NRIs and PIOs across the globe. Under Modi's leadership, overseas Indians have been repositioned not merely as expatriates but as essential partners in the journey of nation-building. Their staggering contribution of $129.4 billion in remittances in 2024 alone reflects not just economic strength but a deep and enduring emotional bond with Bharat.

Another major initiative that has seen critical strengthening under Prime Minister Modi's leadership is the Indian Community Welfare Fund (ICWF). Originally launched in 2009, the fund was designed to assist overseas Indian nationals in distress, particularly in the Gulf and South-east Asian regions. However, it was under the Modi government in 2017 that the ICWF underwent a comprehensive overhaul. The revised guidelines expanded the fund's scope to cover not only emergency services like boarding, lodging, medical care and repatriation of mortal remains, but also long-term welfare initiatives. These included legal and financial assistance in deserving cases, aid to Indian students abroad and support for establishing community and student welfare centres in countries with a significant Indian presence. By empowering Indian Missions with greater flexibility and resources, the Modi government has ensured that the ICWF functions as a proactive and responsive safety net for Indians living abroad – reflecting a shift from reactive diplomacy to citizen-focused outreach.

From New Jersey to Nairobi, from Singapore to South Africa, Indians living abroad have become citizens of the world – yet they carry India in their hearts. Many of them, after walking the halls of the world's best universities or leading global companies, now find ways to give back. Some do it through investments, others by building connections between India and the countries they now call home. Consider Silicon Valley. It's often said the sun never sets on Indian coders. But today, Indian-origin leaders are helping shape the entire global tech landscape—figures like Sundar Pichai at Google and Satya Nadella at Microsoft. What stands out is their continued connection to India's story. Through mentorship, start-up funding and engagement in policy discussions, they are not just exporting innovation – they are helping bring new opportunities home.

In healthcare and academia, too, the diaspora is making a quiet but powerful difference. Many doctors return each year to perform free surgeries in Indian villages. Researchers and professors contribute to curriculum reforms, foster cross-border research and advocate for stronger Indian representation in global forums. Across sectors, these efforts reflect a growing spirit of partnership and purpose.

And when India calls, the diaspora doesn't respond with mere slogans – it rises with solidarity. Time and again, overseas Indians have stood as a resolute second line of defence, amplifying the nation's voice and softening its struggles during moments of crisis – be it natural disasters, pandemic relief or geopolitical challenges. A recent example is the terrorist attack in Pahalgam, Kashmir, where the global Indian community came together in an outpouring of grief and unity. Candlelight vigils were held in cities from New York to Melbourne. Protest marches, solidarity gatherings and prayer services were to honour the victims and condemn the heinous act.

But their response didn't end there. The swift and decisive launch of Operation Sindoor – India's firm retaliation against terrorism – not only reassured Indians at home but also instilled immense pride among the diaspora. From social media campaigns to coordinated public statements, NRIs rallied behind the Indian government's stand, echoing a clear message: the world's largest democracy will not bow to terror. This seamless emotional alignment – between Indians at home and abroad – demonstrates how deeply integrated the diaspora has become in India's evolving national consciousness.

What makes this bond so strong is that it goes beyond transactions – it brings transformation. The diaspora doesn't just give; it builds. It doesn't just visit India; it helps shape its future. Each member of this global community carries India's story with them, influencing how the world sees a country both rich in ancient wisdom and alive with youthful ambition. Their journey is one of resilience and renewal. They left in search of opportunity, but never let go of their roots. And today, in a world hungry for genuine connections, the Indian diaspora stands as proof that heritage and progress can move forward together. As India moves towards the vision of Viksit Bharat@2047, the diaspora will not remain on the sidelines. They will be active partners in this journey. Together, from every continent and corner, they will help script a future where India is not only the *best in the world*, but *best for the world.*

20

Towards a Developed Nation

NAVDEEP SURI

India and UAE: Creating a Dynamic Template for a Viksit Bharat

There is something quite extraordinary that is taking place in India's ties with the United Arab Emirates (UAE). Some seasoned observers have taken note, while many are still caught up in the shibboleths of the past. This is especially true amongst a number of scholars in the West, whose worldview appears singularly incapable of comprehending either the depth or the breadth of the relationship. I have seen this first-hand during my interactions with leading US and European think tanks.

There is, of course, the temptation to offer a kind of 'back to the future' argument, and I should concede that I, too, have occasionally been guilty of overusing this theme because it is just so convenient. After all, as we go back in history, we read about the ancient links between Arab merchants and Indian ports like Surat and Calicut. Then there was the quest of the Portuguese, the Dutch and the

French to establish a lucrative trade monopoly with India on the strength of their naval power, leading them to establish fortifications at strategic locations along the Gulf with the sole purpose of safeguarding their maritime route to India.

The British followed suit in the seventeenth and eighteenth centuries and consolidated their hold over the region through the Trucial States Agreement signed in 1820. This progressively brought the sheikhdoms of present-day Gulf under the protective umbrella of the governor in Bombay and led to a situation where the British political agents and political residents in places like Bushehr, Basra, Bahrain and Sharjah reported to the governor in Bombay and not to London.

The Indian rupee became the dominant currency in the region, a position that started in 1829 and continued until 1959. Fast forward a few decades to the second half of the nineteenth and the early part of the twentieth century, and we recall that the entire economy of the Gulf centred around the pearl trade, and Indian merchants were the lynchpin around which it revolved. Conversations with some of the old Emirati families from Abu Dhabi, Dubai and Sharjah affirm that Mumbai was the big city that residents of the Gulf liked to visit for trade, tourism, education and healthcare.

There is indeed much to be learned from our hoary past, even as we bear in mind that the informal economic integration was largely the outcome of imperial control on both sides of the Arabian Sea. As independent nations acting out of their own volition, we now have other reasons to celebrate our growing proximity. There is the all too visible fact that the 4.3 million strong Indian community in the UAE isn't just the largest concentration of Indian nationals outside India. It is also a community that constitutes around 40 per cent of the total population of the UAE, sends some $23 billion or about 20 per cent of our global remittances and acts as a real bridge between our countries. And over the years, members of this community have played a key role in the remarkable development of the UAE and in positioning that country as India's third-largest trading partner – next only to the US and China and well ahead of G7 economies like Japan, Germany and the UK.

As part of our near-neighbourhood, there is little doubt that the Gulf – and especially countries like the UAE and Saudi Arabia are vitally important for us. But if the Gulf is so important, why did we allow Pakistan to treat the region as its backyard, developing strong political, economic and defence ties while we lamented that it had the advantage of belonging to the same Islamic Ummah? Why did no Indian prime minister visit the UAE for 34 long years since Mrs Indira Gandhi's visit in 1981? Successive Indian ambassadors in Abu Dhabi had conveyed this glaring omission to Delhi, and yet we neglected such a vital part of our neighbourhood?

It wasn't until Prime Minister Modi's historic visit to Abu Dhabi on 23 August 2015 that we started to turn the clock back. I will dwell upon the case of the UAE not just because I had the privilege of serving as India's ambassador there during a critical period in our ties, but also because of the sheer scale of the transformation. In doing so, I will try to provide a flavour of some of the specific aspects that are so vital to India's national interest.

Within a few months after the election of the new government in 2014, it was decided that an outreach to the Gulf was long overdue and that it should be done via the UAE. Preparation for PM's visit was intense but largely carried out quietly through back channels and behind closed doors. The warmth with which he was received by the Emirati side went beyond traditional diplomatic protocols, almost suggesting that a long-forgotten friend had been waiting patiently.

The crown prince (now president), Sheikh Mohamed bin Zayed, was at the presidential terminal to receive the prime minister. So were the other senior members of the royal family. The two leaders quickly established a strong personal chemistry, and Sheikh Mohamed was quick to reciprocate by visiting India in February 2016. India followed up on this early success with the bold gesture of inviting Sheikh Mohamed as the chief guest on our Republic Day in 2017. This was our way of announcing to the world that our newly reinvigorated relationship with the UAE was truly special. It was also reflected in the Comprehensive Strategic Partnership Agreement signed during the visit, a document that encompassed virtually every significant aspect of the relationship and opened exciting new areas for collaboration.

The momentum of the relationship was sustained when Prime Minister Modi went back to Abu Dhabi in February 2018, and Sheikh Mohamed inaugurated a newly built presidential palace complex by hosting the first formal dinner in honour of the Indian leader. The prime minister made a third visit in August 2019 to cement the relationship and also to receive the Order of Zayed, the UAE's highest civilian award. I had the privilege of being our ambassador to the UAE during these visits and observing not just the warm personal equation between the two leaders but also the growing trust and confidence that would catapult the relationship to an entirely different level. Narendra Modi's four subsequent visits to the UAE as prime minister are a clear indication of this intent, as was the virtual summit held in 2022 to make sure that even a global pandemic would not come in the way of the progress we were making. In fact, the virtual summit culminated in a wide-ranging vision statement that set out ambitious targets across the spectrum.

It is instructive to look at some of the key areas in which the high-level engagements have started to make a profound difference, and to soak in the fact that there is now a virtual cycle of commitment and execution. Each successful iteration is an incentive to raise the level of ambition, to venture into new areas, to build trilateral or quadrilateral platforms with like-minded countries. To make things simple, let us break this up into the political, economic, educational, energy and strategic dimensions:

Political

In the relatively short period since August 2015, we have seen the UAE not only embrace the strategic partnership with India but also redefine its ties with our western neighbour. This is partly on account of the changed mindset in the UAE itself after the horrific 9/11 terrorist attacks; the country now proactively opposes any form of militant or radical ideology and has made religious tolerance one of the central pillars of its foreign policy. This is visible in the manner in which the UAE leadership embraced the notion of having the high-profile BAPS Swaminarayan Mandir in Abu Dhabi, and in initiatives like the Abraham Family House, which brings a church, a synagogue and a mosque into the same compound. In this new environment, a strong, stable and secular India became a far more desirable partner than a Pakistan that is legitimately seen as a nursery of terrorist groups and an exporter of their toxic doctrine.

Prime Minister Modi's visit in 2015 came at just the right time and completely flipped the regional dynamics. Who could have imagined the remarkable show of friendship by the UAE in March 2019 when Abu Dhabi was to host the forty-sixth session of the Council of Foreign Ministers of the Organization of Islamic Cooperation (OIC) countries? As the host nation, the UAE exercised its prerogative to invite the Late Mrs Sushma Swaraj, India's minister of External Affairs, to the meeting.

The Pakistanis were caught completely off guard. Their protests were loud and shrill, and they even threatened to boycott the meeting if the invitation was not withdrawn. The Emiratis held firm in the face of intense pressure, and the conference opened with the Indian minister on the podium and the Pakistani seat vacant as they showed their frustration by skipping the opening session. A similar display of solidarity with India was on display a few months later when Article 370 was abrogated. Despite a sustained campaign by Pakistan, the UAE became the first Arab state to describe it as 'India's internal issue' and added insult to Pakistan's professed injury by conferring their highest award on PM Modi. It's active support for India, and quiet backchannel diplomacy was also at play when India retaliated against Pakistan after the terrorist attacks at Pulwama and Pahalgam.

Equally important from both a strategic and a business perspective are the interactions between top CEOs from the UAE and the government of Jammu and Kashmir. As a result of these initiatives, the Emaar group will establish the Mall of Srinagar, accompanied by investments in tourism and hospitality; the Lulu group is setting up a food processing and packaging facility in the valley along with a hypermarket in the Emaar mall and has already started sourcing fresh produce from Kashmir; and DP World are exploring a major inland container port and multimodal logistics facility in Jammu & Kashmir.

Economic

During the visit of Sheikh Mohamed in 2016, the UAE announced its decision to invest up to $75 billion in India. The

Abu Dhabi Investment Authority (ADIA), the world's second-largest sovereign fund, became the first anchor investor in India's National Infrastructure Investment Fund. We have also seen major investments by ADIA into renewable energy, real estate, affordable housing, highways, logistics and the financial sectors. Other Emirati sovereign funds like Mubadala, ADQ and IHCL have invested in the telecom and technology sectors. The Dubai-based DP World has become a major player in the shipping sector with its container terminals in Mundra, Mumbai, Kochi, Chennai and Visakhapatnam and is now expanding into warehousing, cold-storage chains and rail freight. Others like the Sharaf group have also invested in logistics facilities in several states, including Punjab, Haryana and Uttar Pradesh (UP).

The Comprehensive Economic Partnership Agreement, signed with the UAE on 18 February 2022, adds an important new layer to the institutional architecture of the bilateral relationship. It is an ambitious agreement that brings 90 per cent of Indian exports to the UAE under a zero-tariff regime from the very beginning and has already achieved its initial target of taking bilateral trade to $100 billion in FY 2024–25. Given the fact that India's experience with FTAs with some of the ASEAN member states led to an unanticipated surge in trade deficits, this agreement provides for a permanent bilateral safeguard facility and also defines stringent rules of origin norms with a requirement of substantial local processing of up to 40 per cent value addition. CEPA also creates a valuable template that can be replicated with other countries in the Gulf and hopefully provide a fresh impetus to the stalled India–GCC FTA.

Equally important is the template being created via the India–UAE Virtual Trade Corridor (VTC) that seeks to digitize and integrate trade processes, cut down on paperwork and create seamless connectivity between the trade portals of the two countries. It is underpinned by a web-based platform called Master Application for International Trade and Regulatory Interface (MAITRI) that was launched during the visit of the Crown Prince of Abu Dhabi Sheikh Khaled bin Mohamed Al Nahyan, in September 2024. Besides lowering logistics and transport costs, the VTC also aims to become the standard for the larger and more ambitious India–Middle East–Europe Economic Corridor that was announced on the sidelines of the G20 Summit in India.

The establishment of an India Mart in Dubai is another bold initiative that could prove to be of immense value to manufacturers and exporters from India's MSME sector by providing them with a much-needed outlet into global markets. The ability to display actual products at retail outlets in India Mart would be backed by Dubai's highly efficient warehousing, port and shipping facilities and could enable Indian products more competitive access to markets in eastern and southern Africa, as well as to other countries in the Middle East and North Africa (MENA) region. The groundbreaking for India Mart was done during the visit of PM Modi to the UAE in February 2024, and work on this ambitious project is proceeding apace.

There is also a determined effort to link India's RuPay card and UPI with the UAE's instant payments platform to enable seamless cross-border transactions between the two countries. UPI payments are now accepted by 60,000 merchants and at over 2,00,000 point-of-sale terminals across the country, and they are a boon for the large number of Indian tourists and Non-resident Indians who have a UPI linked to a bank account in India.

Energy

India was traditionally a major buyer of crude oil from the UAE and other Gulf countries, with Qatar being a particularly important source of natural gas for the Indian economy. Over the last few years, a simple buyer–seller relationship has turned into a full-fledged energy partnership. In its quest for energy security, ONGC Videsh and other oil majors had ventured from Venezuela to Vladivostok but had never found an opening in the Gulf. But thanks to the prime minister's intervention, India got a stake in the rich Lower Zakum basin. Under the terms of the contract, India has been receiving 2 million tonnes of high-quality crude oil per year for 40 years, starting March 2018. This landmark agreement was followed by a second onshore concession in Abu Dhabi (AD Onshore 1), a virgin site that is soon moving into the production phase. The Abu Dhabi National Oil Company (ADNOC) has also established India's first strategic petroleum reserves in Mangalore and Padur and created a template for more to follow. These would be of immense importance for the Indian economy if a war or some major calamity were to disrupt crude oil supplies from the Gulf.

Education

There are well over 100 'Indian' schools in the UAE that provide affordable education to the offspring of the Indian diaspora within the ambit of the CBSE framework. These are supplemented by the Dubai campuses of reputed educational institutions like BITS Pilani, Manipal, Amity and SP Jain. But the absence of flagship Indian brands like IIT and IIM had often been a sore point. This gap was rectified when IIT Delhi opened its first overseas campus in Abu Dhabi in September 2024 with an inaugural batch of 52 students. IIM Ahmedabad is now following suit with a campus in Dubai.

Strategic

Sometimes, the more important aspects of a relationship lie beneath the surface. We have seen the new Rafale jets getting mid-air refuelling in the UAE as they make their way from France to India. We have also seen the growing range of joint maritime exercises with the UAE and trilaterals with France and the UAE. Each has its significance for maritime security in the Gulf. Discussions on the coproduction of certain platforms and collaboration in cutting-edge concerns like cybersecurity and quantum computing are also an integral part of our engagement. UAE is rapidly positioning itself as a leading hub for AI research that is underpinned by huge data centres, and these are bound to open new avenues of engagement.

But less visible is the intelligence cooperation that India has developed with the UAE and Saudi Arabia. This needs a strong underpinning of trust so that the two sides can share information that is, by definition, highly sensitive. Close collaboration in this area led to the deportation of most-wanted criminals like Dawood Ibrahim's associate Farooq Takla from Dubai. It has led to the interdiction of groups that were aiming to join ISIS. And it has sent out a clear message to our adversaries that terrorists and criminals who target India will not find a haven in the Gulf.

Some Caveats

There is no question that we have accomplished a lot since that breakthrough visit of the prime minister to Abu Dhabi in 2015.

But could we have done better? Personally, I believe that we could have done a lot more to leverage the PM's initiative if our broader systems had been fully aligned with his vision. Let me outline just a few examples:

The $50 billion ADNOC–Saudi ARAMCO mega refinery proposal could have been one of the largest foreign direct investment projects in India. However, the politics of Maharashtra dragged the entire land acquisition process into an unending controversy and the project remains stalled.

ADIA has been enthusiastic about India's renewable energy sector and has invested several 100 million dollars into industry leaders like ReNew and Greenko. But a change in government in Telangana meant that power purchase agreements signed during the previous government's tenure were summarily set aside. The central government argued that this would have an adverse effect on India's investment climate, but to no avail. The ADIA also pointed out for several years that investments worth billions of dollars in India's financial sector were impeded by narrowly defined SEBI guidelines for sovereign wealth funds. These were finally amended in 2023.

Etihad Airways, a company owned by the Abu Dhabi royal family, had a major stake in Jet Airways. During the final months of the Jet saga in 2018, they had indicated a willingness to inject fresh liquidity if the government could indemnify them against lawsuits that might emerge from past actions of the promoters. This was not agreed because our system did not allow for it. The inflexibility of our system not only led to the demise of India's largest carrier but also left a bad taste in influential circles around the royal family, who lost close to a billion dollars in the deal. Etisalat, another royal family-owned company, also faced a difficult situation when it was dragged into our courts and influential Emirati board members were charged under Foreign Exchange Management Act due to the transgressions of Etisalat's Indian partner in the 2G scam.

To be fair, Prime Minister Modi's government did try to address some of these 'legacy issues' that it had inherited from the past, but the perception of India being a relatively tough business destination remained. At a time when Abu Dhabi is positioning itself as the 'capital of capital', it is a sobering reality that the bulk of investment into India has come from the sovereign funds and not from the large private institutions and family offices, which continue to remain somewhat wary.

And finally, some of the ill-advised utterances and violent actions on religious pretexts have tended to create unnecessary controversy. We live in an increasingly borderless world; offensive social media posts and reports of violence against sections of a religious community have a way of making their way into informed circles in the Gulf. Indeed, our adversaries make sure that they reach the most influential quarters to show India in a poor light. It should be a national endeavour across the political spectrum to curb these base instincts, to foster a consensus on our strategic objectives and to take advantage of the political capital invested by the prime minister in deepening India's ties with the Gulf countries. The visits of multiparty and multireligious delegations sent by the government to various countries, including the UAE, Saudi Arabia and Egypt, in the wake of Pahalgam and the clashes with Pakistan were a welcome step in this direction.

Future

21

Energy Security for a Viksit Bharat: Analysing the Evolutionary Journey of India's Public Policy

HARDEEP S. PURI

At its core, public policy involves the study of choices and trade-offs. When dealing with scarce resources, conflicting interests and diverse political/geopolitical views, it sometimes appears difficult to recognize what the right choice is. Fortunately, Indian policymakers have, more often than not, made the right choices. The evolution of public policy in India encapsulates the post-independence experience – rooted in a proud civilizational heritage, but equally, in the pragmatism of a decolonialized state.

In the 1950s, experts in political theory across the world declared that India's democratic experiment was bound to fail. It confounded them that our Constitution provided for universal adult suffrage and other fundamental rights when we faced multiple existential challenges: rampant poverty (80 per cent of the population), low literacy (less than 20 per cent) and food insecurity. Yet, India not only held together but thrived. Much credit goes to the Constituent

Assembly, which displayed exemplary foresight in balancing short-term and long-term objectives.

Its lofty ideals were and continue to be implemented by generations of governments across political divides. Certain periods in our independent history have been testing – most notably, the Emergency, where the deepest foundations of our political system were shaken. Other cracks have appeared over the years. Thankfully, the structural soundness of our democratic construction has prevailed.

If the effectiveness of policy is best judged through outcomes, then observing the long arc of development since 1947 leads one to conclude that India's approach to governance has fundamentally succeeded. India will soon be the third-largest economy in the world; the fastest-growing major economy; the 'voice of the Global South'; a responsible nuclear power; a leading space power; the most vibrant democracy; one of the youngest countries in the world, blessed with abundant human capital and intellectual capabilities; and a vital pillar both in the regional and the global order.

Would we have accepted the current situation nearly eight decades ago? Yes, I think we would have. Indians should revel in the fact that these advances have come against the backdrop of limited resources and room for policy manoeuvrability, particularly in the early years. The challenge was not simply about designing policy but about selecting the best among constrained alternatives. With greater policy room and technical capabilities to work with, the future looks even brighter.

This isn't to say that we have always made the right choices. In the early years, it can be argued that while we succeeded in forging social cohesion and national unity, the chosen economic doctrine imposed high opportunity costs. 'Nehruvian socialism', which sought to incorporate some of the best ideas of post-war socialist thinking, resulted in the Indian economy stagnating at a time when other Asian economies grew tremendously. The long-term inefficiencies which were created were an important factor behind India's failure to alleviate poverty at the desired pace. Nevertheless, if decisions in those first two decades after Independence proved to be sub-optimal for India's economy, at no point could they be termed irrational, especially considering the prevailing distrust of Western capitalism in the newly decolonized Global South.

It was in the 1970s that the constraints and costs of earlier policy choices began to drag growth – and when our leaders failed to correct course. Instead, they doubled down on some inexplicable economic policy choices that left India with the infamous 'license permit raj', an inefficient public sector, a bloated bureaucracy and misguided trade policies. This was compounded by a chastening experience during the period of Emergency when the nobility of India's democratic ambitions suffered a major blow.

The 1991 balance of payments crisis was the inflexion point, forcing India to take sweeping liberalization reforms. These marked a paradigm shift in public policy: moving from control to competition, from state ownership to private enterprise and from import substitution to global integration. This transition was not merely economic; it also reflected the growing maturity of Indian democratic institutions, the pressure of public expectations and the global wave of neoliberal economic thinking. The post-1991 policy landscape introduced a more technocratic, data-driven approach to policy formulation. The role of market signals, entrepreneurship and international trade was institutionalized. India's post-reform policies in the 2000s, particularly since 2014, have focused on inclusive growth, rural employment, large-scale welfare through digital technology, targeted subsidies and public–private partnerships.

Have we come far enough? That's the question scholars and policymakers must ask constantly. It is important to question the past to better inform our policy decisions going forward. Overall, if there were any major black mark, I would say that we haven't done enough to remove the 'gradualism' of India's reforms. Bold policymaking was lacking for much of our post-Independence journey. Perhaps it was the remnant of Nehruvian socialism that has seeped deep into our bureaucracy and political system, which made us innately suspicious of change. Policymakers have found it challenging to tackle certain structural rigidities.

It took a bold 'outsider' – ambitious enough to discount conventional barriers – to bring in bold policymaking. Prime Minister Narendra Modi arrived on the national stage in 2014 with a unique mandate to end the policy paralysis the country had found itself in. I have observed both sides of the Indian policymaking divide: before 2014 and after 2014; first, as an international diplomat representing India, and later as a politician and minister in the government. Prime Minister Modi has transformed policymaking. Where continuity was required, it was maintained. Where radical change was needed, it was introduced decisively.

Nowhere is the boldness more visible than in India's approach to social policy, which has undergone a revolution – from inefficient subsidies to more targeted, rights-based welfare delivery, aided by technological enhancements and deepening digital access. India's integrated service delivery model of governance through a network of instruments such as the Aadhaar, DBTs and mobile platforms, as seen in welfare programmes such as Pradhan Mantri Jan-Dhan Yojana, Ujjwala Yojana and Ayushman Bharat, has become the exemplar for the Global South.

Despite inheriting a 'fragile five economy' and battling various global economic uncertainties, including the pandemic, Mr Modi has guided India to become the fastest-growing major economy in the world. India is expected to register annual growth rates above 6.5 per cent in the near term. There has been a marked reduction in unemployment and poverty; nearly 250 million Indians exited multidimensional poverty.

Under Prime Minister Modi's watch, India has also changed the way trade-offs are viewed. Aspects of social well-being that were generally lost at the altar of 'infrastructuralism', such as inclusion, affordability, environmentalism, gender equality, resilience and heritage conservation, are now front and centre of development initiatives. Legislative maturity has led to nuanced changes in social and economic policy, which are more proactive than reactive, further breaking from the past.

Having been a diplomat for nearly four decades, I can tell you that India's public policy has often reflected and responded to the global order as much as domestic affairs. India's foreign policy choices were initially framed by non-alignment; forced to do so because of severe constraints as much as its idealism to preserve autonomy, particularly during the Cold War. Post 1991, policies such as the 'Look East' (later 'Act East') initiative, deeper engagement with ASEAN and Africa and most importantly, the US, as well as India's proactive role in multilateral forums, reflected a second phase which focused on strategic engagement with a globally integrated worldview. A third phase, beginning after 2014, reflects India's greater confidence on the world stage as it seeks to establish a multipolar world. It has now shed its older hesitations to embrace strategic alliances. A certain strain of autonomy and a distinct, non-interventionist approach to international affairs has remained constant.

After being invited to the cabinet, my interface has primarily been with India's urban development and energy policy. Both these portfolios are indispensable to our economic goals and are also critical in our push towards sustainability and the net-zero transition. In the case of energy, there is the added dimension of geopolitics and geo-economics, which makes deft policymaking not just challenging, but also essential. In this essay, I wish to discuss India's policy framework for building energy security as well as the various internal and external forces at play that determine how we need to fine-tune or even overhaul our approach.

Energy policy in India has been shaped by its historical context, resource endowments and strategic imperatives. India's energy consumption was overwhelmingly based on biomass fuels. The reliance on biomass accounted for nearly 70 per cent of India's energy consumption well into the mid-twentieth century. Coal mining in India began in the late eighteenth century, mainly in Bengal and Bihar. The first oilfield at Digboi, Assam, started production in 1901; however, India's crude oil production remained modest and concentrated geographically, with Assam and later Bombay High offshore fields producing the bulk of domestic crude until the late twentieth century. In 1947, oil represented less than 5 per cent of the energy mix. This reflected the limited industrialization and underdeveloped energy infrastructure at the time.

As India's energy policy confronted the challenge of growing demand driven by industrialization, urbanization and population growth, it became a net importer of crude oil. India currently imports more than 85 per cent of its crude oil and 50 per cent of its natural gas. In the modern world, oil is fundamental to a nation's economic prospects. India is no different. We have nearly 67 million people who visit petrol pumps every day. Our first duty is to them. Total energy demand moves in tandem with GDP growth. This growth-energy correlation is evident as India is now the world's third-largest energy consumer, third-largest LPG consumer, fourth-largest LNG importer, fourth-largest refiner and fourth-largest automobile market in the world. As it grows, so also does its demand for oil. India's oil consumption is forecasted to rise from 5.3 million barrels per day (mb/d) in 2023 to 13.3 mb/d by 2050, a rise that is several times the global average.

The reliance on imports is inconvenient. It stems from historical under-investment in domestic exploration and production (E&P), based on the assumption that imports would remain cheap and abundant. India's import dependence has had significant foreign policy and security implications. For example, dependence on oil imports is a major factor behind the desire to maintain stable relations with the Middle East, which supplies nearly 60 per cent of India's crude oil imports.

Recently, however, there has been a strategic pivot. The government has initiated reforms to stimulate domestic E&P and expand into previously restricted zones. India possesses 3.5 million square kilometres of sedimentary basin, but only 0.5 million square kilometres have so far been exploited. One million square kilometres of the sedimentary basin had been classified as 'No-Go' due to objections from the navy, Coast Guard, Defence Research and Development Organisation and the army, citing operational activity. The prime minister had to directly intervene to override their objections, resulting in the decision to reduce the 'No-Go' areas for exploration by 99 per cent.

Other policy reforms, such as the Oilfields Regulation and Development Amendment Bill 2024, promote domestic production and renewable energy projects. Significant discoveries such as ONGC's Kakinada field, as well as efforts such as the National Data Repository to centralize exploration data and attract global majors like ExxonMobil and Shell, with a target to increase sedimentary basin exploration coverage significantly by 2030 and mobilize $100 billion in upstream investment, highlight progress. India has also diversified its crude supplier base, from 27 in 2014 to 40 today. The establishment of strategic petroleum reserves, currently with a capacity of 5.33 million tonnes, aims to buffer against global supply disruptions.

India's refining and petrochemical sectors are growing rapidly, set to increase from 256.80 million metric tonnes per annum (MMTPA) in 2014 to 450 MMTPA by 2030. Future energy demand growth will originate from Africa and South-east Asia. India is emerging as a global energy export hub due to its advantageous geographical position at the crossroads of Asia, Europe and Africa, making it a gateway to vast and expanding markets in the future.

India stands at the epicentre of global oil demand growth, expected to account for 40 per cent of the overall growth by mid-century. India's energy landscape feeds into the global energy system, which is also undergoing significant transformation, driven by economic growth imperatives, geopolitical shifts and climate commitments. The catch-all phrase for this is 'energy transition' – a widely discussed and disputed term in policy circles. As a student of history, when I look back at the evolution of global energy, I recognize that the very notion of 'energy transition' requires a nuanced understanding.

After the Industrial Revolution, the use of wood did not vanish with the ascendancy of coal; in fact, it expanded in absolute terms. Today's energy transition, similarly, is not about eliminating hydrocarbons overnight but leveraging them strategically while scaling renewables. Even when renewables become the dominant energy sources, oil and gas will continue to play a pivotal role in stabilizing grids, industrial hydrogen and energy storage innovations. Today, fossil fuels constitute about 88 per cent of the world's energy mix and are projected to remain significant by 2050. Clearly, fossil fuels aren't disappearing any time soon, even as the pressure of decarbonizing ramps up. So, how do policymakers balance these opposing forces?

In response to energy security and environmental sustainability concerns, India has pursued an ambitious diversification strategy. The government aims to achieve 500 GW of renewable energy capacity by 2030 and achieve a net-zero transition by 2070 under the Panchamrit agenda. Parallel to hydrocarbons, India is aggressively promoting transitional and cleaner fuels: ethanol blending in petrol has increased from 1 per cent in 2014 to 20 per cent in 2025; natural gas's share in the energy mix is set to rise from 6 per cent to 15 per cent; and LNG terminal capacity is expanding.

Initiatives like the National Green Hydrogen Mission, which aims to produce 5 MMT of green hydrogen by 2030, underscore a multipronged energy strategy. India is now the fourth largest globally in installed renewable energy capacity. India's leadership in the International Solar Alliance (ISA), launched in 2015 with over 100 member countries aiming to promote solar energy adoption in tropical regions, reflects our leadership on this issue. India is also doing its utmost to future-proof energy security. It is strengthening the ecosystem for critical minerals; a recently approved National Critical Mineral Mission, with a total outlay of ₹16,300 crore, aims to strengthen mineral exploration, mining, beneficiation, processing and recovery from products. India is also deliberating on structuring the carbon market in India as the European Union prepares to adopt the Carbon Border Adjustment Mechanism (CBAM).

Strategic investment in the transition must demonstrate balance. India exemplifies this with diversified commitments across hydrocarbons, biofuels, hydrogen and renewables. Related to this is the need to build resilient and equitable supply chains for critical materials like lithium, cobalt and semiconductors. Fragile global supply chains risk a divided transition, benefiting advanced economies while leaving others behind. India's role as a technology hub – with global energy majors operating innovation centres domestically – positions it to contribute significantly to next-generation energy technologies.

As we step further into the twenty-first century, India finds itself at a critical juncture. The world has never been as uncertain since the World War II. Conflicts abound in many parts of the world, including worrisome developments in Ukraine and continued violence in Gaza. President Trump's tariffs and their uneven application could escalate into an economic Cold War; another complication in the global trade disruption is the increasing export controls of critical minerals and technologies. The rules of the 'Great Game' have changed: shifting alliances between the great powers and within regions have left countries scrambling to fortify existing arrangements or seek newer pastures.

India must learn how to navigate this – not just from a security perspective, but also from a policy perspective. Regarding the energy security challenge, this turbulent period has taught us that countries need to pursue energy sovereignty. India has managed to lower retail oil prices over the past three years while developed economies have experienced an average increase of 10 per cent in both petrol and diesel prices. Economic interests have now become central to international relations. As global value chains transform, India must prioritize trade policy, investment promotion and technology flows.

India's primary focus must remain on its domestic constituents and ensuring their continued welfare. Our policies must be oriented towards capitalizing on our demographic dividend – a comparative edge over peers, both among developed and developing countries. This necessarily entails robust investments in education, skilling and health infrastructure. Certain crucial measures have already been undertaken.

—

Formulating public policy is an infinitely complex process that encapsulates every aspect of governance – from the trivial to the profound, and from the infinitesimal to the gargantuan. It reflects the state's efforts to balance growth with equity, autonomy with openness and continuity with reform. India's success in holding together a vast, diverse population within a democratic framework, while lifting millions out of poverty and gaining global stature, underscores the effectiveness of this adaptive policymaking. While not perfect, it has been largely prudent and anchored in the realities of our unique post-colonial context. Going forward, the quality of our policymaking, ultimately, will depend on the ability to continue demanding and making bold, innovative choices. After the Modi years, I don't doubt that it will be as much of a challenge now as it was earlier.

22

State-Level Business Reforms in India: Laboratories for Growth

RICHARD ROSSOW

India's business environment is heavily shaped by both the national government and the regional governments of India's states. After decades of steady reforms by the national government, India's ability to become a significant hub for global supply chains today rests more fully on state governments. A few large states are seizing the moment and securing significant new investments. More states must follow suit.

The longer-term force that could reinforce development is India's slow, steady pace of urbanization. By 2047, a majority of Indian voters are expected to live in large cities. When big cities become the driving force for 'winning' state elections, India's development trajectory will likely accelerate dramatically.

Constitutional Framework: The Ground Rules

The Constitution of India defines the separation of the powers of governance into three categories: the Union List, the State List and the Concurrent List.[37] Foreign trade, banking, defence and interstate commerce fall under the Union's jurisdiction. States control essential inputs for business – power tariffs, water availability, land allocation and law and order. But even in areas of shared jurisdiction like contract enforcement and industrial promotion, states play a defining role. For investors, this means that the business landscape varies sharply across India's geography, not just in cost or convenience, but in policy intent and implementation.

This legal framework is central to understanding India's federal economic architecture. In practice, it translates into distinct patterns of regulatory control that directly shape investment prospects. For example, while FDI policy is a Union prerogative, acquiring industrial land or obtaining electricity connections falls within the state's purview. This duality necessitates bespoke engagement strategies and tailored market-entry plans.

Economic Diversity: Mapping State Economies

A glance at the economic structure of states underscores this divergence.[38] Madhya Pradesh, for instance, contributes over 14 per cent of India's total agricultural GDP. Gujarat alone accounts for more than 16 per cent of the national manufacturing output. In fact, just four states – Karnataka, Tamil Nadu, Maharashtra and Gujarat – together account for over 47 per cent of India's total manufacturing GDP. Conversely, even big states like Uttar Pradesh, Bihar and Madhya Pradesh have disproportionately smaller contributions to the national manufacturing GDP. In services, Maharashtra, Karnataka, Tamil Nadu and Uttar Pradesh lead.

The following table lists the ten largest states by GDP alongside their share of the total national output for specific sectors.

Table 1: States' Share of Total National Output by Sector[39]

State/Union Territory	Agriculture Per Cent	Manufacturing Per Cent	Construction Per Cent	Industry Per Cent	Banking-Insurance Per Cent	Services Per Cent
Maharashtra	8 per cent	13 per cent	11 per cent	11 per cent	26 per cent	15 per cent
Tamil Nadu	5 per cent	11 per cent	13 per cent	11 per cent	9 per cent	9 per cent
Karnataka	7 per cent	7 per cent	5 per cent	6 per cent	7 per cent	10 per cent
Uttar Pradesh	14 per cent	7 per cent	12 per cent	8 per cent	5 per cent	7 per cent
Gujarat*	7 per cent	16 per cent	6 per cent	12 per cent	6 per cent	5 per cent
West Bengal	6 per cent	5 per cent	5 per cent	5 per cent	5 per cent	6 per cent
Rajasthan	6 per cent	4 per cent	6 per cent	5 per cent	4 per cent	4 per cent
Telangana	4 per cent	3 per cent	3 per cent	3 per cent	4 per cent	6 per cent
Andhra Pradesh	6 per cent	4 per cent	4 per cent	4 per cent	4 per cent	4 per cent
Madhya Pradesh	14 per cent	2 per cent	4 per cent	3 per cent	3 per cent	3 per cent

***Note**: Latest available data for states with (*) marked is from 2022–23.

These variations are not anomalies – they reflect long-standing policy choices, historical endowments and regional governance cultures. This diversity creates both complexity and opportunity. It allows states to specialize and compete on their strengths – be it human capital, industrial depth or natural resources. But it also places a premium on tailoring investor strategies to specific state conditions.

At the Center for Strategic and International Studies (CSIS), we closely track all state-level laws and regulations that will have an impact on the business environment in that state or the state's development trajectory with our Indian States weekly update and our Engaging Indian States website.[40] We get to see the types of policy innovations that forward-leaning states have adopted to try to attract investment and create employment. While we realize India is replete with great policies that are not appropriately enacted, smart policies are a good first step.

For instance, experts often consider labour and land deregulation to be the two most politically difficult policy challenges India faces to become a stronger manufacturing nation. Some state governments have been able to adopt investor-friendly policies in these areas.

Foundational Reforms: Labour and Land

Many of the most meaningful state reforms focus on improving the fundamentals of doing business. Below are some highlights of labour and land reforms from across India from the last ten years:

Labour Reforms

- **Madhya Pradesh**: Amid COVID-19, MP passed sweeping labour relaxations.[41] It allowed easier hiring and firing, raised standing order thresholds from 50 to 100 workers and granted exemptions under the Industrial Disputes Act for new factories for up to 1,000 days. Third-party inspections were introduced for small, non-hazardous units.

- **Gujarat**: Building on earlier reforms, Gujarat passed the Industrial Disputes (Gujarat Amendment) Bill, 2020, that raised the threshold for government approval before layoffs from 100 to 300 workers. It also granted the state power to override thresholds for industrial peace and made Special Economic Zones more flexible in workforce restructuring.[42]

Land Reforms

- **Gujarat**: The Dholera Special Investment Region Act facilitates 99-year leases and digital land bank listings.[43] Strategic projects receive expedited clearance via a High-Powered Committee.
- **Haryana**: The Land Pooling Policy (2017) offers voluntary land aggregation, compensates farmers and returns developed plots for commercial use.[44]
- **Maharashtra**: Through its New Industrial Policy 2019–24, Maharashtra developed a vast land bank and streamlined land allotments.[45] Private parks over 10 acres are eligible to receive subsidies up to ₹50 crore and fast-track clearance.
- **Uttar Pradesh**: Under the Industrial Investment and Export Promotion Policy, 2022, UP allows leasing of common and barren land for up to 90 years.[46] Mega investors get fast-track land allocation. Park developers receive capital subsidies, floor area ratio (FAR) relaxations and dormitory grants.
- **Karnataka**: The Karnataka Industrial Areas Development Board drives land acquisition in the state. The Industrial Policy, 2025–30 offers stamp duty and land conversion fee exemptions.[47] PPP-

based parks receive a 10 per cent capital subsidy on infrastructure costs.

These reforms are not merely procedural; they alter the risk–reward calculus for investors. Transparent land allocation and predictable labour laws reduce compliance uncertainty, especially in industries requiring high capital expenditures.

Sunrise Sectors: Targeted State Incentives

Beyond foundational reforms, several states are also drawing investment by crafting incentives for strategic sectors like semiconductors, data centres, drones and space technology. Some notable examples of progressive policies are highlighted below.

Semiconductors

- **Odisha**: The Odisha Semiconductor Manufacturing and Fabless Policy, 2023 offers 25 per cent extra capital subsidy (totalling 75 per cent with central schemes), plus patent cost reimbursement up to ₹10 lakh.[48]
- **Andhra Pradesh**: The Semiconductor and Display Fab Policy, 2024–29 provides 80 per cent subsidy for fabs, including 30 per cent state support.[49]
- **Tamil Nadu**: The Semiconductor and Advanced Electronics Policy, 2024 grants a 25 per cent capex subsidy for prototyping and stacks its scheme atop central incentives.[50]

Data Centres

- **Uttar Pradesh**: The Uttar Pradesh Data Center Policy, 2021, offers a 7 per cent capital subsidy (up to ₹20 crore), 50 per cent land subsidy in backward districts, dual-grid power and state GST refunds.[51]

- **Odisha**: The Odisha Data Centre Policy, 2022 offers 20-year electricity duty waivers, stamp duty rebates and fast-track land allocation. Additionally, the policy also offers a green technology subsidy capped at ₹1 crore.[52]
- **Karnataka**: Through the Data Centre Policy, 2022–27, Karnataka provides green power tariff rebates, FAR relaxations and land subsidy worth ₹3 crore.[53]

Other Sectors

- **Madhya Pradesh**: The Madhya Pradesh Drone Promotion and Use Policy, 2025, offers a 40 per cent capex subsidy (cap ₹30 crore), plus lease rent and training stipends.[54]
- **Karnataka**: The Karnataka Space Technology Policy, 2024–29, targets $3 billion investment and supports 500 start-ups with grants and training for 5,000 individuals.[55]

This is just a sample of some recent state policies. Many other policies preceded these or came later and are now in draft form. While some elements of these policies echo each other, there are always variances. Hence, why Indian states are called the 'laboratories for reform'.

States' Political Risk: Continuity Is No Guarantee

Policies and implementation are, of course, only part of the picture. Doing business in India has other challenges such as political risk, climate vulnerabilities and security.

The first of these three factors – political risk – is an important consideration for investors. Even as re-election rates have risen recently – now averaging well above 50 per cent – many state governments continue to reverse the initiatives of their predecessors.

These reversals are often driven not by legal or public objections, but by political signalling, ideological divergence or simply the desire to claim credit for major developmental projects. Ironically, some of the less developed states – like Bihar, Odisha and Madhya Pradesh – have more political stability than richer and more industrialized states. States such as Goa, Tamil Nadu and Kerala, despite having higher development indices, have seen frequent alternations in government.

A change in a state government can trigger meaningful changes in orientation – and even be damaging to previously adopted policies. Investors must remain vigilant: a project welcomed enthusiastically by one regime may be paused, restructured or even scrapped by the next.

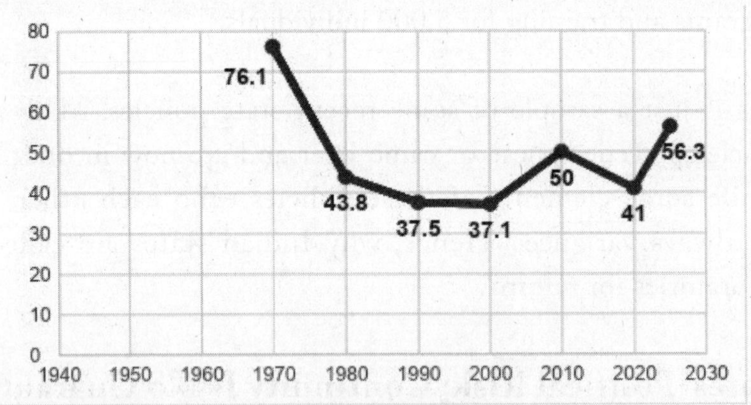

Figure 1: Decade-Wise Evolution of Re-election Rates in Indian states[56]

Consider how successive governments in Maharashtra have retracted and reinstated major infrastructure projects such as the Mumbai Metro depot.[57] Similarly, Andhra Pradesh's long-planned capital city project, Amaravati, has become a political football – launched, shelved and now revived based on which party holds power.[58] In Tamil Nadu, the back and forth between the Dravida Munnetra Kazhagam and the All India Anna Dravida Munnetra Kazhagam governments has led to a cycle of policy discontinuity, from symbolic gestures like state holidays to high-stakes disputes with foreign investors like Nissan over unpaid VAT refunds.[59]

In Rajasthan, major investment memorandum of understandings signed by Vasundhara Raje-led BJP were discarded when Congress, led by Ashok Gehlot, came to power in 2018, disrupting billions in projected capital inflows.[60] In West Bengal, the recent rollback of long-standing industrial incentive schemes by CM Mamata Banerjee illustrates how ideological preferences can override institutional memory.[61]

Political reversals in Indian states aren't just bureaucratic headaches – they can derail investor timelines, trigger legal disputes and damage project viability. For foreign investors, these shifts can mean reputational risks, sunk costs or renegotiations.

To mitigate such outcomes, investors must pair regulatory assessments with political due diligence – understanding ruling and opposition parties' economic agendas and their stance on honouring contracts. Engaging across government layers – from technocrats to ministers – can reduce disruption.

States that offer predictability, even during leadership changes, are better positioned to attract long-term capital. Institutional mechanisms like empowered industrial boards, investment promotion agencies and grievance redressal cells play a crucial role in buffering against electoral volatility. For India to sustain economic momentum, strengthening these institutional buffers may matter as much as new reforms.

Strategic Engagement: Tailoring the Approach

There remains a vibrant debate about the strategy to engage Indian states, whether you are a development partner, investor or other interested party. The debate centres around whether you use a top-down or a bottom-up approach. With top-down, you start with the chief minister or another senior political leader, look for support and the technocrats get behind it. The alternative is to first engage technical leaders and, if required, bring it to their political masters.

The truth is, there is no single correct path. It is dependent on the issue and the state government. Some state governments are known for empowering high-performing bureaucrats to make decisions and move fast – even on contentious issues. For other states, bureaucrats are not comfortable raising contentious issues with their political leaders, and an external partner would be expected to start at the political level.

At the heart of the matter is the fact that, in most states, initiating reforms does not translate into electoral success. The Patnaik government in Odisha took courageous steps to privatize its electric power distribution – and performance parameters quickly improved – yet the government lost its re-election bid last year. Incumbent governments that initiated labour reforms, such as Rajasthan and Telangana, lost their subsequent elections. States considered industrial hubs like Tamil Nadu and Maharashtra rarely see incumbent governments win re-election. But another industrialized state – Gujarat – has had a BJP government for 30 years. That is not to say that big reforms trigger election losses. However, such reforms do not seem to lead to automatic political success, either.

Urban Governance: The New Reform Frontier

India's trajectory toward becoming a $10 trillion economy will be shaped not just by states – but increasingly by cities. By 2047, most Indian voters will reside in urban centres, making city governance a strategic variable in economic planning. Yet most Indian cities today are financially and institutionally weak. They lack autonomy, depend heavily on state and central transfers and operate within fragmented planning and administrative architecture.

Some cities are emerging as outliers. Twelve cities – Ahmedabad, Pimpri Chinchwad, Rajkot, Vadodara, Lucknow, Ghaziabad, Surat, Hyderabad, Vishakhapatnam, Pune, Bhopal and Indore – have successfully issued municipal bonds, signalling maturity in financial governance.[62] Bengaluru and Jamshedpur are experimenting with civic technology and data-driven governance models.[63] Telangana and Maharashtra have piloted urban property tax reforms, improving municipal revenues.[64] However, these successes are exceptions.

Cities account for about 60 per cent of India's GDP, yet they lack corresponding fiscal powers. Few have control over critical urban services like transport, sanitation or housing.[65] Planning is split across multiple parastatals, often with no political accountability. This disconnect inhibits long-term investment and undermines the sustainability of urban growth.

India needs a new compact on urban governance: one that devolves funds, functions and functionaries. States should empower political leaders and enable cities to raise their own-source revenue through reforms to property taxation, user charges and monetization of public assets. Investment in city-level capacity – especially in planning, finance and digital governance – will be critical to unlocking urban potential.

For investors, cities represent the next wave of policy experimentation. Engaging with city leadership – municipal commissioners, smart city CEOs, urban development agencies – can open new channels for infrastructure, logistics, climate resilience and service delivery innovation.

The Outlook

India's federal system is not frictionless – but its dynamism is its strength. Policy reversals are real, but they are often corrected. Some states regress; others reform. The centre sets the stage, but the action is increasingly sub-national. In turn, states' ability to move in the right direction – in empowering cities and offering political stability to policies – will determine India's growth trajectory.

Investors and policy partners must build state-specific playbooks. Success lies in understanding the idiosyncrasies – political, bureaucratic and sectoral – that define each state's appetite and capacity for reform.

Big states like Gujarat, Maharashtra, Karnataka, Tamil Nadu and Uttar Pradesh will remain at the forefront. But fast risers like Odisha, Madhya Pradesh and Telangana are crafting bold new narratives. Urbanization and a recognition of the importance of policy continuity will reinforce this.

India's business future is not anchored in Delhi alone. It is shaped in Gandhinagar, Lucknow, Hyderabad and Bengaluru. States are not merely implementing partners – they are strategic drivers. And as city governance gains traction, a new layer of economic federalism may emerge.

The laboratories of Indian reform are humming with activity. The question is not whether to engage – but how and where to bet. States and increasingly cities are the epicentre.

23

Digital Swaraj: Accommodating Aspirations for Inclusive Growth

ANIL PADMANABHAN

In May 2025, monthly transactions using UPI – India's digital payment mechanism – were a staggering 18.6 billion. Tough to reckon that it was a mere 29,000 in November 2016. Even more impressive is the fact that 60 per cent of the transactions are for less than ₹200. Indeed, if there is a poster child for inclusion in contemporary India, it has to be UPI.

In nine years, the volume of domestic UPI transactions has risen exponentially – and is now acquiring a global footprint with several countries accepting its use, facilitating small-ticket cross-border digital payments. At the grassroots, the network effect of the democratization of payments and the underlying technology is generating unprecedented socio-economic momentum – sufficient to effect a fundamental transformation.

Viewed any which way, UPI and its underlying homegrown Digital Public Infrastructure (DPI) is the compelling story of modern India. It democratized payments, leaving even established international payment gateways like Visa and Mastercard stunned and playing catch-up.

Undoubtedly, UPI has also become the metaphor of India's ability to use DPI to create innovations that can do public good on a staggering scale. It is not just payments. The DPI framework is being adopted to achieve unprecedented transformation in health, e-commerce and social welfare.

In fact, this facet of India's digital economy has become its calling card to the world, with the G20 summit meeting in New Delhi in 2024 adopting it as a global template. The G20 declaration, issued at the end of the summit, said: 'A key area driving this progress is robust DPI. Here, India was decisive in its recommendations, having witnessed the revolutionary impact of digital innovations like Aadhaar, UPI and DigiLocker first-hand. Through the G20, we successfully completed the Digital Public Infrastructure Repository, a significant stride in global technological collaboration. This repository, featuring over 50 DPIs from 16 countries, will help the Global South build, adopt and scale DPI to unlock the power of inclusive growth.'

Data Democracy

Seventy-seven years ago, India became independent by breaking the shackles of colonial rule. In the next 25 years, its people, especially the disenfranchised and the vulnerable at the bottom of the pyramid, will, if all goes to plan, break out of poverty, riding the rails of the new digital economy. To be sure, in the last decade, India has already shrunk the proportion of people living in abject poverty to less than 5 per cent. This was managed to a large extent by leveraging the underlying digital infrastructure powering UPI.

A key part of this was the strategy of banking the unbanked. Imagine, a decade ago, 500 million people did not even own a bank account. Today, they do. Even better, Indians, even those outside the top 1 per cent income bracket, are cumulatively building their digital footprint as they join the formal economy. In future, their data could, for example, be leveraged to access credit. Significantly, a large chunk of these people will be first-time borrowers.

This will be the defining shift for a 'Data Democracy' wherein a billion-plus people can take advantage of their digital footprint to make verifiable claims, and digitally access services, products and opportunities. In short, India is poised for another tryst with destiny.

Democratizing Identity

India's ability to monetize an individual's identity and thereby democratize access to payments, health, social welfare and most recently, COVID-19 jabs is proving to be a game changer. Among other things, it has worked as a force multiplier in reducing abject poverty – UNDP estimated the incidence of poverty in India at 55.1 per cent in 2005–06.

The beauty of this unique digital economy being forged by India is twofold. First, it is based on an open digital architecture. In other words, it provides a state-of-the-art digital highway that anyone, government or private sector, can use to create innovations either for mass or niche use. Second, it enables universal access by lowering the cost of onboarding; thereby building for inclusion and scale, something so critical for India with a population size of 1.4 billion.

The story about India's Data Democracy began in 2009 with the project to set up Aadhaar, the 12-digit unique identity accorded to all those residing in India.

To execute this idea, which originated during the tenure of the National Democratic Alliance (NDA) led by Atal Bihari Vajpayee, the United Progressive Alliance (UPA) led by Manmohan Singh, inducted Nandan Nilekani, the co-founder of Infosys. The project just about survived UPA's tenure, as palace intrigue in the union cabinet all but nixed the idea. Though another way of looking at it is that Aadhaar has bipartisan consensus, having been backed by three regimes – the BJP-led NDA under Atal Bihari Vajpayee, Congress-led UPA under Manmohan Singh and the BJP-led NDA under Modi.

Remarkably, the incoming NDA-led by Modi embraced Aadhaar and weaponized it to tremendous political advantage – especially in using it to identify and reward beneficiaries with economic relief in the two years after the COVID-19 pandemic devastated India and leveraging its power to target the reduction of abject poverty.

Incidentally, Aadhaar was also India's first Digital Public Good (DPG) and has since become the force multiplier in spawning India's digital economy: the three largest public digital platforms in the world today are Aadhaar, UPI and CoWin. In sheer scale alone, India's digital economy is dazzling.

Digital Assets

Built on open protocols, DPGs or digital building blocks – also called the India Stack – are by design interoperable and free for anyone to use. As opposed to the closed platforms like those operated by Facebook and Google that dominate the digital world.

This is akin to building a highway and allowing anyone to use it to ply a vehicle of their choice or to transport goods. In turn, the DPGs have been used to create the Open Digital Ecosystem

(ODE), which permits these digital building blocks to be mixed and matched – either by government agencies or the private sector. In turn, this allows for interoperability – exactly why we can use any payment app to transact with each other.

This feature enables the creation of customized and innovative digital solutions at scale to resolve development challenges like inclusion and social payments. For instance, four years ago, these DPGs were deployed to roll out the national jab programme premised on the principle of 'One Nation, One Jab' – which entailed delivering seamless delivery of 2 billion-plus vaccines. In short, the outcome and scope of this digital economy are compelling.

Democratizing Access

Previously in India, access to most public resources was either a privilege or a favour. In short, India pursued an exceptions-based regime, which fostered cronyism, corruption and sloth. A few examples would suffice to prove the point.

The landline telephone was a rarity and, in fact, a status symbol, while it was meant to be the death of distance. Similarly, withdrawing money from your bank account meant a time-wasting trip to a dedicated branch, braving queues to only suffer the clerical atrocities of the bank teller and their team.

The launch of the cell phone revolution and later the ATMs enabled disintermediation, and worked wonders for the ease of living. However, once again, there was a barrier to universalizing these utilities – more than two-thirds of Indians did not own a bank account.

By weaponizing identity, India solved for Know Your Customer (KYC), enabling low-cost onboarding and thereby dismantling the glass ceiling of access. Today, most Indian households own a bank account – increasing the proportion of adults holding a bank account from 30 per cent in 2014 to 80 per cent at present, a global record.

According to a research paper published by the Bank for International Settlements (BIS), the bank of central banks headquartered in Basel, Switzerland, this kind of financial inclusion will normally take a country 47 years to achieve. Further, the paper argued that this in turn would require per capita income to grow fourfold from $5,000 to $20,000. India managed to achieve this milestone in nine years, even though its per capita income in this period has grown from around $1,500 to $2,700.

Even better, an individual's bank account was combined with their mobile and Aadhaar to create JAM – Jan-Dhan (a no-frills bank account), Aadhaar and Mobile. This, in turn, generated an economic GPS for the government to identify the beneficiaries of social welfare programmes correctly. In fact, the money transfers to 200 million beneficiaries during the lockdown phase of thc COVID-19 pandemic were carried out using this mechanism developed from a DPG.

The Gains

A key aspect of India's digital economy is that it is built to scale – serving 1.4 billion people. By keeping onboarding costs to a minimum, it has been able to achieve inclusion. The gains of its digital economy can be summed up as follows:

- **Disintermediation:** The majority of citizens in India need to interact with the government to receive their social benefits. In the post-COVID-19 phase, this number has grown astronomically and number around 800 million – who continue to receive free food grains. Employing DPGs has ensured the elimination of the middleman – a great example being the DBTs, reducing corruption.

- **Transparency:** By using a DPG, the government has also ensured targeted delivery of services, minimizing leakages. A collateral gain is that this is reducing the trust deficit in public services and resulting in savings to the national exchequer. Cumulatively, DBTs have saved the national exchequer a staggering ₹3 trillion – this is almost double the first COVID-19 relief package rolled out by the government.
- **Frictionless:** It is not just the DBT example, but even in the case of either FASTag or UPI, we see frictionless delivery. Not only does this improve economic efficiency, but it also quietly reinforces the notion of the rule of law. For most of the last 75 years, India has been unfortunately governed by exception, favouring the privileged.

Banking the Unbanked

The worst-kept truth about India is that while it now enjoys saturation in banking, it suffers from chronic under banking, whereby the credit needs of millions remain unaddressed. Remember, credit is key to growing businesses and expanding household budgets.

For example, the unmet credit needs for the cohort of MSMEs are estimated at a staggering $300 billion by the World Bank, and only 8 per cent of MSMEs have access to institutional credit. As a result, they are forced to turn to informal means of credit, which more often than not are on usurious terms.

It is remarkable then that despite this handicap, the MSME sector accounts for 30.1 per cent of gross value added in India's

GDP, a 45.79 per cent share in all India exports and employs 110 million people. Imagine their contribution if the rest of the 92 per cent of the MSME sector too had access to formal credit.

A solution is on the horizon. India is poised to roll out the Universal Lending Interface (ULI) to solve the country's challenge of chronic under-banking. The ULI is another DPG from India. Its architecture is very similar to the Account Aggregator (AA) framework, which is being used to service the credit needs of under-banked, including the MSME sector.

For the uninitiated, the AA is very similar to a financial intermediary. However, there is a big difference. The AA oversees the exchange of an individual's data instead of facilitating money transfers. Their institutional presence secures the privacy of an individual's data and also mitigates against potential misuse by companies.

Typically, this data – capturing cash flows in an individual's bank account, for instance – can be mined to offer non-collateral–based loans. A great example would be how the over 100 million beneficiaries of the nearly ₹1 trillion rural employment guarantee scheme can use their data capturing receipts from the government to avail of loans. At the moment, this is not possible since borrowing is predicated on an individual providing collateral and data from the rural employment guarantee scheme is not shared.

By focusing on a firm's cash flows, AA is working around the challenge of banks that lend against collateral to mitigate commercial risks. At present, the framework has an estimated 90 million users.

In the final analysis, it is clear that DPGs are fundamentally rewiring the nation, altering India's brain chemistry. The change is nothing short of dramatic. In just over a decade, India has brought

500 million people into the banking system, lifted 415 million out of poverty and connected 140 million households with clean cooking gas.

This digital rewiring has reshaped the country's economic mindset. Today, more people are engaged with the economy from within, rather than being excluded and looking in. Their aspirations are no longer distant – they are within reach.

As participants in the formal economy, citizens are now more aware of the power of their vote – because they have more to lose. Many of these new stakeholders are women, whose voices are increasingly being heard and acted upon. Anecdotal evidence suggests that this shift is already redrawing the contours of Indian politics.

This is the emerging political economy of India – one that gives it a better chance to realize its audacious goal of becoming a developed country by 2047.

24

How Public Policy and Public Affairs Can Propel India to Developed-Nation Status by 2047

SUNIL KANT MUNJAL

Few continental-sized 78-year-old nations have achieved as much as India has: when India opened its markets in 1991, its GDP was less than $300 billion – this is roughly the equivalent number of UPI transactions now being processed in a single month!

Today, a cohort of Indian citizens larger than the entire population of Europe surfs the internet, and with e-KYC, the cost of verifying a customer has come down from ₹100 to ₹5 over the last five years. Similarly, approximately $42 billion was the cumulative public money saved in 2024 through India's DBT system once leakages and ghost beneficiaries were eliminated. India is rolling out infrastructure at a frenetic pace. It has expressways that have halved travel time on major roadways, while anecdotal evidence from the country's two operational freight corridors suggests that transportation companies are already seeing 10–15 per cent lower door-to-door logistics bills and sharply shorter transit times.

These are remarkable achievements, and if we can sustain the current pace of progress, there would surely be cause for much celebration when the tricolour is hoisted atop the Red Fort on Thursday, 15 August 2047, for the hundredth time.

India's prime minister has empathetically said that the country should aspire to be a developed nation by 100. Should this become a reality, our per capita income in dollar terms would be at least four and a half times today's levels, R&D investment as a share of GDP would be pegged at least four times higher, most citizens would be literate and health-covered and the majority would be living in homes with round-the-clock power and potable water. When it turns 100, every second member of the workforce would hopefully be a woman, which is the case in most OECD nations today.

The progress over the past three decades has been stunning, and the promise over the next two decades is immense. Yet it is also true that India's per capita GDP in dollar terms is still the lowest among G20 nations; it has risen eight times in the period between 1991. Yet China, another billion-plus economy's per capita income that has grown 38 times over the same period; so, there is clearly work to be done.

To establish a template for inclusive growth that touches many more lives, we need to build and sustain collective will, year after year, for the next two decades. The Indian miracle must percolate from the ground up: whether it means enabling a young expectant mother in a remote Andhra village to receive ₹5,000 maternity benefits directly on her phone, allowing a West Bengal domestic helper to receive her subsidized weekly rations in Delhi, letting a Bihar farmer use his solar pump as a micropower plant, or helping a young coder in Coimbatore to pitch her AIforcotton startup to Silicon Valley investors over an ONDC built platform charging zero commission. The Indian miracle must benefit people from all walks of life.

Mahatma Gandhi once advised policymakers to recall the face of the poorest and weakest before drafting a law. Translating this analogy to modern India, the blueprint for policy and governance must repeatedly run through the prism of ground-level action and relatability. Thus, when we talk about creating a frictionless trade portal for farmers, we must also ensure that farmers are well-versed with the vagaries of sudden weather changes and don't lose their crop. Similarly, while we celebrate the achievements of our quantumcomputing labs, we must ensure primary school children from underprivileged backgrounds are taught in a way that they can clear basic literacy tests.

While we joyfully celebrate our achievements, we must humbly accept and resolutely work on the shortcomings we face as a nation. Therefore, while we applaud the GatiShakti Sanchar Portal for bringing down the right-of-way approvals for telecom fibre from 230 days to under 25, we need to fast-forward development across a fifth of India's panchayats that are still not covered by the Bharat Broadband project. Similarly, while we laud how fast-track special courts have disposed of more than 85,000 cases in 2024 and nearly closed the gap with fresh filings, we must find the resolve, will and ingenuity to close more than 50 million cases that have been pending across our courts for decades. Likewise, while we feel pride that paperless customs and Radio-Frequency Identification–enabled gate passes have reduced port dwell time at Jawaharlal Nehru Port Trust from five days in 2014 to 42 hours in 2025, there is a need to concurrently acquire land at the adjoining multimodal park, which still needs hundreds of clearances. Likewise, we can take some pride in the fact that the recently created Logistics Data

Bank ensures real-time tracking of containers across 17 ports; this saved significant logistics costs in 2024. Perhaps it might be useful to replicate this success across agriculture markets, urban planning and public procurement so that it creates real transformation across India.

The journey towards becoming a developed nation also requires leaps in technological and scientific advancement. Public policies must prioritize increased R&D spending and foster innovation centres, incubators and public–private partnerships. Facilitating technology transfer, cultivating start-up ecosystems and embedding futuristic tech labs (like quantum computing initiatives) across the country can stimulate creative solutions that address local challenges while boosting global competitiveness.

As Indians, we have earned the right to bask in the glow of our remarkable economic transition; we must celebrate the gigawatts of electricity, million cubic metres of storage capacity, terabytes of storage and kilometres of expressways, etc.; yet we must also ensure that we don't get seduced by the big macro numbers. We need to retain our razor-sharp focus on the unfinished tasks. India's journey from developing to developed requires a capacity to create magic at the micro level and across levels, repeatedly. Game-changing reforms and policies must benefit the people for whom they were written in the first place.

To be truly recognized and counted among the league of global leaders, the nation needs to find ways to scale and sustain micro-level successes many times over. This would happen meaningfully when we can prune red tape much faster, by slashing friction costs such as licenses, permits, land titles and judicial delays, while also allowing private capital to compound without being bogged down by uncertainty.

The SMEs are the nation's lifeline; they are responsible for about 30 per cent of GDP and 110 million jobs. It is important to ensure that they spend less time each passing year, wading through overlapping state and central compliances. India's regulatory metabolism has, of course, improved significantly in recent years, yet it remains uneven, and progress has been patchy. Fintech licenses materialize in weeks, whereas gaming start-ups must battle state-wise bans. Harmonizing these speeds is less about deregulation and more about 'smart regulation' – moving from rulebooks that prescribe to dashboards that learn.

At the same time, we also need to respect the reality that ours is a democracy. The journey thus will require parliamentary consensus, tough budgetary decisions, visionary cabinet notes and vocal public debate. As citizens, we would also need to appreciate that the pace of growth will not happen in a hockey stick fashion; public policy will ebb and flow. The pace and quality of public discourse would also be shaped by the capacity, credibility and accountability of our leadership and that of our institutions.

To sustain momentum and traction in this continuing journey, both public policy and public affairs must play pivotal roles and work in tandem. Governments at the centre, state, municipal, panchayat and district levels must strengthen their capacity to work together, think long-term and execute daily. Simultaneously, as businesses, as members of civil society and as informed citizens, we must build pressure and consistently demand accountability – through the media, through our social media groups and our elected representatives – so that all layers of government are continuously on their toes. We need a better fix of whether policy reforms being undertaken at the government level are finding echo, relevance and empathy when it comes to its lowest common denominators:

its citizens, its welfare beneficiaries, its small entrepreneurs and its NGOs.

India needs a dynamic and robust public affairs ecosystem. We need to nurture informed debates, ensure transparent policymaking and propel continuous citizen engagement. These are the connective tissues that hold together the patchwork of public policy. Establishing robust mechanisms for feedback from NGOs, local communities and small businesses keeps policymakers answerable. This involved approach can fine-tune reforms to ensure they work at the brass tacks and bridge the gap between bold national visions and everyday realities.

A meaningful, dynamic and relatable form of transparent dialogue between leaders and citizens builds trust. It also creates a virtuous cycle where policies are both visionary and deeply grounded. In this context, PM's Mann Ki Baat, which has completed 122 episodes at the time of writing, has been quite mind-shaping and transformational.

To borrow a metaphor from the construction industry, if public policy is the scaffolding that will be used to erect Viksit Bharat, dialogues around public affairs must become the mortar mix that will cement the building and keep it strong. Public policy should further invest in and expand digital platforms that improve service delivery, reduce verification and compliance costs and monitor governance dynamically and in real time. Simplifying administrative processes by reducing redundant filings, converging licensing procedures and creating clear, uniform compliance protocols can pave the way for private capital investments and entrepreneurial energy. This would fuel economic productivity and build public trust in a system, making it less burdensome and more efficient.

Of course, we are fortunate that India now has a set of leaders who understand that good economics makes for excellent politics, and sound governance leads to rich electoral pickings; they understand and appreciate the importance of working on multiple fronts at once.

Achieving the big pivot – from macro to micro, a helicopter view to a granular view, grand policy showcasing to nuts and bolts management, pronouncements to measuring real impact on the ground, state-driven research to ecosystem-led, private sector propelled research – these are some of the trickiest reforms of all, but also the ones that unlocks more doors and opens more windows.

In 1991, India opened its doors to the world. In the decades since, and especially over the last 10–15 years, the world has been entering through these doors in large numbers. What the world once called chaos, India turned into a billion-person democracy at work. In the 1990s, India found its economic voice. In the 2020s, millions are learning to sing in harmony – with tech, ambition and scale. Thirty years ago, we were a nation of missed calls, but today, we are a nation of digital wallets, segueing from queues for ration to clicks for online delivery.

Yet, the journey is only half complete. We need to take the best Western and Eastern success stories, put them in a cauldron filled with the right ingredients of public policy and public affairs, and serve up an Indian model that is truly wholesome, sustainable and people-centric. Such a model must be aligned with the country's unique history, geography, diversity, ethnicity and political structure; once this happens, we might find our rightful perch on the 'Developed Nation' tree even sooner than we can imagine.

25

The Role of Institutions in Promoting Economic Growth

T.K. ARUN

The 2024 Nobel Prize in economics went to three economists who have articulated a view that explains economic growth or the absence of it in terms of social and political institutions and how they are formed. Daron Acemoglu, James A. Robinson and Simon Johnson won the prize not for saying that institutions matter in economic performance – World Bank economists who initiated the 'ease of doing business' rankings should have got the prize, if that was all there was to it. India ranks at the bottom of the league table on, for example, contract enforcement, thanks to the tardy and inefficient judicial process, and that cripples the economy in multiple, and obvious, ways.

The point that the Nobel laureates make is best illustrated by an example they provide. After defeat at the hands of the US in the nineteenth century, Mexico ceded large swathes of land to the US, including California, Nevada, Utah, parts of Arizona and four other states. A town called Nogales in Mexico's Sonora was divided into two, the northern part becoming part of Arizona. Trump's idea of building a wall between America and Mexico had a precedent in Nogales, with a fence being built in 1918 by the US Army. The fence separated the American and Mexican parts of Nogales.

The people of Nogales have the same geographical benefits and constraints, whether in Arizona or Sonora. They have the same cultural bequest from Spanish colonization of Mexico, and constant and, often, hostile, engagement with gringos. Yet, northern Nogales is distinctly more prosperous than the part in Mexico.

The reason is that the residents of northern Nogales are governed by the relatively more enabling and inclusive institutions of the US, while the residents of southern Nogales are subjected to the relatively more corrupt, crime-ridden and discriminatory institutions of Mexico. American Nogales has functional markets, a level playing field, enabled by a legal system less amenable to capture by drug cartels and other powerful vested interests. Children of American Nogales are inspired by the 'American Dream' and have access to America's education system.

While Americans can point out plenty that is wrong and non-inclusive in the American legal system and American society, compared to the way things are in Mexico, the residents of northern Nogales are way better off than their cousins south of the border.

Let us look at some of the non-inclusive or exclusionary characteristics that inhibit economic growth.

Drastic inequality of income and wealth can kill opportunities for the majority in multiple ways, starting from blighting access to quality education, denying jobs to those who are not networked into the power structure, creating hurdles in the path of obtaining government permits and clearances or obtaining bank loans or justice from the legal system. All over the world, the wealthy enjoy privileged leverage over different organs of the state, but not entirely arbitrarily or without constraints, as can happen in parts of India removed from urban centres and media exposure.

The government has been keen on stamping out left-wing extremism but is less attentive towards eliminating the exercise of social power differentials in a way that oppresses tribal populations, which has created space for Maoists to thrive.

Weak property rights or weak enforcement of theoretically strong property rights favour those who can exercise more power in society. Kolhapuri slippers can be sold by Prada, without the artisans in question even getting to know the fame their product has acquired, let alone gaining financially from such fame.

Arbitrary decision-making, corruption and a weak, biased or inefficient judicial system can thwart economic activity for those with reduced access to power. In India, the bulk of prison inmates are undertrials, not convicted criminals. They remain incarcerated because they lack the resources to employ decent lawyers, or the courts take way too long to decide their cases.

Poor governance can be crippling in general, particularly for the delivery of enabling services. India's dysfunctional education system, starting with the primary schools, bars the vast majority from accessing modern economic opportunities. Taking part in significant patches of globalized economic growth calls for a working knowledge of English. Schools fail to impart that facility to most children who study in government schools. In a fast-changing and technologically evolving economy, the workforce needs to have learned to learn at school and be engaged in constant upgradation of their knowledge and skills. Since the school system focuses on learning a finite number of things, rather than on instilling intellectual curiosity, constant skill upgradation eludes most.

Culture, broadly defined, is a social institution, encompassing the effects of social structure, belief systems and socially legitimized conduct. India's traditional culture, based on the caste system, is positively inimical when it comes to broadening the base of entrepreneurship or innovation. Traditionally, different groups in society were assigned different occupations and skills based on their varna or caste. Taking on risk and investing money to produce additional income used to be the legitimate domain of only a small group. The lingering effect of this in modernizing India can be seen in the societal castigation of failure, fear of which dissuades a considerable proportion of the population from plunging into entrepreneurship. While the groups, for whom risk-taking was deemed legitimate, thrive and take advantage of new opportunities thrown up by advances in technology, endless possibilities of their application in different contexts and access to venture capital, making reliance on inherited wealth or capital sourced from a kin network redundant, the vast majority of society still hold themselves back from venturing into the terrain of risk. Hence, the premium on getting a steady job.

Culture inhibits innovation in another fashion. Respect for authority and fear of challenging an established hierarchy of power are an integral part of the caste system. This shapes the top-down structure of the classroom, in which the teacher passes down wisdom, and the student feels that to question the teacher is to question authority and thus endanger the social system. Intellectual curiosity and critical thinking are casualties. This is reinforced by another strain of traditional culture. The traditional understanding of knowledge holds the Vedas to be the repository of all knowledge. In other words, knowledge is finite and pre-existing. The original Sankaracharya, the eighth-century philosopher and proselytizer of Advaita from Kerala, had been bestowed with the title 'Sarvagna', meaning one who knows everything.

Creating new knowledge almost seems sacrilege in this scheme of things. Yet, research and development, the pursuit of new knowledge and its application to different human needs, is at the core of the modern economy.

A segmented rationality that cannot but crimp critical thinking is imposed on a bright student, who learns all about the physics of heavenly bodies, but is forced by custom and familial notions of good conduct, to observe Rahu kaal, Rahu being a giant serpent that periodically swallows and regurgitates celestial bodies, creating inauspicious and auspicious intervals throughout the day.

It is possible to hypothesize an explanation as to why Indians are such an excellent workforce for R&D at Global Capability Centres, even as they find it difficult to come up with research ideas and original problems to solve through research. If some foreigner commits the sacrilege of assuming there is new knowledge to be developed, and the Indian researcher is paid to carry out the needed research, he or she is just doing their job, and doing one's job well is part of one's moral obligation to society.

Caste culture is inimical to modern economic growth in another fashion as well. Only those born to social groups at the apex of the social hierarchy were expected to excel at learning. Some numerically large groups were deemed unworthy of knowledge. The value different caste groups attach to learning is still influenced by this traditional prejudice, and that affects scholastic outcomes, constraining the supply of workers needed for the knowledge economy.

Competition is an enabler of excellence and the spread of knowledge, especially when competition lures workers from advanced firms to join firms struggling to catch up with market leaders, and knowledge and know-how spread. Competition is a key driver of innovation, superior efficiency in production and lower costs, all vital ingredients of economic success.

When the government favours certain companies, and other companies face unequal access to funds, government clearances and other support, competition suffers, afflicting the economy as a whole with a lack of dynamism. Unequal societies and privileged access to the levers of power for a few can lead to the stifling of competition.

Let us leave societal institutions at the macro level and focus on some micro-level institutions that govern economic life. Here, we also see large dysfunction.

India is proud of being a democracy. Yet, it lacks an institutional system of financing the political parties that make democracy work. Competitive politics is an expensive business. It is not only at election time that parties need huge amounts of money. The party establishment must be paid for, regular party workers must be paid, party offices across the country need money to run, leaders need to travel and party publications and publicity material are expensive to produce in the quantities required. Print and digital advertising on a steady basis, and the creation and maintenance of a visible social media presence, call for oodles of money, far beyond what is available through open contributions formally made and accepted.

Parties mobilize their funds not through a mass of small contributions from the people, but from companies, big and small. Money is extracted through extortion, sale of patronage and loot of the exchequer. For files to move and to prevent bad things from happening to you, you must pay – that is extortion. In the licence permit raj, the sale of patronage was relatively straightforward: multiple entities applied for a small number of licences on offer, and some were chosen to receive the licence for reasons that have little to do with superior ability to convert the licence into a thriving business. Even in the liberalized economy, subtle and not-so-subtle forms of patronage continue. Some companies receive regulatory latitude, while others do not. Even after the allocation of some resources at the state's disposal came mandatorily to be transacted through open, transparent methods, others remain the subject of patronage.

The formula for choosing the winner in a competitive bid can be fixed in such a fashion that only those with access to the levers of power can bid freely and aggressively, guaranteeing victory. In airport privatization, for example, the bid parameter is how much revenue can be shared with the government, whether as so many rupees per passenger or as a share of the total revenue. Those who are certain about being able to raise airport development charges and other similar levies, via their clout with the powers that be, can bid aggressively, beating the competition that cannot assume any such contingency. Making railway rakes available for transporting imported coal from the port to an inland power project moves from the realm of the routine to that of patronage, when there is a scarcity of rakes and there is no mechanism for prioritizing the different demands for rakes.

The absence of a vibrant market for corporate bonds is a source of corruption and patronage. A competitive market for bonds entails frequent analysis of bond pricing, taking into account project costs, execution capability of the bond issuer and past credit record, by multiple stakeholders in the security ecosystem. In the absence of a functional corporate bond market, companies rely on bank loans. Credit decisions of banks can be influenced by the powers that be. When only a committee of bankers needs to be convinced as to what the realistic project cost is, cost padding is relatively easy, as compared to when national and international analysts of different funds and brokerages have to be persuaded that a claimed project cost is accurate and not exaggerated.

While India has a good number of independent regulators, and many of them have a decent track record of doing a good job, a structural weakness in the regulatory framework is accountability. Who would hold the regulators to account?

If a regulator is made accountable to the line ministry, true autonomy becomes a casualty. If the regulator is accountable only to the professional ethics of the personnel staffing the body at different levels, that might fall short of the needed level of accountability.

What is called for is to make regulators accountable to the relevant committees of Parliament. Regulators should periodically testify to their respective supervisory committees of elected representatives, as happens, for example, in the US. Right now, regulators often testify before committees of Parliament, but that is optional, not compulsory, as the previous incumbent of the chairman of the markets regulator SEBI showed, when she skipped a scheduled testimony.

The institutional mechanism for funding basic and applied research in India is highly flawed. Universities continue to be, in the main, the teaching shops the British designed them as, during colonial rule, leaving actual research to specialized laboratories in the public sector. This must change. Universities must become hubs for generating new knowledge. Research labs must shed their sclerotic bureaucracy. Funding for basic research must become more liberal, the resources for which could be found by rationalizing assorted subsidies.

Private companies must step up their outlays on research and development. India's R&D spend is just 0.64 per cent of GDP, a shade above Gambia's. China spends almost 3 per cent of its much larger GDP, the US a little more, Israel 5.5 per cent of GDP and South Korea 5 per cent of GDP.

These are all vital institutional deficits that must be made good to enable fast growth. But these matter only if society has essential coherence that allows it to function, without occasional eruptions of violence and disruption. Such social coherence is under strain now, with the onset of sectarian and exclusionary politics. Sectarian, divisive politics is to be rejected with the same vehemence as with which irresponsible populism is to be rejected.

Is this listing of what is missing and what is desirable merely an exercise in wishful thinking? It need not be. And that is also an insight from Acemoglu, Johnson and Robinson, who advocate political mobilization in favour of the institutional changes that are desired,

While the actual shift in policy that brings about change has to be carried out in the realm of politics, preliminary groundwork to mobilize public opinion in favour of the desirable changes and against entrenched interests that refuse to budge from the status quo falls plump in the domain of public affairs professionals.

Notes

1 Samreen Wani and Vignesh Radhakrishnan, 'School dropout rates go from bad to worse in Bihar and Assam', *The Hindu*, 4 January 2025, https://www.thehindu.com/data/school-dropout-rates-go-from-bad-to-worse-in-bihar-and-assam/article69056787.ece.

2 'Part 4. Education, the Power that Shaped a Global Korea', KBS World, 21 March 2025, https://world.kbs.co.kr/service/contents_view.htm?lang=e&menu_cate=history&id=&board_seq=457431.

3 Abhishek Waghmare, 'Education levels in India', Data for India, 6 June 2024, http://dataforindia.com/education-levels-in-india/.

4 'Economic Survey 2024–25', Government of India: Ministry of Finance, January 2025, https://www.indiabudget.gov.in/economicsurvey/doc/echapter.pdf.

5 Hasmukh Adhia, 'India Needs Public Policy Education, Hasmukh Adhia', *The Hindu*, 30 March 2023, http://thehindu.com/opinion/op-ed/india-needs-public-policy-education/article66675629.ece.

6 'Mandate of the Commission', Capacity Building Commission, https://cbc.gov.in/.

7 'Capacity Building Commission', User Experience Design and Technology, http://uxdt.nic.in/documents/logos/capacity-building-commission/.

8 'About Karma Yogi Bharat', Karm Yogi, https://karmyogiup.in/.

9 'Annual Report 2024–25', Public Affairs Forum of India, https://pafi.in/panel/assets/images/reports/17482563985623.pdf.

10 Angus Maddison, The World Economy: Historical Statistics, Organisation for Economic Co-operation and Development, 2023. p. 259; 'GDP of India', *Statistic Times*, https://www.statisticstimes.com/economy/country/india-gdp.php.

11 Arpan Sheth, Sur Shah, Neera Nundy, Ami Misra and Prachi Pal, 'India Philanthropy Report 2025', Bain and Company, February 2025, https://www.bain.com/insights/india-philanthropy-report-2025/.

12 Ibid.

13 Rakesh Rajani and Tim Hanstad, 'Helping NGOs and Funders Make the "Big Shift" to Working with Government', *Stanford Social Innovation Review*, 5 May 2025, https://ssir.org/articles/entry/big-bet-philanthropy-government-scaling. p. 6.

14 For instance, using World Bank PovcalNet data from 135 countries for the period 1974–2018, Katy Bergstrom has estimated that 90 per cent of changes in poverty can be explained by changes in average income. See Katy Bergstrom, 'The Role of Income Inequality for Poverty Reduction', *World Bank Economic Review*, August 2022, https://hdl.handle.net/10986/34507. pp. 583–604. See also in this regard, David DollarTatjana Kleineberg and Aart Kraay , 'Growth still is good for the poor', *European Economic Review*, January 2016, https://doi.org/10.1016/j.euroecorev.2015.05.008. pp. 68–85.

15 Karthik Muralidharan, Accelerating India's Development: A State-Led Roadmap for Effective Governance, Penguin Random House India, 2024, pp. 30–33.

16 Rajani and Hanstad, 'Helping NGOs and Funders Make the "Big Shift" to Working with Government'. p. 1.

17 'ASER 2024 – Rural', PRATHAM, 28 January 2025. https://asercentre.org/wp-content/uploads/2022/12/ASER_2024_Final-Report_25_1_24.pdf

18 https://api.theconvergencefoundation.org/uploads/reports/1740635507344-systemic-impact-exemplars.pdf

19 Aart Kraay and David McKenzie, 'Do Poverty Traps Exist? Assessing the Evidence', *Journal of Economic Perspectives*, 2014, https://pubs.aeaweb.org/doi/pdfplus/10.1257/jep.28.3.127. DOI: 10.1257/jep.28.3.127. pp. 127–48.

20 'Hindu rate of growth: Where does the term come from and what it means', *Business Standard*, 6 March 2023.

21 'World Development Report 2024: The Middle-Income Trap'. World Bank, 2024. https://www.worldbank.org/en/publication/wdr2024.

22 Laura Silver, Christine Huang and Laura Clancy, 'Key facts as India surpasses China as the world's most populous country', Pew Research Center, 9 February 2023, https://www.pewresearch.org/short-reads/2023/02/09/key-facts-as-india-surpasses-china-as-the-worlds-most-populous-country/.

23 'India's Growing Focus on Youth and Sports', Government of India Press Information Bureau, 1 February 2025, http://pib.gov.in/FactsheetDetails.aspx?Id=149107; Silver, Huang and Clancy, 'Key facts as India surpasses China as the world's most populous country'.

24 This definition was revised in the National Youth Policy 2014, replacing the

earlier 2003 policy which classified youth as individuals aged 13–35.

25 'Draft National Policy', Ministry of Youth Affairs & Sports, 29 April 2022, https://static.pib.gov.in/WriteReadData/specificdocs/documents/2022/may/doc20225553401.pdf.

26 'Expenditure budget', Union Budget of India 2025–26, https://www.indiabudget.gov.in/doc/eb/allsbe.pdf.

27 'Key highlights from the CSDS-KAS Report 'Attitudes, anxieties and aspirations of India's youth: changing patterns', Lokniti, https://www.lokniti.org/media/upload_files/KeyfindingsfromtheYouthStudy.pdf; Damini Nath, '48% of govt. buildings in States, 8% of public buses made accessible', *The Hindu*, 20 February 2022, https://www.thehindu.com/news/national/48-of-govt-buildings-in-states-8-of-public-buses-made-accessible/article65068360.ece.

28 'Youth Act 2017', Ministry of Culture, Government of Finland, https://okm.fi/en/legislation-youth.

29 'The Apparel and Footwear Sector and Children in Vietnam', UNICEF Vietnam, http://unicef.org/vietnam/sites/unicef.org.vietnam/files/2018-07/Footware%20Report%20Eng%20revised.pdf.

30 'Women bearing brunt of Covid-19's impact on RMG sector: ILO', *Daily Star*, 21 November 2020, http://thedailystar.net/business/news/women-bearing-brunt-covid-19s-impact-rmg-sector-ilo-1998605; 'Women's Health, Decent Work and the Electronics Industry', Good Electronics, 11 March 2019, https://goodelectronics.org/womens-health-decent-work-and-the-electronics-industry/.

31 'Twelfth Malayasia Plan', RMKE12, https://rmke12.ekonomi.gov.my/en.

32 'The analysis of gender equality mainstreaming elements in national strategic orientation documents on socio-economic development and financing period 2021-2030', 11 January 2023, http://vietnam.un.org/en/214776-analysis-gender-equality-mainstreaming-elements-national-strategic-orientation-documents.

33 Ibid.

34 'Malaysia government offers tax exemption for women who return to work', *People Matters*, http://peoplemattersglobal.com/news/diversity/malaysia-government-offers-tax-exemption-for-women-who-return-to-work-20054.

35 'Breaking Barriers: Toward Better Economic Opportunities for Women in Malaysia'. September 2019. chrome-extension://efaidnbmnnnibpcajpcglclefindmkaj/https://openknowledge.worldbank.org/server/api/

core/bitstreams/a6743617-94a4-5c2e-aa8a-bd152dd8e4e4/content.

36 'State of Discrimination: Legal barriers on women's right to choose work in India', Prosperiti, https://prosperiti.org.in/wp-content/uploads/2025/03/Prosperiti-_-State-of-Discrimination-_-Legal-barriers-on-womens-right-to-choose-work-in-India-_-February-2025.pdf.

37 'The Constitution of India', Legislativ.gov, 1 May 2024, http://cdnbbsr.s3waas.gov.in/s380537a945c7aaa788ccfcdf1b99b5d8f/uploads/2024/07/20240716890312078.pdf.

38 'Handbook of Statistics on Indian States', RBI, 2024, http://rbi.org.in/scripts/AnnualPublications.aspx?head=Handbook+of+Statistics+on+Indian+States.

39 Ibid.

40 'Engaging Indian States', CSIS, http://indianstates.csis.org/; 'Indian States Weekly', CSIS, http://indianstates.csis.org/.

41 'Indian States Ease Labor Laws, Letting Companies Fire at Will, Extend Hours', Bloomberg, 8 May 2020, https://www.bloomberg.com/news/articles/2020-05-08/indian-states-ease-labor-laws-as-economy-reels-from-lockdown.

42 'The Industrial Disputes (Gujarat Amendment) Bill, 2020', PRSI India, http://prsindia.org/files/bills_acts/bills_states/gujarat/2020/Bill%2016%20of%202020%20Gujarat.pdf.

43 'SIR Act 2009', Dholera.Gujarat, https://dholera.gujarat.gov.in/sir_act.

44 'Haryana Land Pooling Act', *Haryana Govenrment Gazette*, 6 September 2022, http://tcpharyana.gov.in/Policy/Gazette_36-2022_14338.pdf.

45 'महाराष्ट्राचे नवीन औद्योगिक धोरण - 2019', Maitri.Mahonline.Gov, https://maitri.mahaonline.gov.in/PDF/Maharashtra%20New%20Industrial%20Policy-2019.pdf.

46 'Uttar Pradesh Industrial Investment and Employment Promotion Policy 2022', Invest Up, https://invest.up.gov.in/wp-content/uploads/2023/02/Uttar_Pradesh_Industrial_Investment_Employment_Promotion_Policy_2022-en.pdf.

47 'Karnataka Industrial Policy 2025–30', Invest Karnataka, https://investkarnataka.co.in/wp-content/uploads/2025/02/IndustrialPolicy2025_PrintPagesSingle_.pdf.

48 'Semiconductor Manufacturing and Fabless Policy 2023', IT Odisha, https://it.odisha.gov.in/news/semiconductor-manufacturing-and-fabless-policy-2023.

49 'Andhra Pradesh Electronics Manufacturing Policy 4.0 (2024–29)',

Andhra Pradesh Industrial Infrastructure Corporation, https://apiic.in/wp-content/uploads/2024/12/Andhra-Pradesh-Electronics-Manufacturing-policy-4.0-2024-29.pdf.

50 'Semiconductor and Advanced Electronics Policy 2024', Investing in Tamil Nadu (Guidance Tamil Nadu), https://investingintamilnadu.com/DIGIGOV/StaticAttachment?AttachmentFileName=/pdf/poli_noti/SCP_2024.pdf.

51 'Uttar Pradesh Defence Corridor Policy 2021', Invest UP, https://invest.up.gov.in/wp-content/uploads/2021/09/DC-Policy-2021-Eng-final_page-f.pdf.

52 'Odisha State Data Center Policy 2022', Invest Odisha, https://investodisha.gov.in/download/Odisha-State-Data-Center-Policy_2022.pdf.

53 'Data Center Policy 2022–2027', Scribd, https://www.scribd.com/document/849506492/data-center-policy-2022-2027.

54 'Drone Promotion and Utilisation Policy 2025', Invest Madhya Pradesh, https://invest.mp.gov.in/wp-content/uploads/2025/02/Drone-Policy-2025-1.pdf.

55 'Karnataka Space Policy 2024–29', NammaKPSC, https://www.nammakpsc.com/affairs/karnataka-space-policy-2024-29/.

56 Based on the author's calculations and data from the Election Commission of India.

57 'Shinde-Fadnavis govt reverses half a dozen decisions of MVA dispensation', *Business Standard*, https://www.business-standard.com/article/politics/shinde-fadnavis-govt-reverses-half-a-dozen-decisions-of-mva-dispensation-122102300099_1.html.

58 Amarnath K. Menon, 'How Jagan Reddy's Andhra tri-capital plan got a shot in the arm', *India Today*, 30 November 2022; 'Return of TDP is the return of Amaravati as Andhra Pradesh's sole capital', *News Minute*, 12 June 2024.

59 Migrator, 'Tamil Nadu Day to be celebrated on July 18, not Nov 1, says Stalin', *DT Next*, 30 October 2021, https://www.dtnext.in/tamilnadu/2021/10/30/tamil-nadu-day-to-be-celebrated-on-july-18-not-nov-1-says-stalin; 'Nissan sues India over outstanding dues; seeks over $770 million', CNBC, 1 December 2017, http://cnbc.com/2017/12/01/nissan-sues-india-over-outstanding-dues-seeks-over-770-mln.html.

60 Dev Ankur Wadhawan, 'BJP lashes out at Rajasthan govt's decision to cancel MoUs', *India Today*, 8 January 2019, https://www.indiatoday.in/india/story/bjp-lashes-out-at-rajasthan-govt-s-decision-to-cancel-mous-1426643-2019-01-08.

61 'Bengal govt revokes old incentive schemes, to formulate modern one to set up industries', *The Print*, 20 March 2025, https://theprint.in/india/bengal-govt-revokes-old-incentive-schemes-to-formulate-modern-one-to-set-up-industries/2555410/.

62 'Municipal Bonds', SEBI, 31 May 2025, https://www.sebi.gov.in/statistics/municipalbonds.html.

63 'IIIT Bangalore announces GoK funded 'Digital Governance' and 'Data-Driven Planning' Initiatives', IITB, 3 July 2022, http://iiitb.ac.in/media/iiit-bangalore-announces-gok-funded-digital-governance-and-datadriven-planning-initiatives; 'Jamshedpur-Kalinganagar Corridor – DELTA Microplanning', TATA Trusts, http://tatatrusts.org/our-work/digital-transformation/data-driven-governance/jamshedpur-kalinganagar-corridor.

64 Sunny Baski, 'GMHC plans GIS-based survey to track taxes', *Times of India*, 1 March 2024, https://timesofindia.indiatimes.com/city/hyderabad/ghmc-to-conduct-gis-based-survey-to-track-taxes-and-improve-property-recovery/articleshow/108123272.cms; 'Maharashtra pushes GIS mapping of properties to fill civic coffers', *Indian Express*, 17 May 2017, https://indianexpress.com/article/cities/mumbai/maharashtra-pushes-gis-mapping-of-properties-to-fill-civic-coffers-4659307/.

65 'Cities as Engines of Growth', NITI Aayog and Asian Development Bank, May 2022, niti.gov.in/sites/default/files/2022-05/Mod_CEOG_Executive_Summary_18052022.pdf.

Acknowledgements

The story of strategy is always, in the end, the story of those who shaped it.

The idea for this book came to us about eight months ago, while far from Delhi, looking at India from a distance, thinking deeply about the forces shaping its policy landscape. What began as a quiet exchange of thoughts soon became a calling. The more we spoke, the clearer it became: this was not just a book we wanted to bring out, but a story that needed to be told.

This book, *The Policy Pivot: Inside India's Strategic Shift,* is dedicated to the public affairs and advocacy fraternity in India – the professionals who navigate change before it makes headlines, and who turn uncertainty into opportunity. Public policy practitioners are, above all, builders of trust – weaving relationships across governments, industries, media and civil society, often in moments of great tension. Their work is invisible to most, but essential to the health of our democracy and the progress of our economy.

Imagine this: a phone rings in the middle of the night – an urgent overseas call. Breaking news flashes of a trade dispute, while a draft crisis statement waits on the screen. Meetings with state officials, quiet talks with regulators, media briefings, CSR reviews, stakeholder dialogues – all in a single day. Geopolitics shifts. Markets react. Uncertainty endures. And yet, the work carries on.

To our contributors – this book is yours.

From that moment, the support we received was overwhelming. All twenty-five contributors, without hesitation, offered their time, wisdom and experience. They brought not just their expertise, but their hearts – filling these pages with honesty, insight and a belief in the power of engagement. Their voices represent the diversity, depth and richness of India's public affairs community, and together they have created a living record of a fraternity that has come of age. It is to them that we owc the soul of this work.

Your essays capture the sleepless nights, the high-stakes negotiations, the shifting political and economic landscapes, and the unwavering belief in the power of dialogue. You have shown that in a world of competing interests, it is still possible to find common ground and forge solutions for the greater good.

Our gratitude to **Shri N.K. Singh** for his inspiring foreword at short notice, and to **Minister Hardeep Singh Puri** for his thoughtful essay and enduring friendship with the PAFI.

To PAFI's co-founders, past presidents, Managing Committee and members – you have built more than an organization; you have built a family, a safe harbour for this profession. To the PAFI Secretariat, especially the tireless Jeeva Kharb – thank you for holding every thread together and ensuring we reached the finish line.

And to Swati Chopra and her incredible team at Juggernaut — you have turned our vision into pages we can hold, and our purpose into something that will endure.

Here's to our fraternity – may we continue to build trust, shape policies that matter and find common ground in a world that needs it more than ever.

Ajay Khanna and Rahul Sharma

A Note on the Contributors

T.K. Arun is a Delhi-based journalist and columnist. He writes extensively on a range of subjects overlapping political economy, accessible at htttp://tkarun.substack.com. He has been the resident editor of the *Economic Times* in Delhi, headed the economy bureau and looked after the editorial page of the paper in the past. He had been with the paper from 1994 till contractual disengagement at the end of 2021, except for a two-and-a-half-year stint with the Dotcom world. He has worked as a technical adviser for the Kerala State Planning Board before beginning his career in journalism in 1992 at the *Observer of Business and Politics*. He has a rich experience of advising students at the PhD level and has a number of students both in India and abroad.

Chandrajit Banerjee is the director general of CII, India's apex industry body. With over 35 years in the organization and serving as its director general since 2008, he has been instrumental in driving policy advocacy, industry competitiveness and international collaboration. He is a member of several key government advisory bodies and serves on the boards of institutions including the Institute of Economic Growth, Global Innovation and Technology Alliance, Invest India and IIM Ranchi. He also supports numerous bilateral CEO forums constituted by the Government of India. Chandrajit Banerjee has received several international honours, including the China–India Friendship Award, Spain's Knight Commander decoration and Italy's Cavaliere dell'Ordine della Stella d'Italia. He holds a postgraduate degree in economics from the University of Calcutta and honorary doctorates from Amity University and Xavier Institute of Management. Through his leadership, CII continues to serve as a vital bridge between Indian industry, government and global stakeholders.

Laveesh Bhandari is president and a Senior Fellow at CSEP. Dr Bhandari has published widely on subjects related to sustainable livelihoods, industrial, economic and social reforms in India, economic geography and financial inclusion. He received his PhD in economics from Boston University, for which he was awarded the Best Thesis in International Economics. He has taught economics at Boston University and IIT Delhi. Apart from applied economics research, Dr Bhandari has built, seeded and exited from three companies in the research, analytics and digital domains, including Indicus Analytics, a leading economic research firm. Currently, he is researching issues of inclusion, India's energy transition and how it will impact the government as well as the economy.

Aparajita Bharti is a founding partner at The Quantum Hub (TQH) and co-founder of the Young Leaders for Active Citizenship (YLAC), an initiative that empowers young people to engage meaningfully with democratic processes. Her work spans gender, technology policy and the integrity of India's democratic institutions. Before founding TQH and YLAC, Aparajita was manager, Corporate Affairs and Communications at Snapdeal, where she led media strategy and policy engagement for the digital commerce sector. She began her public policy career as a legislative assistant to Rajya Sabha MP, N.K. Singh.

Aparajita holds a master's in public policy from the University of Oxford. She was one of four Indians selected for the prestigious Faiths Act Fellowship by the Tony Blair Faith Foundation in 2011. As an undergraduate at the College of Business Studies, Delhi University, she co-founded Manthan, a street theatre platform for spreading social awareness, which has now grown to cities across India. She is also a World Economic Forum Global Shaper from the New Delhi hub, actively contributing to policy conversations at both grassroots and national levels.

A.K. Bhattacharya is the editorial director of *Business Standard* and one of India's most respected economic journalists. He has previously served as the editor of *Business Standard* and *The Pioneer*, and held senior editorial roles at the *Financial Express* and the *Economic Times*. Known for his long-running column, Raisina Hill, he writes incisively on government policy, economic affairs and development issues. He is a distinguished fellow at the Ananta Aspen Centre and a member of CII's Economic Affairs Council. A former general secretary of the Editors Guild of India, he received the Shriram Lifetime Achievement Award for Excellence in financial journalism in 2017. He is the author of *The Rise of Goliath* and a three-volume series on India's finance ministers, published by Penguin Random House, India. Bhattacharya is a regular commentator on policy forums and media platforms and is based in New Delhi.

Ajay Bisaria is a strategic adviser and commentator on international affairs, with over three decades of experience in diplomacy and global policy. A distinguished fellow at the Observer Research Foundation, he also chairs a task force on green steel for the Ministry of Steel and advises global firms such as OMERS and

NEO Asset Management. A former Indian high commissioner to Canada and Pakistan, he has served in key diplomatic roles across Europe, North America and Central Asia, and was a senior aide to Prime Minister Atal Bihari Vajpayee. His expertise spans geopolitics, trade and Eurasian affairs, and he regularly writes and speaks on these themes. His acclaimed book, *Anger Management*, explores India–Pakistan diplomatic ties. Mr Bisaria holds degrees from St Stephen's College, IIM Calcutta and Princeton University, and has been recognized with distinguished alumnus honours.

Vijay Chauthaiwale is in charge of the Foreign Affairs Department and a member of the National Executive of Bharatiya Janata Party (BJP). In this role, he coordinates with the Indian diaspora globally and also the 'Know BJP' initiative to enhance the party's global outreach. Before joining the BJP, he was the vice president (R&D) at Torrent Pharmaceuticals Ltd., Ahmedabad. He holds a PhD in microbiology from the University of Pune, and was a post-doctoral fellow in the USA for four years, including three years at the National Institutes of Health, Bethesda, MD, USA.

He attended executive management programmes at IIM Bangalore and London Business School. He has authored several peer-reviewed papers in international scientific journals, co-invented global patents, co-edited three books and penned articles on contemporary topics. He has been a swayamsevak of RSS since childhood.

Ashish Dhawan is the co-founder of Centre for Effective Governance of Indian States (CEGIS) and the founder–CEO of The Convergence Foundation (TCF). He is also the founding chairperson of Ashoka University and the Central

Square Foundation and serves on the governing board of the Bill and Melinda Gates Foundation. Before his second career as a philanthropist, Ashish was among India's most successful private equity investors. He founded and ran ChrysCapital, the country's leading private equity firm. Ashish graduated from Yale University and received his MBA from Harvard Business School. He is also on the India Advisory Board of Harvard and a member of Yale's Development Council.

Co-authors:

Swagato Ganguly is a senior fellow at TCF and works closely with the strategic communications team. He has switched disciplinary streams, moving from a degree in electrical engineering at IIT Kanpur to a doctorate in comparative literature and literary theory at the University of Pennsylvania. Thereafter, he moved to journalism and has worked across the editorial pages of newspapers, most recently heading the *Times of India's* editorial page for 12 years.

Praveen Khanghta leads the Strategy and Investments team at TCF. With over a decade of experience in strategy and programme management, he has worked across diverse sectors, including philanthropy, non-profit and education. Before joining TCF, Praveen held senior roles at the Central Square Foundation, where he contributed to strategic initiatives aimed at improving educational outcomes across India. He also served as an adviser to the secretary, School Education, at the Ministry of Human Resource Development. His journey in the social sector began as a fellow with Teach For India, where he worked on grassroots education challenges. Praveen holds a BTech in engineering from the National

Institute of Technology, Kurukshetra, and is an alumnus of the Young India Fellowship at Ashoka University.

Shubhashis Gangopadhyay is a leading economist with a PhD from Cornell University. He began his academic career at the Indian Statistical Institute, becoming a full professor in 1991. He founded the India Development Foundation in 2003 and currently serves as its managing trustee and research director. Dr Gangopadhyay has played a key role in establishing institutions such as the Indian School of Public Policy, Shiv Nadar University's School of Humanities and Social Sciences and the School of Liberal Studies at UPES. He has held academic positions at the University of Groningen and the University of Gothenburg, which awarded him an honorary doctorate in 2006. In 2008, he was appointed adviser to the finance minister of India during the global financial crisis. His work spans economic policy, finance and law, with contributions to major reforms in India's energy and pricing sectors. He continues to advise governments, multilateral institutions and academia globally.

Pooja Sharma Goyal is the founding CEO of the Udaiti Foundation, which is dedicated to closing the gender gap in India's workforce and enabling India's vision of becoming a $30-trillion economy by 2047. Her work blends personal conviction with professional insight, shaped by her experiences as a corporate leader, entrepreneur and caregiver.

A serial entrepreneur, Pooja co-founded *Avishkaar*, which set up 2,500+ robotics labs globally, and *Intellitots*, later acquired by KLAY. She began her career at Adobe in the US, where she led global business units and billion-dollar portfolios. Her journey highlighted systemic barriers limiting women's economic participation, prompting her to drive change.

At Udaiti, she leads initiatives to increase women's workforce participation, promote gender-responsive infrastructure and drive financial inclusion. Through the flagship 'Close the Gender Gap 30x30' initiative, she works with industry and government to raise women's formal workforce participation from 18 per cent to 30 per cent by 2030.

Pooja is a recipient of the Women Transforming India Award, an angel investor and a founding member of Plaksha and Ashoka University. She is also a limited partner at Appreciate Capital. She holds a BTech from IIT Delhi and an MBA from INSEAD.

Amitabh Kant is a distinguished civil servant and policymaker who served as India's G20 Sherpa during its presidency year, playing a pivotal role in shaping global policy discourse. Before this, he was the CEO of NITI Aayog, the Government of India's premier policy think tank, where he led transformative national initiatives. He has also served as secretary of the Department for Promotion of Industry and Internal Trade and is a member of the Indian Administrative Service (Kerala cadre, 1980 batch).

Mr Kant has been the driving force behind several landmark campaigns such as Make in India, Startup India, Incredible India and God's Own Country, which significantly enhanced India's and Kerala's global image as leading investment and tourism destinations. These initiatives integrated infrastructure development, public–private partnerships and strategic branding, earning global recognition and numerous awards.

In his career, he has held key positions including secretary, Tourism, Kerala; joint secretary, Ministry of Tourism, Government of India; district collector, Kozhikode; and CEO, Delhi–Mumbai Industrial Corridor Development Corporation.

He is the author of *Branding India: An Incredible Story* and *Incredible India 2.0*, and editor of *The Path Ahead: Transformative Ideas for India*, reflecting his deep engagement with India's growth and innovation agenda.

Chetan Krishnaswamy brings extensive public policy and business expertise, shaped by leadership roles in some of India's most complex corporate policy environments. He joined Amazon after nearly seven years at Google, where he built a high-performing team, developed strategic partnerships with the central and state governments and significantly enhanced the company's reputation among key political and policy stakeholders. Before Google, Chetan served as director of Corporate Affairs at Dell India and led public policy at Intel, where he was a technical assistant to the president and received the prestigious Intel Achievement Award – an honour awarded to less than 1 per cent of Intel employees. He began his career in journalism, reporting for leading Indian publications, including heading the technology bureau at the *Times of India*. Chetan's cross-sectoral experience uniquely positions him at the intersection of technology, policy and governance.

Rajiv Kumar is chairman of Pahlé India Foundation, a policy think tank he founded in 2013. He is the former vice chairman of NITI Aayog and currently serves on the Global Leadership Council of GASP, New York. He chairs the board of governors at the Giri Institute of Development Studies, Lucknow, and was formerly chancellor of the Gokhale Institute of Politics and Economics, Pune. Dr Kumar has held senior positions across academia, government, industry and multilateral institutions. He has worked with ICRIER, IIFT, CPR and held key roles in the Ministry of Finance and the Ministry of Industry. He spent a decade at the Asian Development Bank in Manila and later served as chief economist at CII and secretary general at FICCI. He has been a board member of both RBI and SBI. Dr Kumar holds a PhD in economics from Lucknow University and a DPhil from Oxford University.

Shashank Mani is a member of Parliament from Deoria, Uttar Pradesh, and a senior leader of the Bharatiya Janata Party (BJP), where he serves as the party whip and National Niti Pramukh of the Swavalambi Bharat Abhiyan, a movement promoting entrepreneurship and self-reliance. An IIT Delhi graduate with an MBA (Hons) from IMD Lausanne, he began his career at Schlumberger. He later became a senior partner at PwC, leading national initiatives such as Mission Karmayogi and the $5 Trillion Economy Committee. Shashank is the founder of the Jagriti Yatra, the world's largest entrepreneurial train journey and the Jagriti Enterprise Centre – Purvanchal, a rural innovation hub. A recipient of the IIT Delhi Distinguished Alumni Award, he is also a published author of *India: A Journey Through a Healing Civilization* and *Middle of Diamond India: National Renaissance through Participation and Enterprise*. Residing in Barpar village, he remains deeply committed to grassroots development and youth-led nation-building.

Luis Miranda is chairman and co-founder of the Indian School of Public Policy, and also chairs the Centre for Civil Society and CORO. A passionate advocate for social impact, he co-founded Take Charge, a mentoring initiative for Catholic youth in

Mumbai, and supports numerous non-profits, including Educate Girls, Sunbird Trust and SNEHA. Luis and his wife, Fiona, are #LivingMyPromise signatories, having pledged to donate over half their wealth to charity. Professionally, he chairs ManipalCigna Health Insurance, advises Morgan Stanley and L&T-SuFin and sits on the board of L&T Technology Services. He played a key role in building HDFC Bank and IDFC Private Equity, stepping down as CEO of the latter in 2010. A chartered accountant and MBA from Chicago Booth, he serves on several University of Chicago boards. A prolific writer, Luis contributes to *Forbes*, *IDR* and *Thrive Global*. He lives in Mumbai with Fiona; their children are pursuing creative and research careers abroad.

Sunil Kant Munjal is a business leader, institution builder and social entrepreneur. Former joint managing director of Hero MotoCorp and currently chairman of Hero Enterprise, he is deeply engaged in education, healthcare and capacity-building initiatives through various family trusts. He is the founder of Serendipity Arts Foundation and president of Ludhiana Sanskritik Samagam, both of which promote the arts across India.

Munjal serves on the boards of leading institutions including ISB, IIM Ahmedabad, SRCC and The Doon School, and is associated with organizations such as Bharti Foundation and the Coca-Cola India Advisory Board. A former president of CII and AIMA, he was a member of the Prime Minister's Council on Trade & Industry and has led key studies on skill development, vocational training, CSR and tribal development.

He played a significant role in policy formulation as a member of the Narasimhan Committee on banking reforms and the Kelkar Committee on indirect taxes, which laid the groundwork for VAT and GST. His inputs on red tape and skills development have informed major national policy changes, including the Ease of Doing Business and Skill India initiatives.

Nandan Nilekani is the co-founder and chairman of Infosys Technologies and the founding chairman of the Unique Identification Authority of India (UIDAI), where he led the Aadhaar initiative from 2009 to 2014. He co-founded and chairs EkStep Foundation, which leverages technology to improve foundational literacy and numeracy for children. In 2023, he was appointed co-chair of the G20 Task Force on Digital Public Infrastructure.

A graduate of IIT Bombay, Nilekani has received several accolades, including the Padma Bhushan (2006), the Joseph Schumpeter Prize (2005) and the Economist Social and Economic Innovation Award (2014). He has been featured on *TIME* magazine's list of the 100 most influential people (2006, 2009 and 2024 for AI) and was named Asia's Businessman of the Year by *Fortune* in 2003. He also received the Lifetime Achievement Award from EY (2017) and *Business Standard* (2022), as well as the Nikkei Asia Prize for Economic & Business Innovation (2017).

He is the author of *Imagining India* and co-author of *Rebooting India* and *The Art of Bitfulness*. A visionary in digital governance, Nilekani continues to champion inclusive and tech-enabled transformation in India.

Anil Padmanabhan has been a journalist for the last 38 years. He has worked in various news publications, including the *Press Trust of India*, *Business Standard*, *India Today* and *Mint*. He was awarded the Nieman fellowship in 2001, after which he was hired by *India Today* to be based out of New York as their chief of bureau (till September

2006). Since 2020, he has opted for freelancing and writes for the *Economic Times*, *Moneycontrol*, *NDTV.com*, *Russia Today*, *Khaleej Times*, *NRI Focus* and *The Open*, and he features regularly on national television. Anil also writes a weekly column, *Capital Calculus*, on Substack and does a weekly show on *StratNews Global*, which looks at policies and developments through the intersection of politics and economics.

Hardeep Singh Puri is an Indian politician, former diplomat and author. He was inducted into the Council of Ministers as minister of state (independent charge) for Housing and Urban Affairs in September 2017. He was given the additional charge of minister of state (independent charge) for Civil Aviation and the minister of state for Commerce and Industry in May 2019. He was sworn in as union minister in July 2021 and was the minister of Housing and Urban Affairs and Petroleum, and Natural Gas. He was sworn in as union minister in July 2024, and currently, he is the minister of Petroleum and Natural Gas. A 1974-batch Indian Foreign Service officer, he served as the permanent representative of India to the United Nations in Geneva and New York and served additionally in Tokyo and Colombo.

Richard Rossow is senior adviser and holds the chair on India and Emerging Asia Economics at the Centre for Strategic and International Studies (CSIS) in Washington, D.C. He has over 25 years of experience working on US–India relations, with a particular focus on economic policy and sub-national engagement with Indian states. Before joining CSIS in 2014, he was director for South Asia at McLarty Associates, where he continues to be affiliated. He previously worked at New York Life Insurance as head of International Governmental Affairs, overseeing global policy and M&A strategy, including engagement with India. From 1998 to 2008, he served as deputy director of the US–India Business Council, managing sectoral policy initiatives in energy, IT, insurance, media and telecom. Through these roles, he has helped shape business and economic ties between the two countries. He holds a BA from Grand Valley State University, Michigan.

Sanjoy K. Roy, an entrepreneur of the arts, is managing director of Teamwork Arts, which produces over 33 festivals in 42 cities and 17 countries, including the world's largest literary gathering – the Jaipur Literature Festival and international editions of JLF. He is a founder–trustee of Salaam Baalak Trust, working to provide support services for street and working children in the inner city of Delhi, where over 1,30,000 children have benefited from education, training and residential services. Roy is the co-chair of FICCI's Art and Culture Committee and a former president of the Event and Entertainment Management Association. He lectures at and works in collaboration with leading universities across the world and has been conferred the honorary degree of Doctor of the University honoris causa by the University of York, UK, in recognition of his outstanding contributions to the arts and society.

Navdeep Suri is a distinguished fellow at the Observer Research Foundation and professor of eminence at Guru Nanak Dev University, Amritsar. A former diplomat, he served in the Indian Foreign Service for 36 years, holding key postings in Cairo, Washington, London and as consul general in Johannesburg. He was India's high commissioner to Australia and ambassador to Egypt and the UAE, where he was awarded the Order of Zayed II, the UAE's second-highest civilian honour. Known for pioneering the use of social media in public diplomacy, he received two prestigious awards for his efforts. Navdeep holds a master's degree in economics and is fluent in Arabic and French. He writes on India's foreign policy, the Middle East and public diplomacy, and co-edited *A 2030 Vision for India's Economic Diplomacy*. He has also translated his grandfather Nanak Singh's Punjabi novels into English, with works published by Penguin Random House and HarperCollins.

Ajay Tyagi is a distinguished expert in the financial sector, with extensive experience in energy and environmental policy. He served as chairman of SEBI from 2017 to 2022, where he oversaw key reforms to strengthen investor protection and market development. A former Indian Administrative Service officer, his 33-year career included senior roles in the Ministries of Finance, Environment and Petroleum, and he represented the government on the boards of the Reserve Bank of India, Bharat Petroleum Corporation Ltd. and GAIL (India) Ltd. He also held top positions in the Himachal Pradesh government across finance, planning and industry portfolios. Currently, he serves as an independent director on several prominent corporate boards and is a distinguished fellow at the Observer Research Foundation. A prolific writer and speaker on economic and financial issues, he has published more than 40 articles in leading publications. Mr Tyagi holds degrees from Delhi College of Engineering, IIT Kanpur and Harvard University.

T.S. Vishwanath has expertise in analysing multilateral and bilateral trade agreements, global economic policies and regulatory frameworks over three decades. He has an in-depth understanding of competitiveness and policy dynamics across sectors. His leadership roles at VeK, a policy advisory and research firm, and ASL-Legal, a law firm specializing in trade law, combined with his extensive experience engaging with Indian government departments and international organizations, position him as an expert in navigating policy and regulatory challenges. With a rich background as a former senior director at CII and a trade policy expert, Vishwanath brings the strategic vision and stakeholder engagement capabilities essential for driving successful projects.

Co-author:

Adhiraj Gupta is a senior associate at VeK, where he applies rigorous, evidence-driven methodologies to tackle today's most pressing policy challenges. With a background in public policy and regulations, his previous and current areas of work span international trade, housing and urban development, sustainable mining policy and regulatory frameworks, with a focus on translating in-depth research into clear, impactful recommendations. He believes that research-driven writing not only uncovers nuanced insights but also helps shape policy discourses with clarity and purpose.

A Note on the Editors

Ajay Khanna is a leader in public policy and public affairs, advocacy, stakeholder engagement and strategic thinking, working across diverse sectors. In a career spanning more than 45 years, he has focused on ethical and value-based leadership. He writes regularly in major newspapers and has been a member of several high-level government delegations, committees and task forces. Ajay leverages his experience, expertise and network to advise, mentor and support several organizations and initiatives across various domains. The co-founder of the Public Affairs Forum of India, he is strategic adviser and ombudsperson of Jubilant Bhartia Group; senior adviser with The Convergence Foundation, Urban Land Institute (India), Internet and Mobile Association of India, Catalyst 2030 and Teamwork Arts; and member of the advisory board of SaveLIFE, Pahlé India foundation and National Association of Innovators and Social Entrepreneurs. Ajay is a professor of practice with the Indian School of Public Policy and an expert member of the Grievance Redressal Board of the Digital Publisher Content Grievances Council. He is a trustee on the Board of India Development Foundation. A member of the WEF Global Alliance for social entrepreneurship, Ajay has been associated with the World Economic Forum and the Schwab Foundation for Social Entrepreneurship for over three decades. For over 35 years, he has been a regular participant at the WEF annual meeting in Davos.

He led the Social Entrepreneur of the Year award initiative of the Schwab Foundation and Jubilant Bhartia Foundation in India for 15 years. Ajay was the founding chief executive officer (2002–06) of India Brand Equity Foundation (IBEF). He spent 27 years with CII as the deputy director general and held several national and global positions from 1981 to 2008. He was a partner with Accenture India. Ajay has a degree in law from the Faculty of Law and is an alumnus of the Shri Ram College of Commerce, both celebrated institutes under the University of Delhi.

Rahul Sharma is a co-founder and past president of PAFI. He had a long career in international and Indian media before switching to public affairs, advising large global and Indian corporations and other entities on policy issues and strategic business communications. An alumni of the Fletcher School of Law and Diplomacy, Rahul is currently the managing director of the US–India Business Council (USIBC), the industry bridge between US and Indian business that is now in its fiftieth year. He has written for several publications and earlier co-edited *A New Cold War: Henry Kissinger and the Rise of China (2021)*. He continues to closely follow the world and the many new challenges it faces. An amateur photographer, he loves to travel and read books, many of which he gladly gives away to those who want them. In his free time he blogs about things that matter.